Structuralist analysis in contemporary social thought

International Library of Sociology

Founded by Karl Mannheim

Editor: John Rex, University of Warwick

Arbor Scientiae
Arbor Vitae

A catalogue of the books available in the **International Library of Sociology** and other series of Social Science books published by Routledge & Kegan Paul will be found at the end of this volume.

Structuralist analysis in contemporary social thought

A comparison of the theories of Claude Lévi-Strauss and Louis Althusser

Miriam Glucksmann

Routledge & Kegan Paul

London and Boston

First published in 1974
by Routledge & Kegan Paul Ltd
Broadway House, 68–74 Carter Lane,
London EC4V 5EL and
9 Park Street,
Boston, Mass. 02108, U.S.A.
Printed in Great Britain by
Unwin Brothers Limited
The Gresham Press
Old Woking, Surrey

ISBN 0 7100 7773 4

Library of Congress Catalog Card No. 73–86572

Contents

Preface

This book was originally presented as a Ph.D. thesis to the University of London in 1971.

Much of the financial burden of changing the thesis into a book was borne by a grant from the Leicester University Research Board, for which I am very grateful.

Introduction

Structuralism reached the height of intellectual fashion in France in the mid 1960s, and reached Britain in the late 1960s, propagated principally by 'Marxish' intellectuals who saw it as a possible solution to both theoretical and political problems. In the absence of an alternative coherent framework, other perhaps than phenomenology, which also enjoyed a new vogue, the adoption of structuralism as a homogeneous system of thought was not surprising. However, the enthusiasm for structuralism is conjunctural and must be seen in its historical context. The generation of students who went through the student movement realized the need for theory, both as the basis for a critique of bourgeois ideology, and as the foundation of their own political activity. Structuralism seemed to fulfil this need in several ways. First, it stressed rigorous theory, and maintained that a scientific epistemology was a necessary precondition for non-empiricist and objective knowledge of the social formation as well as its cultural and psychological dimensions. This emphasis on explicit premises contrasted with the empiricism and woolly theory of academic thought, and provided the concepts for a critique of sociology and anthropology in particular. Second, structuralism was neither reductionist nor economic determinist, but examined contradictions within the capitalist-imperialist system other than the classic ones, and also attempted a non-reductionist theory of the superstructure. Finally, the apparently political character of the structuralists, all of whose analyses implied a critique of conventional orthodoxy, promised some practical relevance for the theory, and a link between social analysis and political action of which bourgeois thought is incapable.

Both individually and collectively, the structuralists provided a coherent framework for social analysis, in the absence of alternatives.

Lévi-Strauss's approach to kinship and primitive thought produced insights which were inconceivable within an evolutionary or functionalist problematic. His critique of history and evolutionism implies an anti-imperialist stance, and the structuralist orientation towards his material points the way forward for theoretical anthropology in a post-fieldwork era. The applicability of his method to data conventionally thought to be the preserve of other disciplines breaks down the barriers between the study of literature, language and culture on the one hand, and economics, sociology and anthropology on the other, especially with his consideration of communication in all its guises.

Similarly, Althusser's critique of Hegel and of historicist variants of Marxism could culminate in a rigorous structuralist analysis of different social formations and their component substructures and internal contradictions, without succumbing to humanist philosophy or millennial predictions about the collapse of capitalism. His militant interpretation of Marx and Lenin brings into focus the political relevance of their epistemology, and provides the groundwork for a theory of contemporary capitalism by formulating necessary concepts. His political standpoint brings into question the relationship between Marxist theory and revolutionary political practice.

Lévi-Strauss, Althusser, Lacan, Barthes and Foucault produced similar critiques of empiricism, historicism and reductionism—critiques which any scholar in their fields now has to face and answer. But the homogeneity of structuralism can be discerned only by overemphasizing the epistemological and methodological aspects of their work. There are important philosophical and political differences between the structuralists, which are becoming increasingly evident with the continuing development of their ideas, and in time these may override the existing epistemological similarities. Althusser remains a Marxist militant, but his recent writings and those of his followers entail a theoreticism, intellectual elitism and virtual contempt for political practice which were not apparent in his earlier work. Lévi-Strauss's physiological reductionism has reached its full expression only in the last volume of the *Mythologiques*, and makes nonsense of his earlier claims to provide a theory of the superstructure, complementary to Marx's analysis of the base. Politically and philosophically, Althusser and Lévi-Strauss are poles apart, but this is only now becoming manifest.

The conjunctural nature of structuralism as a distinctive problematic does not necessarily mean that it is only of temporary significance. The epistemological critique of bourgeois thought remains one of the most coherent; and the enthusiasm for the structuralist approach should bear fruit in Britain during the next few years with the production of theories of contemporary capitalism, and other social formations, as well as structuralist analyses of art, music, film and literature.

It was in the context of confusion in Britain about the difference between structural and structuralist thought, and the lack of attention paid to Althusser, in contrast to Lévi-Strauss, that I decided to compare these two theorists, and to tackle the issue of the homogeneity and heterogeneity of structuralism. The method used was largely a structuralist one, concentrating on textual analysis, and sought to isolate their conceptual apparatus, its component parts, and the internal contradictions within it. This then seemed to have the advantage of rigour, clarity and avoided the impossibility of reductionism, but on the other hand, a textual comparison has few criteria of its own by which to determine overall similarities and comparisons. I started working on it at the time when structuralism seemed a homogeneous alternative to bourgeois sociology, and the progress of the work implicitly reflects the developments and divergences within structuralist thought that emerged between 1967 and 1972.

1 The approach to structural and structuralist theory

Introduction

The term 'structure' is as old as social analysis itself. It stands with other such terms as 'organization', 'function', 'institution', 'norm', 'value', as one of the key words which sociologists use to designate the social —non-individual—characteristics of human life. It has been widely used by the classical theorists of sociology and anthropology: Weber, Durkheim, Marx, Pareto, Simmel and Radcliffe-Brown, to name only a few. Recently it has come into wide use again in several of the social sciences, and many of its proponents feel that their use of it is analogous and that they are all to be considered 'structuralists'. The main areas where it has regained currency are the social anthropology of Lévi-Strauss, Althusser and his school in Marxism, Godelier in economic anthropology, Poulantzas and Glucksmann in politics, Lacan and others in psychoanalysis, Barthes in semiology, Macherey in literary criticism, and Foucault in the history of ideas.

The aim of this work is to attempt a critical exposition of 'structuralism'. I shall examine the similarities and differences in the use of the term 'structure' by different theorists and investigate whether its proponents all work with a similar conceptual framework, paying particular attention to Lévi-Strauss and Althusser. The substantive way in which their theories converge will be examined and an attempt made to construct a coherent framework based on them. The relationship between their theories and the use of 'structure' by classical sociology will also be examined, and I shall investigate how, in the various fields, the 'structuralist' orientation departs from alternative ones; for example how Althusser's contribution to Marxism differs from the humanist or historicist orientation, and the impact of Lévi-Strauss's theories of kinship or myth on anthropological conceptions of the primitiveness of primitive man. The

1

contribution of structuralism to sociology will be assessed in terms of the extent to which it helps solve persistent theoretical problems and what new problems it raises in turn.

Because of the enormous variation among structuralists in theoretical apparatus, field of study, use and meaning of the concept 'structure', an investigation of their substantive work cannot be based merely on a comparison of what they say about the things which they are studying, or in isolation from their total system of ideas. To locate the exact similarities and differences between the various theorists, it is essential to examine their whole conceptual system, of which 'structure' is just one element, and to determine whether or not different 'thought structures' are implied, which would account for the differences in outlook towards the subject matter.

Approach to the theory of theory

In sociology there are no accepted procedures for studying theory, nor is there a 'theory of theory' which could help us analyse social theory into separate frameworks and within these, into its component parts and levels. The examination of theory has been confined mainly to the philosophy of science or to the sociology of knowledge. The former tends to refer either to the procedure of scientific investigation, or to the process of scientific change, rather than to the internal structure of scientific theories and their morphological relationship.[1] The sociology of knowledge attempts to situate particular types of thought, such as politics, religion or literature, within their socio-historical environment and to show how they arose to pose or solve problems or express group interests in particular social conditions (see e.g. Mannheim, 1952 and Gouldner, 1967). However, there has been little work on the internal analysis of thought systems, as opposed to the examination of their external referents, especially of those concerned with social phenomena.

It is likely that the similarities between structuralists will be discovered at a more abstract level than their empirical use of the term 'structure' in concrete studies. Accordingly the first step in this study must be to define the main terms to be used and to discuss the methodological problems involved in the study of theoretical systems.

The first problem is that of the approach towards theory, how to analyse it structurally rather than developmentally or with reference to its social setting alone. I shall assume that a theoretical system is not a series of elements but a structured unity of concepts, and that a change, addition or removal of one element will affect all the others, and hence the structure of the framework as a whole. Without morphological analysis it may be possible to achieve only a history-of-ideas picture which sees certain aspects of theoretical development only, but does not treat the concepts themselves as part of a system.

The terms 'problematic' and 'thought structure' will be used interchangeably to denote the system of concepts through which particular terms become meaningful and in terms of which concrete texts may be examined. What I shall be investigating is whether or not a common 'structuralist problematic' exists. The notion of a problematic, though not well known in sociology, has in fact been used by both Althusser and Lévi-Strauss in their attempts to define particular theoretical systems.

Althusser's concept of problematic

Althusser means by the term 'problematic' a defined theoretical structure of conceptual framework which determines the forms of the posing of all problems and what is seen as relevant to the problem (Althusser and Balibar, 1970, p. 25):

> This introduces us to a fact peculiar to the very existence of science: it can only pose problems on the terrain and within the horizon of a definite theoretical structure, its problematic, which constitutes its absolute and definite condition of possibility, and hence the absolute determination of the forms in which all problems must be posed, at any given moment in the science.

The problematic includes particular theories, concepts and methods. Objects and phenomena which do not have necessary links with the field defined by the problematic are excluded so that internal limits are placed on what is studied. Althusser elaborates the point that it is the fundamental questions,[2] the outlook, that determine the results and the conclusions of any study (1969a, p. 67):

> What actually distinguishes the concept of the problematic . . . is that it brings out within the thought the objective internal reference system of its particular themes, the system of questions commanding the answers given by the ideology. If the meaning of an ideology's answers is to be understood at this internal level it must first be asked the question of its questions.

Althusser developed the notion of the problematic in his attempt to define what was specific about Marx's theory. One basic controversy within Marxism relates to the continuity between Marx's early idealist and humanist writings and his later works. For Althusser the problem is the consistency between Marx's Feuerbachian writings in the period 1843–5, and his later work which rejected Feuerbach. Althusser suggests that a change in problematic—based on the abandonment of humanism—accounts for this. Marx points out that Feuerbach's attempt to invert Hegel by placing the essence of man in materiality rather than consciousness merely recreated Hegelian idealism with changed terms. Althusser concentrates on Marx's claim to have merely 'inverted' Hegel, in this light, to discover the difference in conception implied. The mirror-image relation of Feuerbach and Hegel means that both used the same concepts of totality and contradiction. Marx used the same words, but the concepts changed. He rejected Feuerbach's history and politics based on man, which assumes that there is a universal essence of man and that this is an attribute of each individual man, and he rejected Hegel's concept of the totality as homogeneous and revolving around one central contradiction. Althusser claims that the confusion of Marxist humanists who see a direct continuation between the early and later works is due to too superficial a reading— to get to the problematic it is not enough to read what is written and accept it at face value; rather it is essential to reconstruct the system of concepts behind the words. The discovery of the outlines of a problematic amounts to a production of knowledge, rather than a surface reading, and to distinguish it Althusser (Althusser and Balibar, 1970, p. 28) calls it 'a symptomatic reading'. It attempts to discover the undiscovered, or what is latent in the texts. Thus when studying Marx (Althusser, 1969a, p. 66):

> We must go further than the unmentioned presence of the thought of a living author to the presence of his potential thoughts, to his problematic, that is, to the constitutive unity of the effective thoughts that make up the domain of the existing ideological field with which a particular author must settle accounts in his own thought.

The notion of problematic is just as useful when Althusser comes to examine the differences between the English classical economists and Marx. Though certain findings and emphases were common to both, especially the stress on production and the discovery of value, Althusser contends that because they belonged to different problematics these were quite differently thought of in the two cases. In his view, the classical economists failed to see the implications of the concept of production because their problematic concentrated on individual facts and embodied a latent anthropology; their 'subject' of study was real individuals, and distribution, consumption and production were interpreted as based on the 'needs' of economic men, which required the assumption of a 'homo œconomicus' and that economic 'facts' are immediately given. Marx, on the other hand, allied his recognition that circulation, distribution and consumption are inseparable from production to a concept of 'mode of production' existing as a system independent of individual capitalists and workers. Thus the object of study was defined as the workings of a mode of production, not as one of its elements. In a similar way, he studied value as a general category, not its particular forms. The subject of the process was the relations of production, the definition and distribution of the places and functions in different systems, not the concrete functionaries themselves. This change of outlook had repercussions on Marx's ideas on the history of economic development and his explanation of the workings of the capitalist system. Althusser summarizes this by saying that Marx had a new problematic in relation to the classical economists and could see what Smith for example could not see, i.e. the problematic could integrate new findings into the new framework they demanded.

The concept of problematic as used by Althusser thus brings order into the examination of social thought, especially in the case of Marx, whose work has given rise to many interpretations. Other approaches tend to analyse his work in terms of 'elements' which suggest spontaneous associations with other theorists, such as Feuerbach and Hegel, and often their latent aim is to 'prove' that the theories of the commentator were present in the original Marx, so that their reading of the texts becomes teleological. Certain elements only are examined, usually materialism and idealism, and the interpretation fails to grasp the global meaning of a text or to come to terms with a theoretical system other than its own. Althusser (1969a, p. 57) considers such approaches eclectic and unscientific since they presuppose that it is possible to reduce theoretical systems to their elements and to compare these individually with elements from other systems in isolation from the significance they have within their own system.

Althusser's overall aim is to produce a theory of the production of knowledge, and where better to start than a systematic exposition of the philosophical framework of Marx's work? In view of the confusion besetting other approaches, it was necessary to start afresh, and to develop concepts separate from the subject matter, with which to analyse it. The 'problematic' was one of these (Althusser, 1969a, p. 32):

> The examination of the status of this declaration called for a theory and a method—the Marxist theoretical concepts in which the reality of theoretical formations in general (philosophical ideologies and science) can be considered must be applied to Marx himself. Without a theory of the history of theoretical

formations it would be impossible to grasp and indicate the specific difference that distinguishes two different theoretical formations. I thought it possible to borrow for this purpose the concept of a 'problematic' from Jacques Martin to designate the particular unity of a theoretical formation and hence the location to be assigned to this specific difference.[3]

Lévi-Strauss's use of the problematic

Lévi-Strauss also makes implicit use of the concept of a problematic. His work on the various forms of primitive thought such as classification systems, totemism, systems of naming, myths, points to the wealth of information of the natural environment at the disposal of 'primitive' men and the highly complex methods that they have evolved for assimilating it in order to hand down their knowledge in the absence of writing. The principles of classification they use form an internally coherent system, as complex as the Linnaean scheme, but which differs from 'scientific' classifications because of the different and wider functions it fulfils in primitive society. Totems constitute one of the major means by which non-literate men can exercise their intellectual faculties, and are therefore 'good to think'. But in addition the classification of the external world also imposes order on human society. The differences between animal species are applied to human groups, and the difference between one human group and another is felt to be of the same order as the difference between one animal species and another. Totems as codes are often accompanied by rules of conduct in relation to totemic emblems; the differences between animals which man abstracts from nature and applies to culture are adopted as emblems by groups of men to reduce their own similarities.

However, Lévi-Strauss's emphasis is on the formal character of totemic thought—the verbal categories used to classify flora and fauna serve as codes capable of assimilating any kind of content (1966b, p. 75):

> The operative value of the systems of naming and classifying commonly called totemic derives from their formal character; they are codes suitable for conveying messages which can be transposed into other codes, and for expressing messages received by means of different codes in terms of their own system.

Similarly, the prime function of myths is to help solve intellectual problems and the basic paradoxes of human life such as the origin of the world, the differences between men and animals, and between sisters and wives. They have a role in primitive society analogous to that of religion or philosophy in other societies. Natural phenomena here are 'the medium through which myths try to explain facts which are themselves not a natural but a logical order.' (Lévi-Strauss, 1966b, p. 95.) Lévi-Strauss argues that magical thought, totemism, and myths constitute a coherent way of looking at the world, responsive to the exigencies of primitive life which constitutes a legitimate alternative to science. They belong to a different problematic from European natural sciences, and the differences between them are to be seen on this basis (ibid., p. 13):

> Magical thought is not to be regarded as a beginning, a rudiment, a sketch, a part of a whole which has not yet materialised. It forms a well-articulated system, and is in this respect independent of that other system which constitutes science . . . it is better, instead of contrasting science and magic, to compare them as parallel modes of acquiring knowledge.

The disparity of concrete knowledge acquired is to be explained in terms of the different objective and multi-functional character of primitive thought, which is a mode of scientific thought but operating at the level of perception and imagination, whereas 'modern' science operates at a remove from this.

In Lévi-Strauss's view, the primitive problematic has a different objective in relation to knowledge and cosmology, and uses different means for producing that knowledge. Classifications and systems of naming work by means of a limited number of categories and established rigid and formal relations (oppositions, inversions, homologies) between the phenomena they deal with. Myths work from an awareness of oppositions to their mediation. These operations correspond to the conceptual apparatus included in Althusser's definition of the problematic.

According to Lévi-Strauss (1966b, p. 22):

> Mythical thought, that bricoleur, builds structures by fitting together events, or rather the remains of events, while science, 'in operation' simply by virtue of coming into being, creates its means and results in the form of events, thanks to the structures which it is constantly elaborating and which are its hypotheses and theories . . . the scientist creating events (changing the world) by means of structures, and the 'bricoleur' creating structures by means of events.

Lévi-Strauss thus works with the hypothesis that primitive thought and science are distinct systems, alternatives to be distinguished on the basis of different questions asked, that is, the different functions of classification and storytelling in primitive and modern societies, and the different conceptual apparatus each uses.

At the moment I am not concerned whether Althusser and Lévi-Strauss are correct in their definitions of particular problematics. It is possible that Althusser's claim that Marx's later work represents a rupture of problematic with his early work is not validated by the evidence, or that Lévi-Strauss's distinction between primitive and scientific modes of thought is over-general. I am concerned only to demonstrate that the problematic is a fruitful approach to the study of social thought, and this is independent from the correctness of conclusions its proponents have reached.

To summarize, a problematic or a thought structure is a particular way of looking at the world, defined by the fundamental question asked, and which includes concepts, methods and theories. To isolate a problematic requires more than a simple reading of the texts, but depends on making explicit concepts that are often only latent, and investigating their interrelationship within a total system.[4]

The notion of the problematic thus provides us with a guiding question around which to orientate our study, though it still needs to be refined. There are certain other methodological assumptions and hypotheses underlying this project which must also be discussed.

A general problem for the analysis of thought structures is that there is no constant relationship between a term and its denotation, between signifier and signified. So we have to be wary of accepting undefined uses of the term 'structure' and take care not to assimilate different empirical uses of it too readily without examining its place within the general approach. It is only to be expected that at any given time there will be a pool of terms whose meaning is precise to their users but may not be to the social science community at large; they may have been borrowed, recently invented or returned to fashion after a lapse into obscurity. Thus the same term may be used in different ways to denote different concepts—the use varying both over time and between different problematics. To put it more succinctly, the same signifier may be used in quite different systems of signifieds. This problem of definition is only too obvious, but can be easily forgotten. That this is the case with the term 'structure' is more than likely especially in view of its very wide use, and will be examined in the next chapter.

Structural analysis of theory

Another presupposition of the approach adopted here is that theoretical frameworks can be considered as distinct entities, capable of analysis from the outside; that the results of analysis of problematics are independent of the theories of the analyst of theory; and that it is possible to attempt a sociology of thought systems without raising the problem of the determinacy of thought, a problem undermining many concrete studies in the sociology of knowledge, which refer too readily to origins and external determinants. A corollary of this is the necessity to produce concepts independent from the subject matter to which they are to be applied, so as to avoid the teleological approach that Althusser criticizes. We cannot accept that thought structures contain their own principle of intelligibility or that they can be understood solely in terms of the concepts they provide. However, scientific concepts appropriate to describe the nature of particular thought systems cannot be postulated in advance of detailed textual analysis. In this sense the analysis itself rests on theoretical production, and must involve a dialectical movement between the concepts of the text and what the investigator wishes to get out of them. That reality and the scientific description of reality are not the same is self evident, but this recognition has to be incorporated into the method of study of thought systems just as for more concrete social products. For example, one facet of Hegel's problematic may be very briefly summarized as follows: society is viewed as a homogeneous totality revolving around one central contradiction (monism); constituent elements are dissolved into an undifferentiated unity, and the possible relevance of internal contradictions and interrelationships of specific levels and elements within a given social formation is not examined. This indicates the basic structure of concepts and the limitations they impose. But the discovery of Hegel's monism and homogeneity requires a 'symptomatic' rather than visual reading. The primacy of morphological analysis is implicit in the notion of a problematic. But this is not intended as a substitute for the other possible types of analysis: historical, that is, the development of the problematic and the origin of each of its elements; sociological: examination of the external, especially social, referents of the theory, and how it is located within the social structure; or an evaluation of its validity. Morphological analysis has a more limited aim than these, merely to establish a morphology. Any attempt at a 'total' explanation would have to combine all four of these aspects.

Definition of levels

But how exactly are we to embark on the task of analysing thought structures as structured unities of concepts? The need to develop independent concepts to express the substantive characteristics has been mentioned, but these cannot be established *a priori*. In addition, it is necessary to study the total structure of theoretical systems in general, and to consider the number of possible different levels and types of operation of which they are composed, and the way these interrelate. Here certain guidelines can be postulated in advance, since thought structures must possess certain characteristics merely in order to constitute thought structures. The following levels are fairly obvious:

(1) epistemology: theory of knowledge and how it is to be acquired. Views on what sort of knowledge of the social world we can hope to achieve.

(2) philosophy: substantive and generalized world view, which incorporates certain values and puts limitations on the substantive theoretical postulates which also form part of the system.

(3) theory: substantive hypotheses to account for and explain observed facts, phenomena and events.

(4) methodology: lower level prescriptions as to the methods to be used in research e.g. hypothetico-deductive method, subjectivism.

(5) description, or field of study, actual method of describing observations.

This is not an exhaustive list, and the numbering refers to descending levels of abstraction rather than a hierarchy of determinacy. The number of levels and areas may differ for different kinds of orientation, and they may be separate or combined; each coherent thought system includes the five mentioned in some form, if it is to analyse specific data and assess the significance of hypotheses made to account for them in terms of its own theory of what constitutes knowledge. However, the relations between the parts of the theoretical system are not predetermined nor the same in each case. They must be established by detailed examination rather than taken as given. I shall attempt to show that the structuralism of Althusser and Lévi-Strauss embodies an epistemology which transforms the usual relation between conceptualization, description and explanation. It is unlikely that the relations between the various levels of the system are strictly determined, probably they determine only limits of compatibility and incompatibility, the exact nature and degree of which may vary between different parts of the same system.

Certain theories may be similar at face value but belong to different epistemologies and vice versa; the same epistemological framework may be compatible with varying lower level theoretical propositions.

Thus in order to analyse a theory completely, it is not enough to accept it as 'independent' and self-sufficient. In most cases theoretical hypotheses and the methods for testing them are embedded in a wider 'problematic', linked with distinctive epistemological and philosophical premises which confer extra meaning on them.

The term 'theory' becomes overloaded if we look at it in this way, and we can distinguish two separate meanings that it has already acquired:

(1) customary meaning as substantive hypothesis to account for and explain particular social phenomena;

(2) a whole conceptual framework embodying different levels and areas of which theory in the first sense is just one.

The term 'theory' will be reserved for the first, and 'problematic' for the second.

Examples

I hope that this framework will be generally fruitful in the study of the history of social thought. Taking sociological theory, for example, as ' "raw" material', some current orientations—for instance, the descriptive empirical approach—seem to rest on description and lower level theory alone (elements 4 and 5 above), although a more careful examination may reveal that it is based on the premises of positivist epistemology, which makes certain assumptions about the logical status of explanations and about the predictability of social life. On the other hand, some orientations may consist of only elements 1 and 2, epistemology and philosophy, embodying a magnificent metatheory but with little relationship to the problems of studying actual social phenomena. Alternatively, there may be systems with all five levels well articulated but not linked to one another operationally so that the empirical results are not seen to rest on the professed epistemology and philosophy. Such perhaps is the case with Parsons, and the apparent disjunction between particular observations and explanations of them on the one hand (studies on religion and the family for example), and his systematic metatheory on the other.[5]

Some of the controversies concerning particular theories could also be made more systematic by looking at their constituent parts separately. Different conceptions of what functionalism is, can be seen in this light; whether it is merely a method for examining social life and synonymous with sociology itself as Davis (1959), claims or whether it is a normative view of society. In the first case it would be compatible with other types of explanation and the attention paid to functions would not predetermine the conclusions of the study, as for example in Bateson's study (1936) of the 'naven' ceremonies; in the second case it becomes a philosophy of society, with ideas about the necessary integration of the parts of society and the functional nature of this for the survival of society. Malinowskian-type func-tionalism is based on the notion of social and individual needs, and of the 'harmony' of society, and these have implications for the observations of the social arrangements of particular societies. Different users obviously make use of the theoretical apparatus at their disposal in different ways, but it is more helpful to see these as

11

different thought structures or different combinations of numbers of elements rather than different uses of an undifferentiated functionalism. In this case, the more inclusive variety which incorporates a general world view approximates to the ideal construct of a thought structure more closely, while the other type more narrowly a 'theory' in the sense above.

Evolutionism could be examined in the same way—at its most general it embodies a conception about change, both in the natural and the social world, based on a philosophy of progress. Yet it is compatible with many different specific theories; unilinear or multilinear theories of development, stage theory, 'structural differentiation', and others, all of which may differ as to the actual process of change, the mechanisms and the determinacy of the process. However, they are all basically evolutionist, and uphold the notion of progress, though they may accept to a lesser or greater degree the cultural bias implicit in this. This philosophy again has inevitable repercussions on description and method, though its relation to epistemology is not very clear.

The problem of structuralism

The analysis of 'structuralism' will be a way of testing the usefulness of the approach outlined in this chapter, especially in view of the general confusion that surrounds the subject. Many theorists query whether 'structuralism' is a meaningful category and there are as many different interpretations of structuralism as there are interpreters; it is seen variously as substantive theory, formalism, linguistic method, idealism or merely a French fashion. Yet the majority of commentaries are confined to Lévi-Strauss and the semiologists, and only rarely examine the Marxists and psychoanalysts.[6]

The confusion is greatest in relation to Lévi-Strauss and Althusser. The first reading of their texts may reveal great similarities, and the next major differences. Which of these gives the correct impression? The similarities are most evident in their attitude to the historical dimension, and conception of the social whole as a complex structured unity capable of objective analysis into its parts. Yet the differences seem sufficient to invite the conclusion that they are studying incomparable subject matter and with different objectives. Lévi-Strauss is concerned to show that the social organization, kinship networks, cultural products and thought structures of 'primitive' men are coherent, organized structures and are, all over the world, variations of a limited number of possible patterns. What he studies are particular kinship systems among the Nambikwara or Murngin, and specific myths of types of face painting.

Louis Althusser, on the other hand, is a philosopher and Marxist. His aim is to show that Marx's mature writings embody a distinctive epistemology of which he was more or less unaware and which was not presented as such. Althusser hopes to fill this gap by providing the concepts to express Marxist epistemology, to reinterpret Marx's postulates in these new terms and to show their significance within the corpus of Marxist thought. Much of his work, therefore, takes the form of a detailed textual analysis of Marx.

Although the substantive conclusions of Althusser and Lévi-Strauss may be compatible, what they are studying does appear to be incomparable. Both use the term 'structure' but in different ways. The basis of Althusser's theory is 'materialist' in that, for him, the economy is determinant 'in the last instance', and one of his major preoccupations is to show how Marx departed from Hegelian idealism, and the contemporary disjunction between 'scientific' and 'humanist-historicist' Marxism. But for many of his critics, Lévi-Strauss is an idealist who sees actual social structures and cultural phenomena as mere instantiations of some platonic and essential structure of the mind which is natural and universal.

Given these differences, it is clear that the relationship between Lévi-Strauss and Althusser ought to be studied at the level of problematic rather than the textual use of the term 'structure'. I shall attempt to establish the epistemological and philosophical framework of each, their respective views of the construction of social reality, and the appropriate methodological approach to this, and the place of 'structure' within this. The most fundamental differences have been stressed here, and it will be the task of what follows to look afresh at the works without preconceptions to reconstruct the thought structure of each.

In the light of the problems of method discussed here, we may conclude that in the examination of social theories based on the concept of 'structure' it will be essential to determine:

(1) whether the same concept is being used in all cases;
(2) if it is, whether it belongs to the same problematic.

We shall have to consider how meaningful it is to talk of 'structuralism', old or new, at the level of theory, or whether it would be better to consider different varieties of 'structuralism' as different problematics and total conceptual systems which involve differences also in 'theoretical' positions, and in terms of which particular authors may be situated and compared.

Thus the aim of this work is wider than the critical exposition of a particular framework. In order to examine the structuralist problematic it is also necessary to develop a systematic method to study theoretical systems. The apparatus on which the primary investigation rests has also to be produced. In so far as the methods used in this approach are based on ideas drawn from the writings of modern 'structuralists', where they are often only implicit and not put to the test, it is also a case study in structuralism, an application of structuralist theory to itself.

2 Meanings and uses of the term structure

Introduction

The word 'structure' derives from the Latin 'structura', from the verb 'struere', to construct. Its meaning was exclusively architectural until the seventeenth century when its use was extended to the study of anatomy and grammar. The arrangement of the organs of the body came to be viewed as a kind of construction, and language was understood as the arrangement of words in speech having a 'structured' character. The term always designated a whole, the parts of a whole and their interrelations and it was this focus that appealed to the developing 'exact' sciences. In the nineteenth century, the term was introduced from biology to the new 'sciences of man' by Herbert Spencer (Gurvitch, 1957). Although he insisted on the difference between the social and biological organism, the conception of social structure that developed was, perhaps inevitably, tinged with naturalism. The original analogy between organic and social structures has important methodological consequences. It implies that in both cases, the structure is the organization of the observable parts of the whole, a bias which orientates social structure studies in a specific direction by defining the area and level of abstraction at which they operate, and what constitutes a 'complete' analysis.

The naturalistic limitations characterizing the system of ideas that runs from Spencer to Durkheim and Radcliffe-Brown have predisposed some modern users of the term 'structure' to seek descent elsewhere, notably from the anthropologist Lewis Morgan. It was he, Lévi-Strauss claims, who first analysed data in terms of what he called 'systems', unhampered by the analogy with organisms and the privilege accorded to observed phenomena.[1] Who actually introduced the term is not important, but the possibility that there are two lines of descent does throw light on the different notions of structure that have emerged.

There are additional influences on twentieth-century structural thought; the Hegelian idea of totality applied to society by historians and German idealist philosophers who understood societies as the embodiment of certain ideas; Gestalt theory in the psychology of perception which operationalized the philosophical idea of totality and attempted to prove empirically that the whole was different from the sum of the parts; Saussurean linguistics rejected the atomism of classical grammar and distinguished between language as the total fund of linguistic apparatus available, and speech, understood as particular actualizations of language and inexplicable without reference to it; Marx's analysis of social formations as resting on the complex interaction of a number of elements; the development of cybernetics and communications theory since the 1930s have also played an important role in setting higher standards of rigour to be achieved in the analysis of social phenomena. Nowadays structure has a very extensive use in sociology and new derivations, such as macro- and micro-structure, infra and superstructure, de- and restructuration, express its various shades of meaning.

But to list influences is not to analyse their specific contribution to structuralism in sociology and anthropology. I shall attempt to establish a more precise genealogy for each of the various structuralisms. The point here is simply to highlight the advantage that modern definitions have from developments in related areas, and that differences between newer and older versions are only to be expected.

One of the difficulties of examining the various definitions of 'structure' has already been encountered; it is always allied to a general conception of method, of the aims of sociology and to a philosophical orientation. Hence the problem of extricating it from the studies of specific data where it is found, and from its theoretical context. To make matters worse, some theorists do not use the term itself although their work undoubtedly has a structural aspect. In this chapter I shall examine the use and meaning that 'structure' has had in British social anthropology, and French sociology, before looking at its contemporary use. The fundamental question is whether the term has the same meaning in all cases, or to what extent distinct varieties of 'structuralism' may be distinguished.

To make the task of comparison easier and more rigorous several questions should be kept in mind: its derivation; whether or not it is a key concept; the degree to which it is *theoretically* defined; how it is related to the scientific pretensions of the author; whether it is considered to be observable; the level of abstraction it refers to; whether attention is paid to the internal organization of structure; how it is allied to the conception of society as a whole.

Radcliffe-Brown and British social anthropology

The British school of anthropology of the first half of the twentieth century is renowned for its meticulous observation and description of native customs and ways of life, and its rigorous analytic approach to the data thus collected, both being considered necessary groundwork for the discovery of laws of social life which has its ultimate aim. In this project, the term 'structure' is one of their fundamental conceptual tools.

Radcliffe-Brown is the best exponent of this school. In his earliest study, *The Andaman Islanders* (1922), Radcliffe-Brown used the term 'structure' to describe the regularities inherent in kinship relations, economic organization and religious customs which he observed as recurrent individual events and used it as a matter of course, unselfconsciously. It was only later, in 1935–40, that he felt the need to define the terms 'structure', 'function', 'institution', 'organization', and 'role', which he had used in the analysis of fieldwork, and to indicate their underlying theoretical premises. His definitions were methodical and undogmatic, clarifying issues rather than propounding philosophical positions. What he said about the nature of science and the role of theory in the social sciences is in any case implicit in his actual studies.

In Radcliffe-Brown's view, social anthropology is a branch of natural science and has similar methods of study. Science in general is empirical in the sense that the fundamental relationships between phenomena are observable or can in some way be ascertained through the senses (1952, p. 190):

> My view of natural science is that it is the systematic investigation of the universe as it is revealed to us through the senses. . . .
> Social phenomena constitute a distinct class of natural phenomena. . . . Social structures are just as real as individual organisms.

The analysis of social life is to be based on direct observation and 'social structure' relates to actually existing social relations observable to the field workers.[2]

The ultimate aim of anthropology should be to classify structures so as 'to learn as much as we can about the varieties, or diversities, of structural systems' (ibid., p. 194). The concept of structure was a method for the analysis of social relations and comparison of the societies of which they were a part. Radcliffe-Brown's aim was to establish an inductive 'natural science of society' on the model of the natural sciences, which could discover laws applicable to all societies at all times because they expressed man's place in nature.

In the definitions, it is individuals who are the basic unit of analysis, and it is their actions and beliefs which form the basis from which the social structure is to be elaborated (Radcliffe-Brown, 1952, p. 10):

> When we use the term 'structure' we are referring to some sort of ordered arrangement of parts or components . . . the units of social structure are persons, and a person is a human being considered as occupying a position in a social structure.

and (ibid., p. 194):

> we cannot study persons except in terms of social structure, nor can we study social structure except in terms of the persons who are the units of which it is composed.

Social structure is thus assimilated to the arrangement of persons and social relations between them, relationships being distinct from activities. Social structure is used to designate (ibid., p. 11):

> an arrangement of persons in institutionally controlled or defined relationships, such as the relationship between king and subject, or that of husband and wife, and social organisation [to] refer to an arrangement of activities.

Radcliffe-Brown appears somewhat uneasy about this definition, and to denote the continuity of interpersonal relations through time as distinct from the social relations between particular individuals, he introduced a distinction between structure and the 'form' of the structure, which remains relatively constant over time. That is, structure in the sense of actual social relations between particular individuals changes over time, and 'structural form' now means what was previously called 'structure'. Structure is now the set of actually existing relations at a given time which link persons together, and 'structural form' is the general form of a relationship, which is relatively permanent, abstracted from the variations of particular instances.

Thus in Radcliffe-Brown's view, anthropology is an empirical science whose object of study consists of phenomena whose regularities can be perceived and reformulated in more abstract terms. It provides the basis for a specifically sociological approach to ethnographic material which does not rely on psychology or history as had so much of the early anthropology with its speculative history. Social structure in Radcliffe-Brown's sense is not reducible to the psyche,[3] and the lack of historical data is not a hindrance since natural laws apply at all times and can be discovered at any time.

But the definition of social structure raises more questions than it solves largely because Radcliffe-Brown takes it as so unproblematic. In the first place, he does not distinguish at a theoretical level between structure, organization and arrangement so that, although at first structure was defined as a specific entity, it is later assimilated to the other two as an arrangement or organization of relations between individual persons. In fact, one is left with the impression that 'social structure' is a residual term having no denotation other than this. Radcliffe-Brown obviously felt this as a problem but located it at the level of time rather than that of abstraction.[4]

Apart from this ambivalence, Radcliffe-Brown's definition of social structure is questionable from another point of view. While it is certainly true that persons can be understood only in their relation to social structure as a whole, the reverse is not necessarily so, although Radcliffe-Brown assumes it as a matter of course. Of course, social structure is to be observed only in the interaction between individuals but this does not mean that their interaction explains it fully. It is possible that a correct explanation of the workings of a society may consist in discovering systems of relationships existing at a more abstract level which govern the observed social relations. Radcliffe-Brown's position implies that in the last analysis the workings of society as a whole are explicable as the sum of empirically existing interactions, and the possibility that underlying principles of operation exist, not discernible in the social relations, but nevertheless determinant, is not conceivable within his framework. This raises two problems in Radcliffe-Brown's definitions. First, that such a system of relations, more abstract than observed interactions, requires a more theoretical analysis which departs at some point from the observed data in order to postulate underlying principles. But Radcliffe-Brown was bound by his naturalistic bias of 'viewing through the senses' to analyse only observed phenomena or abstractions based on them.

The other problem is that of the relatively concrete or abstract nature of social reality: in Radcliffe-Brown's notion, what is real is observable, social relations are observable and hence real. Conversely what is not observable is not 'real' in the same way. Explanations of observed data on the basis of principles of operation or systems of relationships which are not amenable to the senses are for him not as 'real' as explanations based on personal interactions, and can only be, at the best, models, and at the worst, conjectures in the mind of the anthropologist. This view implies that appearances and reality coincide. The point is not that Radcliffe-Brown was unable to theorize on the basis of his data. His essays (1951, 1952) on the relationship between mother's brother and sister's son, and on the meaning of the relationship between totems and social groups, are admirable examples of his method at its best. But even his theory is directly inferred from observations.

Thus for Radcliffe-Brown the concept of structure was not

problematic, but there were serious inadequacies and problems in his definition; the distinction between structure and social relations, the role of theory in anthropology and the question of whether observation of concrete individuals can provide a sufficient basis for laws of social life.

Radcliffe-Brown's definition of social structure was generally accepted by British social anthropologists. In most cases their definitions were developed in close relation to empirical research and this explains small differences in emphasis. Evans-Pritchard's view that social structure consists of relationships between groups is clearly drawn from his observations of Nuer society and its complex organization of descent groups (1940, pp. 262–3):

> Structural relations are relations between groups which form a system. By structure we therefore mean an organized combination of groups. The social structure of a people is a system of separate but interrelated structures.

Firth, from his study of the Tikopia, considers social structure to be composed of certain key relationships (1951, p. 31):

> The essence of this concept is those social relations which seem to be of critical importance for the behaviour of the members of the society, so that if such relations were not in operation, the society could not be said to exist in that form.

Nadel, on the other hand, defines it more abstractly, using the concept of role (1957, p. 12):

> We arrive at the structure of a society by abstracting from the concrete population and its behaviour the pattern or network (or 'system') of relationships obtaining 'between factors in their capacity of playing roles relative to one another'.

Despite differences in conceptualization, all contain a central reference to relations between actual, empirically given social phenomena whether these are individuals, groups, or roles. These relationships are either given in the facts as observed directly, or are arrived at by abstraction from them. Thus 'structure' refers to little more than the actual organization of society. Reality and appearances are coterminous.

This is not to say that Radcliffe-Brown has been without critics in Britain. Evans-Pritchard has always been critical of Radcliffe-Brown's view of anthropology as natural science. Fortes' essay on 'Time and Social Structure' (1949), which was intended as a sympathetic extension to Radcliffe-Brown's work, in fact revealed some of the difficulties of his definition of social structure. But the major theoretical reaction to Radcliffe-Brown's orthodoxy has come from

Leach and Needham in Britain, and from Claude Lévi-Strauss in France, who claims to have transformed the concept of social structure completely.

Evans-Pritchard (1951) disputes the scientific pretensions of anthropology and the possibility of establishing universally valid laws in Radcliffe-Brown's sense. For him, on the contrary, anthropology is more akin to history, and should make the patterns of social organization explicit through the method of 'descriptive integration'. Social structure is conceived not in naturalistic terms but as deriving from the order existing in societies, which is expressed through groups. Societies are, for Evans-Pritchard, moral rather than natural systems; if societies are not part of nature they cannot be subject to laws. So he pays attention to laws, moral and jural norms and uses the term 'social structure' to refer only to persistent social groups such as nations, tribes or clans which retain their continuity and identity as individual social groups despite changes in membership.

Fortes (1949, p. 56) criticizes Radcliffe-Brown's conception of social structure for different reasons:

> Structure is not immediately visible in the 'concrete reality' . . . when we describe structure we are already dealing with general principles far removed from the complicated skein of feelings, beliefs etc. that constitute the tissue of actual social life. We are, as it were, in the realm of grammar and syntax, rather than of the spoken word. We discern structure in the 'concrete reality' of social events only by virtue of having first established the structure by abstraction from the concrete reality.

Structure and structural form are reformulated by Fortes as complementary ways of analysing the same data, referring to its quantitative and qualitative aspects respectively. However, Fortes' concern with the analysis of particular cases seems to have prevented him from elaborating further this view of social structure which has remarkable similarities with that of Lévi-Strauss.

The best known critic of Radcliffe-Brown's type of structuralism is Edmund Leach.[5] In *Rethinking Anthropology* (1961b) he contends that the aim of social anthropology should be generalization rather than comparison, and challenges Radcliffe-Brown's conception of both social structure and the comparative method. He opposes comparison on account of its initial bias in being undertaken from the point of view of one aspect of society alone, and the fact that it has no logical limits; typology makers never make clear why they are using a particular frame of reference, and given the almost infinite number of possible comparisons, there is a difficulty in assessing their relative significance. Leach believes that anthropology

21

should focus on types of relationship and arrangements rather than individuals and individual social relationships, and that the anthropologist should examine the relations between the parts of society, and the way these vary in type and degree of connectedness in different societies (Leach, 1961b, p. 7):

> Our task is to understand and explain what goes on in society, how societies work. If an engineer tries to explain to you how a digital computer works he does not spend his time classifying different kinds of nuts and bolts. He concerns himself with principles, not with things.

Since classification can only reassert something already known, if anthropologists want to learn anything new, they should pay attention to principles of organization and the relative connectedness of relationships. This can be done by thinking of the organizational ideas in society as constituting a mathematical pattern, and of society as an assemblage of variables expressed through principles, not observable things. He takes an analogy from topology; if lines are drawn on a rubber sheet to symbolize the relations between phenomena, and the sheet is then stretched, the manifest shape of the geometrical figure will change yet it will still be the same figure. In the same way there are general structural patterns which are not restricted to any one society.

Having got this far though, Leach does not really explain his rejection of the nuts and bolts approach to anthropology on specifically methodological grounds but rather presents his critique as a means of rejuvenating anthropology. The examples he gives to illustrate the potentialities of his approach are concerned more with the *degree* of connectedness and ways of measuring it, than with different types of connectedness.

Though trenchant, the criticisms of Radcliffe-Brown by Evans-Pritchard, Fortes and Leach are not as strong as Lévi-Strauss's redefinition of the term 'structure'. Complementary to these explicit critiques is the work of Needham and Turner, who have both, in different ways, transformed the empiricist conception of structure in their work on kinship and ritual respectively.

The major differences between Radcliffe-Brown and Lévi-Strauss concern empiricism, the nature of reality and the philosophical connotations of the concept of structure, which will be examined in detail in the section on Lévi-Strauss. Radcliffe-Brown's conception of social structure was naturalistic, empiricist, and allied to a particular type of comparative method, all of which Lévi-Strauss rejects.[6]

The structural approach was for long the unifying theme in British social anthropology. The idea of structure is a concrete and straightforward one; it is assumed to relate directly and virtually without mediation to the empirical reality of social life, and is a property of the observable. The notion is derived from biology and societies are thought to have a structured organization much as the body does.

The down-to-earth character of British anthropology can only be understood in relation to the conditions affecting its development. Two of these are quite clear: the first is the isolation of anthropology as an academic discipline from both philosophy and sociology (indeed anthropology preceded sociology as a specific discipline), a fact inconceivable in France or Germany. The isolation was so great that philosophical or epistemological problems never entered the realm of discourse of anthropology, and questions such as whether observed phenomena constitute 'reality' or only 'appearances', or what sort of knowledge can be reached through the senses were not in the mind of anthropologists. The second fact is the very strong bias to fieldwork which has characterized British social anthropology since its inception, and which must in turn be related to anthropologists' role as auxiliary to the colonial administrator.[7] Fieldwork has assumed the status of an initiation rite, obligatory to a career in anthropology. The exigencies of having to give a general and theoretical form to the particular events and relationships experienced in the field demanded of anthropologists the ability to give immediate patterns a structured form. The first task of the anthropologist has always been, as Fortes says (1945), 'to give an account of the social structure of the people he has studied'. The principal concern of social anthropology has been with the problem of social order: how is it that, once the field worker has accustomed himself to the bewildering mass of strange impressions, the social life of the people he is studying presents itself as a stable ordered repetitive reality? The small scale social system of primitive societies presented a unique opportunity to study the coherence of society in microcosm and to establish the bases of social integration. Hence the emphasis on cohesive aspects of society as embedded in norms, kinship regulations and so on, rather than its divisive characteristics, and the presupposition of an isolable 'primitive' totality. Both of these rested on the possibility of revealing the empirical existence of a social structure, and explain to some extent the emergence of a concept of structure which is highly empirical in scope.

Durkheim, Mauss and the Année Sociologique school

The differences in orientation and outlook between British anthropologists and their French counterparts are to be seen, to a certain extent, in relation to their different institutional circumstances and philosophical traditions. In France, sociology has never been separate from social criticism or philosophy, and it was only in the 1920s that anthropology came to be thought of as distinct from sociology. (Mauss introduced the term 'social anthropology' into French in 1938 (Lévi-Strauss, 1967c).) In the nineteenth century sociology was considered a scientific method which could be applied to all sorts of data. Hence the close co-operation between sociology and law, history, economics and linguistics. Separate academic fields still interpenetrate today to a far greater degree in France than in Britain, as is evident in Lévi-Strauss's anthropology. In Durkheim's work sociology and anthropology were indissoluble for an additional reason: his conviction that the analysis of social phenomena could result in an explanatory synthesis which would show how modern forms of social life have grown out of older ones—a belief which did not altogether promote the successful co-operation between the subjects since the data of one was inevitably reduced to that of the other.

This institutional setting prevented the sheltering of anthropology from the discussion of methodological problems of the social sciences. From its inception, French sociology was characterized by a concern with its scientific nature, and the transition from auxiliary method to autonomous discipline around the turn of the century required, as a charter, the elaboration of a specific methodology. This was provided in Durkheim's *Rules* (1938), which represented a major step in getting sociology recognized as worthy of study in its own right in France.

The analytical philosophy long predominant in France was an additional factor shaping the character of social analysis. Durkheim and Mauss display a constant concern with objectivity, with using scientific definitions elaborated according to the essential internal properties of the phenomena under consideration rather than through conformity to ideal notions. They evolved a highly analytic approach, manipulating vast amounts of data to isolate social facts from their various cultural forms, and establishing complex classifications.

Both British and French sociology were based on the biological analogy, but whereas the British tended to analyse individual organisms and postponed the task of comparing them and establishing laws based on them to a later stage, French anthropology started with an attempt to define the characteristics appropriate to the species. Their neglect of fieldwork, their more theoretically orientated outlook and search for features common to many societies were a consequence of this.

The term 'structure' was not so central to their technical vocabulary as it was to Radcliffe-Brown's. Durkheim argued in *Rules*

(1938, p. 13) that the sociologist should investigate 'social facts' which he defined as:

> Every way of acting, fixed or not, capable of exercising on the individual an external constraint; or again, every way of acting which is general throughout a given society, while at the same time existing in its own right independent of its individual manifestations.

Social events with a demographic aspect were among the most important social facts: birth, death, marriage and suicide rates for example. The aim of most of Durkheim's earlier writings was to define and explain a particular social fact such as the incest taboo, suicide or the division of labour.

While the category of social fact had a lasting significance in Durkheim's work, his early concern with unprejudiced definitions and the empirical investigation of social facts gave way to an increasingly philosophical outlook and use of *a priori* categories. The idea that society exerts a force over its members independent of their actions, assumed increasing importance, though he retained interest in the same problems, particularly social integration. However, the conclusions of particular studies such as the *Elementary Forms of Religious Life* (1915) were predetermined by the philosophical categories which came to dominate his view of social life: the distinction between sacred and profane, individual and collective consciousness, the antinomy between society and the individual, and the equivalence of society and religion. As Lévi-Strauss says (1946, p. 528):

> Durkheim struggled between his methodological attitude, which makes him consider social facts as 'things', and his philosophical formation which uses those 'things' as a ground on which the fundamental Kantian ideas can be firmly seated. Hence he oscillates between a dull empiricism and a prioristic frenzy.

Despite this change of focus, Durkheim nevertheless laid the foundations for structural analysis. He always held that the first step in sociology must be to establish a social morphology, to determine the fundamental forms of social life in particular societies and in society in general, and to analyse the way these interconnected, both functionally and structurally, to constitute a social whole. His evolutionary perspective, however, detracted from the success of this project since he was convinced that complex forms are only agglomerations of more simple ones and to be explained in terms of their origins in simple and prior types. Hence a constant search for origins, attempting to reduce the complex to the simpler, an approach which was based on the confusion between simple, elementary and

25

prior. Lévi-Strauss comments on this aspect of his work (1946, p. 519):

> One may criticize the methodological principles on which Durkheim built up his typology: 'Societies are made up of parts put together . . . which themselves are simpler societies'. One may doubt the validity of any genetic morphology making it possible to follow the way in which a society 'composes itself with itself, and its components put together'. Even in the simplest society we may find each and every element of the more complex. But if Durkheim did not succeed in discovering the foundations of a sound social morphology, he was at least the first to undertake, with a clear conception of its paramount importance, the basic task of formulating one.

Durkheim undertook to get behind observed phenomena to their essential components which could then be used as part of a general classification. For example, he dissolved the initial category of suicide into several irreducible constituent types. 'There is not one suicide, but suicides', and, to account for the different varieties, developed an explanatory principle relating to the integration of the individual to the group. Similarly his study of the division of labour was not a historical or monographic account, but an attempt to isolate such abstract categories as 'mechanical solidarity' and 'organic solidarity', which were intended to make intelligible the data although they were not immediately given in them. Mauss's work has a similar aspect, which is 'structuralist' in Lévi-Strauss's sense even though the term is not much used. When Mauss compared the different types of gift, it was to discover, behind the diversity of types, the fundamental idea of reciprocity, and when he studied the transformations of the psychological conception of 'ego' it was to establish a relationship between social forms and the concept of personality.[8] Thus Durkheim and Mauss sought to establish abstract categories and concepts to express essential properties inherent in the phenomena studied rather than give empirical descriptions of particular cases. This assumed that the social actors' definitions of social life are inadequate and that the first and most obvious theorization of data is also likely to be the most superficial. Their constant aim was to get behind the layman's and social actor's categories to underlying components. Hence also their concern with the details of problems of method, particularly the correctness of definitions and the distinction between scientific and unscientific fact (Lévi-Strauss, 1946, p. 524):

> They have attempted . . . to reach behind (categories) those hidden fundamental elements which are the true components of

phenomena. . . . Indeed one could say that the entire purpose of
the French school lies in an attempt to break up the categories
of the layman, and to group the data into a deeper, sounder
classification. As was emphasised by Durkheim, the true and the
only basis of sociology is social morphology.

The penchant for theory and aversion to fieldwork enabled the
Durkheimians to claim that their approach alone was truly sociological since they made abstract propositions accounting for observed
phenomena. Their raw material was the data already collected and
sifted by other anthropologists and their work represents a second
level theorization in relation to Radcliffe-Brown's 'social structure'.
They could afford to be selective in their use of the comparative
method and concentrated on a limited number of facts, usually
choosing one society as an exemplary case. Durkheim's theory of
religion was based on material from Australia, Hubert and Mauss's
study of sacrifice was based on Hebrew and Hindu texts. Ethnographic material of other regions was used only to determine whether
conclusions reached in the one area of intensive study had a more
general validity or what divergencies had to be accounted for. However 'laws' established on this basis were of dubious validity,
especially in Durkheim's case, since all divergences somehow always
turned out to be 'secondary variations' which could be easily
dismissed.

The work of Durkheim's disciples gives the clearest indications of
the contribution of French sociology to modern 'structuralism'.
Much of it was undertaken in response to problems which were
insoluble within Durkheim's framework. The most outstanding of
the group were Mauss, Hubert, Hertz, Bouglé and Fauconnet. They
were active in the years before the First World War, and published
their work, mostly in the form of monographs, in the annual *Année
Sociologique*, edited by Durkheim and Mauss. Much of their work
has a preliminary character, analyses of particular rites or customs
which were later to be integrated into general theories of religion,
magic or expiation.[9]

Unlike the 'Maître', their work was not hampered by an infinite
regression in explanation, and confusion between simple and elementary forms which had been implicit in Durkheim's evolutionism.
Mauss, for example, analysed primitive societies not because they
were earlier forms of life but because they exhibited phenomena in
relatively uncontaminated forms. The elementary could therefore
be just as complex as the developed forms. Mauss is quoted
(Lévi-Strauss, 1946, p. 527) as saying that 'it is easier to study the
digestive process in the oyster than in man; but this does not mean
that the higher vertebrates were formerly shell-fish'. Mauss's studies

27

of the gift, Eskimo social organization, sacrifice, magic rites and other topics are models of the attempt to reduce the complexity of data into more 'elementary structures'.

Durkheim's followers were also free of his increasingly pre-dominant conviction that society and individual are the only levels of analysis, that society is external to and above the individual, and the sociological determinism that this entails. This prevented him from examining levels intermediate between the individual and the totality and the various distinguishable spheres of social life, and his tendency to draw universal conclusions from a single case embodied a disdain for the analysis of ethnographic material.

Mauss, on the contrary, based his work on the realization that the social is composed of different elements: linguistic, symbolic, psychological, religious and so on. For him the totality is a foliated structure of interlinked layers intermediate between individual and society, each worthy of analysis in its own right. He took some of Durkheim's most interesting ideas, operationalized them and made them less rigid, at the same time bridging the chasm between theory and ethnographic investigation. Durkheim's notions of totality and social fact are transformed into Mauss's 'total social fact', a way of expressing the recognition that social activities such as gift exchange or sacrifice are significant on several planes (Lévi-Strauss, 1967c, p. 12):

> In the theory of the total social fact, the notion of totality is less important than the very special way in which Mauss conceived of it; foliated as it were and made up of a multitude of distinct yet connected planes. Instead of appearing as a postulate, the totality of society is manifested in experience . . . it does not suppress the specific character of phenomena, which remain at once judicial, economic, religious and even aesthetic or morphological, so that the totality consists finally of the network of functional interrelations among all these planes.

So, for example, in *The Gift* (1966), Mauss used two detailed ethno-graphic descriptions of primitive systems of ritual exchange (Malinowski's Trobriand kula and Boas's Kwakiutl potlatch) as the foundation for a broad generalization about the nature of social action. He examined the different types of exchange as examples of the larger structure of reciprocity; the 'gift' or material thing which passes between individuals expresses their relationship and helps maintain it since the recipient has to reciprocate as well as receive. The gift has significance on many levels (symbolic, individual and social) and in many of the spheres of social life (religious, economic, legal and moral).

Mauss, Hertz and Hubert eschewed Durkheim's aim to establish universal laws and attempted a different type of explanation which made the various facts intelligible by showing that their meaning lay in their interrelation rather than in taking each one singly. Individual facts were to be explained as parts of an integrated cultural complex (Lévi-Strauss, 1946, p. 538):

> The kind of relation he [Mauss] aims at discerning is never between two or more elements arbitrarily isolated from the culture, but between all the components; this is what he calls 'faits sociaux totaux'.

This approach approximates Evans-Pritchard's 'descriptive integration', and he has, in fact, been the greatest champion of the Année Sociologique school in Britain.[10]

Mauss's concern with the interrelation between phenomena and the obligation of the sociologist to confine himself to revealing meaning within the phenomena studied is admirably expressed in his definition of sociology in *La Grande Encyclopédie*, where he contrasts, for example, historical and sociological modes of explanation (Mauss and Fauconnet, 1887, p. 171):

> While historians describe facts without explaining them, sociology attempts to offer a satisfactory explanation. It seeks intelligible relationships between them, rather than temporal sequences. It attempts to demonstrate how social facts are produced and by which forces . . . and is not satisfied with general causes, which may be insufficient and only indirectly linked to the facts. As social facts are specific, they can be explained only by causes of the same nature as themselves. Sociological explanation thus links one social phenomenon with another, and establishes relationships only between social phenomena.

Mauss, unlike Durkheim, laid great stress on the synthetic aspect of sociological analysis; Durkheim's philosophical education was probably such that he considered a study complete when the phenomenon in question had been analysed into its simplest forms and these rearranged in an evolutionary series. Mauss, however, always attempted to resynthesize the analysed data into a totality, and argued that a sociological explanation should account for differences as well as correlations, a point also made by Lévi-Strauss.

A few examples may illustrate the methodological innovations of the Année Sociologique school. Hubert and Mauss analysed sacrifice in much the same way as Mauss had examined the gift. Hebrew and Hindu texts were the primary source of data though others are referred to in an attempt to demonstrate the unity of the sacrificial system. Sacrifice in general is defined (Hubert and Mauss, 1964, p. 13)

29

as 'a religious act, which, through the consecration of a victim, modifies the condition of the moral person who accomplishes it or that of a certain object with which he is concerned'. They proceed to analyse the scheme of sacrifice which applies to all empirical cases: the preparation of participants for a sacred act centring on the elimination of bodily imperfections, the attribution of sacredness to the victim and the means by which this is bestowed (mainly through purification again), the act of sacrifice itself, followed by the gradual dissolution of the sacred character conferred on the participants, again with the aid of specific rituals. Ritual actions result in a rising crescendo of sacredness, consummated in the killing of the victim, and which slowly declines again. They go on to discuss the various functions of sacrifice: sacralization (creating something sacred out of something initially neutral in the sacred-profane continuum), expiation, desacralization (for example, of the first fruits), and the various types of sacrifice: on behalf of persons, objects (such as in house building, agriculture) and the ultimate sacrifice—of the God. They conclude that there is not one single original sacrifice as previously thought (for example, by Robertson-Smith, but this would also have been Durkheim's conclusion), but (Hubert and Mauss, 1964, p. 95) 'of all the procedures of sacrifice, the most general, the least rich in particular elements, that we have been able to distinguish are those of sacralization and desacralization'. In this way they explain the data in terms of its underlying structure rather than its origins. Sacrifice is a unitary system though the diversity of ends that may be pursued account for variations in observed procedures (ibid., p. 97):

> But if sacrifice is so complex, whence comes its unity? It is because, fundamentally, beneath the diverse forms it takes, it always consists in one same procedure, which may be used for the most widely differing purposes. This procedure consists in establishing a means of communication between the sacred and profane worlds through the mediation of a victim, that is, of a thing that in the course of the ceremony is destroyed.

Many of the notions which underlie the study are Durkheimian: the distinction between sacred and profane and the emphasis on the psychological aspects of the ceremony and symbolism, but in method it departs significantly from Durkheim.

Robert Hertz's essays (1960) on death and on the pre-eminence of the right hand are also examples of the attempt to show that the meaning of observed facts lies in their interrelation. For instance, the double disposal of the dead cannot be understood without some knowledge of beliefs concerning the ghosts of the dead and the rules of mourning. Hertz discovers a pattern in three aspects of death (corpse, soul and mourners): they all express the idea of transition. On the basis of this, certain other facts concerning the dead in Indonesia, which Hertz took as his main example, become intelligible: why the death of rulers cannot be announced, and why the corpses of very young children and very old people are not accorded the same treatment as others. Comparisons can be made between mortuary rites and other *rites de passage*, such as initiation or marriage. Events which appeared incomprehensible when analysed separately were shown to be part of a meaningful whole. Again the method involves an appeal to abstract principles underlying observed activities.

In the other essay, Hertz suggests that the polarity between right and left in man symbolizes the widespread belief in the duality of all aspects of the universe, and natural and social life, where one pole is strong and good and the other weak and fallible (sacred versus profane again). The hands have become symbols of polarities in thought and values because the duality of the universe must be centred on man who is the centre.

To summarize, French sociology and anthropology did not define the term 'structure' in such a specific way as the British did. Nevertheless, the concept is present in a more abstract and philosophical form. Social structure is no longer the abstract form of observed social relations but resides in principles of operation underlying observed data, and governing relationships and procedures which may be observed. The Année Sociologique writers in particular focused on the variety of elements and levels of the social whole and their interrelationships. Their concern with 'getting behind the facts' reveals an awareness of the possible disparity between the actor's conscious model of the workings of society and the 'real' structure, of which there may be no conscious awareness, and this entails an attitude of suspicion towards apparent 'reality'. Thus, their ideas are pre-structuralist in relation to Lévi-Strauss's later definitions, both in method and substantive themes.

The use and meaning of structure in the work of Lévi-Strauss

The concept 'structure' is more difficult to analyse here than in the previous cases, since Lévi-Strauss uses the term at all levels of his work, from the minute dissections of individual myths to general philosophical speculations, and yet it is never satisfactorily defined. His style makes it all the more difficult since it is (often deliberately) ambiguous, and it requires a much more thorough reading to arrive at a definition of structure than was the case for Radcliffe-Brown or the Durkheimians. Even where 'structure' is defined, it is really more confusing than helpful as what he says he does and what he actually does are not in all cases the same.

Lévi-Strauss starts his long essay on 'Social Structure' (1968b) by pointing out that, for him, 'social structure' has more to do with models based on empirical reality than with empirical reality itself. As a model, it fulfils certain requirements (ibid., p. 280):

> First, the structure exhibits the characteristics of a system. It is made up of several elements, none of which can undergo a change without effecting changes in all the other elements. Second, for any given model there should be the possibility of ordering a series of transformations resulting in a group of models of the same type. Third, the above properties make it possible to predict how the model will react if one or more of the elements are submitted to certain modifications. Finally, the model should be constituted so as to make immediately intelligible all the observed facts.

He goes on to discuss several distinctions seminal to structural studies: observation and experimentation, conscious and unconscious models, structure and measure, and mechanical and statistical models, and to outline the various types of social structure: social morphology or group structure, communications structures, and the structure of structures. Throughout there is an emphasis on the analysis of social phenomena into their constituent elements and the theoretical reconstitution of these into a model which represents their working (ibid., p. 284).

> What makes social structure studies valuable is that structures are models, the formal properties of which can be compared independently of their elements. The structuralist's task is thus to recognize and isolate levels of reality which have strategic value from his point of view, namely, which admit of representations as models, whatever their type. It often happens that the same data may be considered from different perspectives embodying equally strategic values.

Social structure studies have a dual nature. First (ibid., p. 285) they:

> aim at isolating strategic levels, and this can be achieved only by 'carving out' a certain constellation of phenomena. From that point of view, each type of structural study appears autonomous, entirely independent of all others and even of different methodological approaches to the same field.

Second (ibid., p. 286) they

> construct models the formal properties of which can be

compared with and explained by the same properties as in models corresponding to other strategic levels.

This essay on social structure is one of the most misleading of Lévi-Strauss's writings. His definition is abstract, never illustrated by particular examples, and corresponds only vaguely with the notion of structure which emerges from his studies of specific topics. His approach is much better expressed in the method he outlines for the study of totemism (Lévi-Strauss, 1964c, p. 16):

The method we adopt, in this case as in others, consists in the following operations:
  (1) define the phenomenon under study as a relation between two or more terms, real or supposed;
  (2) construct a table of possible permutations between these terms;
  (3) take this table as the general object of analysis which, at this level only, can yield necessary connections, the empirical phenomenon considered at the beginning being only one possible combination among others, the complete system of which must be reconstructed beforehand.

Here the emphasis is on discovering the fundamental relations between the constituent elements of the phenomenon in question. There is no mention of models, and in any case the term model, customarily understood as a heuristic device for relating unobservables, is quite inappropriate to describe Lévi-Strauss's structures.[11]

In view of this, an attempt to define the meaning of 'structure' for Lévi-Strauss can only be based on the way it is in fact used in his work, and in spite of his explicit definitions. The best way to approach it is from an examination of the influences which he himself acknowledges. One of these is Morgan whom Lévi-Strauss claimed was the first 'structuralist'. He refers to Morgan whenever he wants to distinguish the origins of his approach from those of Radcliffe-Brown, and explains that Morgan's studies of kinship among the Iroquois were structuralist, although he used the term 'system' rather than 'structure'. Spencer introduced the term 'structure' but his work was certainly not structuralist (Bastide, 1962, p. 145).

In this way Lévi-Strauss distances himself from the origins of positivism in sociology. Marxism and Gestalt theories are also mentioned briefly in a list of influences. But there are several others which he does not acknowledge explicitly. Freud's discovery of the unconscious, and the distinction between the conscious and unconscious mind, are at the basis of Lévi-Strauss's insistence that the conscious models of society of social actors are often inaccurate and mask the actual social relations (Lévi-Strauss, 1968b, p. 281):

> When the structure of a certain type of phenomena does not lie at a great depth, it is more likely that some kind of model, standing as a screen to hide it, will exist in the collective consciousness . . . the more obvious structural organization is, the more difficult it becomes to reach it because of the inaccurate conscious models lying across the path which leads to it.

His study of the Bororo of Central Brazil shows the importance of looking beyond the actors' model of society. Anthropologists have taken the view that much of primitive life is organized in terms of a dual principle of symmetrical and reciprocal relations, and the Bororo seemed an ideal example ostensibly organized in this way. However, Lévi-Strauss discovered that the dual layout of the village and the image people had of its workings only helped to mask other principles, which were less egalitarian and on whose basis the society was in fact organized; in particular the distinct status of men and women and the subdivision of the moieties into four intermarrying clans, distinguished on the basis of wealth. Lévi-Strauss concluded that the real structure was triadic and asymmetrical and not dualistic at all. However, the various manifestations of dualism such as the spatial division into two groups and the apparent exogamy of these masked the actual hierarchy of the structure from the natives.[12] In this case, as in others, what Lévi-Strauss calls the 'structure' of the society are the underlying principles on which it operates, which are real though they may be unobservable and unconscious.

Another influence on Lévi-Strauss's concept of structure may be called 'geological'. He is concerned to differentiate the various layers existing in society, the levels at which it can be analysed, and the way these interlock to form a whole. He is always at pains to make clear the level to which he is referring (1968b, p. 312):

> The anthropologist considers the social fabric as a network of different types of orders. The kinship system provides a way to organize individuals according to certain rules; social organization is another way of ordering individuals and groups; social stratification, whether economic or political, provides us with a third type, and all these orders can themselves be ordered by showing the kinds of relationships which exist among them, how they interact with one another, on both the synchronic and diachronic levels.

This concern with distinguishing levels, elements and their spheres of relevance applies not just to the analysis of society in general but also to its various parts, including cultural products such as myth, art, and face painting. The analysis of the story of Asdiwal (1967b) is a good example of this. Lévi-Strauss distinguishes the different 'schemata' of the myth: geographical, cosmological, integrative and sociological, and analyses the way these interrelate with one another and with Tsimshian social life. He hopes in this way to achieve a total explanation of the myth, to show why each element occurs and what it means. The same is the case with the analysis of tote-mism, primitive classifications, and marriage regulations. The whole project rests on the assumption of a highly structured but knowable social reality.

A third influence, also evident in the essay on social structure, is that of communications theory and linguistics, both methodologi-cally and substantively. One of the paradigms for the type of detailed formal analysis that Lévi-Strauss undertakes is to be found in the structural linguistics of Saussure, and in Jakobson and the Prague school. Lévi-Strauss argues that the data of anthropology are of a quantity and complexity similar to those of linguistics and sus-ceptible of a similar treatment. Saussure's distinction between language and speech reappears, in altered form, in Lévi-Strauss's dictum that empirical cases are to be explained as manifestations of a pre-existing underlying structure. The analogy with language is also one of substance: social relationships are seen as communica-tions or exchanges of information. In his view there are three main types of communication in society, women, goods and services, and messages, and it is the anthropologist's job to analyse the structures within which these operate. It is not social relations between indi-viduals that should interest the anthropologist, but the impersonal principles on which these are based. Linguistics, economics and anthropology (Lévi-Strauss, 1968b, p. 298):

> consist exclusively of the study of rules and have little concern with the nature of the partners (individuals or groups) whose play is being patterned after these rules . . . what is important is to find out when a given player can make a choice and when he cannot.

The communication orientation thus provides anthropology with a unifying concept. The concern with assimilating different types of data and constructing relations of transformation between them is one of the major preoccupations of Lévi-Strauss's structuralism. It also results in a more interdisciplinary approach than was the case for the British or French sociologists. The ultimate aim of Lévi-Strauss's linguistic orientation is (ibid., p. 301) 'to reach a depth where social structure is put on a level with other types of mental structure, particularly the linguistic one'. These influences clarify, to some extent, the orientation of the 'Social Structure' essay, yet, taken in isolation it still remains an extremely misleading text. The specific nature of his approach is best seen in contrast to earlier French and British anthropology.

Unlike the earlier French anthropologists, Lévi-Strauss uses the term 'structure' all the time. Nevertheless, from a certain point of view, his use of the concept appears simply as a logical extension of the type of analysis inaugurated by Mauss and the Année Sociologique school. Like them he starts with data about similar institutions or cultural products from several societies, dissects them into their constituent elements with the aim of establishing their fundamental relations, so that characteristics general to several societies can be revealed from a small number of cases. However, he goes further than Mauss in 'foliating' social phenomena, in approaching the dissection with more formalistic precision and in attempting to reach universal characteristics of a more general nature which pertain to the human mind rather than to the solution of particular social problems. For example, he argues that totemism is but one specialized variety of a universal human activity, the classification of social phenomena by non-social means, and, when examined in this perspective, caste systems can be seen as logical inversions of totemic groups (1966b, chap. 4). Totemic groups are based on the postulate of homology between the relationship of natural to human groups so that Clan 1 is to Clan 2 as bear is to eagle. Caste societies apply the homology to the terms rather than to the relations between them so that Clan 1 *is* bear and Clan 2 *is* eagle. In the first case, social groups are distinct but parts of a whole; in the second, the diversity between social groups is all important, and it becomes difficult to maintain links with the other groups. In this way, data and types of society previously thought incomparable and quite distinct, from a comparative or evolutionary point of view, are seen to be logically related.

To a greater extent than the Année Sociologique school, Lévi-Strauss is concerned both with the detailed analysis of particular cases and with the universal properties inherent in them. The different empirical instances of similar activities found in different societies are conceived as variations of one another such that, by a mathematical or logical operation, one can be seen as the transformation of another. The structure is what unites these various instances: it is the syntax of transformations which pass from one variant to another and is known as the 'combinatory'. To take the musical analogy, of which Lévi-Strauss is so fond, empirical cases of, say, a particular type of marriage regulation or a particular myth are variations on a theme and the structure is the underlying theme although it may never be manifested in a pure form. All the theoretically possible variants are rarely realized in practice, but a consideration of them permits the definition of their common underlying structure.

Thus Lévi-Strauss is less concerned than Radcliffe-Brown with determining the actual social organization of particular societies, and more with the manner of arrangement. He recognizes the possibility of several modes of arrangement of the same activity or function, as did Mauss, and attempts to establish relations which give to the terms they unite a position in an organized whole. To Lévi-Strauss an organization is a combination of elements intelligible only when its internal arrangement can be seen as one amongst others. This is how distinct social phenomena, such as totem and caste, can be shown to be closely related on a formal level, and structural possibilities can be visualized even if they do not exist empirically. Lévi-Strauss argues, as does Leach in his critique of orthodox structural anthropology, that the features of totality and interdependence that characterize anthropological data necessitate an analytic rather than a classificatory approach. Hence Lévi-Strauss's opposition (1967c, p. 21) to the comparative method as used by Radcliffe-Brown.

Lévi-Strauss's conception of structure differs from that of traditional anthropology, and often appears to the latter as more akin to speculative philosophy than anthropology (see e.g. Leach, 1961b and Forge, 1967). According to Lévi-Strauss the determinant relations constituting 'structure' are unlikely to be immediately observable; hence his assumption that anthropological propositions rest on theoretical statements rather than empirical generalizations. He is always very careful to emphasize that anthropology rests on two distinct stages of study, the first of which consists in the observation of social relations, and the second in theoretical statements about the structural properties inherent in these (Lévi-Strauss, 1968b, p. 280):

> Many discussions on social structure revolve around the apparent contradiction between the concreteness and individuality of ethnological data and the abstract and formal character generally exhibited by structural studies. This contradiction disappears as one comes to realize that these features belong to two entirely different levels, or rather to two stages of the same process.

Thus what we read in Lévi-Strauss's treatises about structures are not accounts of observations made in the field but second order theorizations, so to speak, made on the basis of such raw material. Meticulous observation can be the only sound basis for his type of analysis and hence his sympathy with the difficulties of the fieldworker overcome by the strangeness of native life. Lévi-Strauss's criticism of empiricism is directed not against ethnographers but against those who tend to confuse the two distinct stages of analysis.

For example, Radcliffe-Brown confused social relations with structure by taking what he saw 'on the ground' as equivalent to its fundamental constituent properties. Lévi-Strauss associates this misconception with Radcliffe-Brown's inductive view of science and his ambitions for anthropology on this model, described above. Thus, many of the controversies between Radcliffe-Brown and Lévi-Strauss over the interpretation of particular data have a more than substantive interest, for example their opposed definitions of the kinship unit. Radcliffe-Brown defined it thus (quoted in Lévi-Strauss, 1968a, p. 51):

> The unit of structure from which a kinship is built up is the group which I call an 'elementary family', consisting of a man and his wife and their child or children. . . . The existence of the elementary family creates three special kinds of social relationship, that between parent and child, that between children of the same parents (siblings), and that between husband and wife as parents of the same child or children. . . . These three relationships that exist within the elementary family constitute what I call the first order. Relationships of the second order are those which depend on the connection of two elementary families through a common member, and are such as father's father, mother's brother, wife's sister and so on.

Lévi-Strauss is critical of this definition partly because Radcliffe-Brown treats the biological family as the elementary unit, while for him kinship systems are arbitrary systems of representation existing in the human consciousness. In addition, Radcliffe-Brown treats relations which Lévi-Strauss considers as first order, as secondary and derived. For example, the mother's brother is a necessary constituent element in Lévi-Strauss's definition of the basic unit of kinship. But the difference is more one of theoretical explanation: Radcliffe-Brown's 'theoretical' reflections on the facts of kinship result in an empirical definition of the elementary unit based on the observation of what appear to be basic attributes of the family. In this sense, he is influenced by the ubiquity of the biological family, and his concentration on immediate biological ties results in an acritical nominal definition. Nowhere does he attempt to penetrate given biological reality to see if the apparently irreducible substratum of kinship ties is illusory.

The discussion between Radcliffe-Brown and Lévi-Strauss on the avuncular is of similar methodological interest. Radcliffe-Brown was the first to account sociologically for the relationship between mother's brother and sister's son. He argued that the relationship takes two forms: in the first, the maternal uncle has authority over his sister's son and certain parental rights and obligation in respect of him, and this is correlated with a relationship of familiarity with the father. In the other form, the reverse obtains: the son fears and respects his father who has familial authority, while the relation to the maternal uncle is one of warmth and familiarity. Radcliffe-Brown accounts for these differences in terms of the type of descent system: in patrilineal societies where authority is vested in the father's descent group, the father has authority, and in matrilineal societies the uncle assumes authority in relation to his sister's offspring.[13] Lévi-Strauss proposes an alternative explanation on the grounds that Radcliffe-Brown has isolated only two elements of a 'global structure' which presupposes four terms: brother (uncle), sister (mother), nephew (son), brother-in-law (father). The correlation between the forms of avunculate and descent types does not always hold and Lévi-Strauss claims that, regardless of the mode of descent, if all four terms of the relational system were taken into account, an organic connexion exists between the four fundamental types of relation within it: brother and sister, husband and wife, father and son, and mother's brother and sister's son, such that, if one pair of relations is known, it is possible to infer the forms of the others. For Lévi-Strauss this group of four is the most elementary kinship unit and any kinship unit must presuppose this irreducible structure of first order relationships (1968b, p. 46): 'The presence of the maternal uncle is a necessary precondition for the (elementary kinship) structure to exist: The error of traditional anthropology was to consider the terms and not the relations between the terms.' In Lévi-Strauss's definition, the maternal uncle is essential because of the universal existence of the incest taboo which, sociologically, means that a man must obtain a woman from another man outside his immediate kinship group.

Thus whereas Radcliffe-Brown begins and ends with the mother's brother/sister's son relationship, and attempts to relate regularities in its forms with other empirical regularities, notably the mode of descent, Lévi-Strauss takes the analysis to a different level. He tries to locate the avuncular relationship in an integral structure whose elements are empirically manifest and hence open to observation, but which do not appear as systematically related. Organic connexions can be shown to exist between them but only by going beyond observable patterns.

Lévi-Strauss thus agrees with Marx that scientific analysis would be superfluous if the phenomenal appearance and the essence of things coincided. We can see now more clearly why he rejects Radcliffe-Brown's distinction between structure and structural form. 'Structure' for Radcliffe-Brown is what Lévi-Strauss considers observable and calls 'social relations', and 'structural form' is of dubious theoretical value: as abstraction from relatively permanent social relations it can only formalize manifest properties and is incapable of disclosing their inner 'structure'. Thus Radcliffe-Brown is criticized for theorizing too soon, and for being dominated by observed impressions. For Lévi-Strauss, traditional anthropology as a whole has been subverted by a methodology which assumes that reality is a property of the observable. What is 'real' for traditional anthropology is at best a clue to the underlying structure brought into theoretical consciousness by Lévi-Strauss's type of structuralism. So, for Lévi-Strauss, structural analysis consists in reducing a given phenomenon in social or cultural anthropology to its fundamental properties, and examining these along with other examples as variants of a more inclusive and general 'structure'. The 'structure', or 'combinatory', is not empirically given, nor amenable to observation, and it is held to have a real existence. The word 'structure' is used confusingly by Lévi-Strauss to refer both to the detailed relationships within a specific phenomenon and to the general case of which they are one example, so that it is both the formal relations of particular variants and the 'syntax of transformations'.[14]

Both Radcliffe-Brown and Durkheim are forerunners of Lévi-Strauss's approach and he acknowledges his debt to them. The differences between them are briefly the following: Lévi-Strauss continues the path laid by Mauss and his colleagues in reaction to Durkheim's sociologism and quest for totalizing syntheses, in paying attention to the distinct spheres of social life and search for principles underlying apparently disparate events. Lévi-Strauss and Radcliffe-Brown differ in important respects: one derives his structuralism from Morgan and the 'systematic' approach, the other from Spencerian naturalism; Radcliffe-Brown pays attention to individuals, concrete social relations and the visible workings of social organization, Lévi-Strauss to principles of organization which are not visible and often unconscious; the concept of structure in the one case refers to empirically given social relations or abstractions based on them, and in the other to general principles of organization only manifested through empirical phenomena. Most important, they have different conceptions of what constitutes 'reality'.

Lévi-Strauss's idea of structure raises many problems: what is the difference between models and structures? In what sense do structures 'exist'? Do they really lie 'behind' appearances as behind a curtain? Do they imply a psychological universalism? I shall examine these questions in later chapters, but first I shall consider other contemporary uses and meanings of 'structure'.

Other contemporary uses of structure

Structure has become a central concept in several disciplines in recent years, among them Marxism, psychoanalysis and semiology.

Marxism

In the interpretation of Marx by Althusser, Balibar, Godelier and others, historical materialism is viewed as a theory of 'structures' based on certain fundamental concepts such as forces of production, relations of production, economic base, political and ideological superstructures. These are related in a complex manner in any given social formation. History is the development of structures and their transformation. In *Capital*, Marx analysed the preconditions and the consequences of the interplay of these relations and illustrated his argument from the history of the English economy. The 'structure' was formulated in terms of the concepts of labour power, socially necessary labour time, surplus value and others which were the reality of the capitalist mode of production in the sense of being the underlying principles necessary to the perpetuation of the system. It is constantly emphasized that these realities are not observable but had to be reached by theoretical discovery. It is in this that the scientific nature of Marx's approach resides. Marx emphasized that the scientific description of society cannot rely on immediate observations, and that conscious models of the working of society were often discrepant with the reality. For instance, in the analysis of capitalist exploitation, Marx argued that value is created by labour, and that profit is that part of value (surplus value) not returned to the worker. Yet at the most immediate level, wages are seen, both by workers and capitalists, as payment for work done, and profit is seen as the product of capital rather than unpaid labour. This illusory conception is caused by a structure that mystifies social relations: capitalism relates men to each other not directly but through the commodities they exchange; the social relation between men 'assumes, in their eyes, the fantastic form of a relation between things'. (Marx, 1951, I, p. 72.) With feudalism, exploitation, in Marx's sense of extraction from the product of labour, is immediate; the peasant pays dues directly to the lord. Under capitalism, exploitation is just as prevalent but not in such an immediate form.

Thus Marx, like Lévi-Strauss, probes beneath surface phenomena in an attempt to discover the structures which underlie social relations. It is necessary to work through what seems to be given fact both because reality is not as simple as it appears and because of the inadequacy of the concepts of the social actors.

The Althusserians emphasize that, in any case, the type of knowledge that science aspires to cannot be based on observation. For Marx, the economic system is not perceivable as such but only through other levels of society. However, this does not detract from its efficacy. Surplus value, for example, expresses capitalist relations of production but it is a concept and measurable only in its effects:

prices, profit, and rent. However meticulous the scrutiny of such economic facts, the structure is not to be found by observation.

Marx also has a 'geological' approach to social formations: they are composed of several interlocking layers, each relatively autonomous and to be studied in its own right. However the fundamental elements constitutive of a mode of production are not peculiar to a particular social formation but, like Lévi-Strauss's 'syntax of transformations', are considered as the explanatory principles of several modes. Thus different modes of production are seen as specific combinations of the different elements necessary to all production. The Althusserians call this a 'combinaison articulée' (articulated combination), a system of five elements which coexist and define themselves reciprocally. They are labour force, means of production, non-worker appropriating the surplus, the process of production and property relations. These five are necessary to any mode of production and each is a result of a different combination of these. Marx's attention to the various modes of articulation between these elements approximates to Lévi-Strauss's consideration of structural variations.

Freud

Freud's work has recently been reinterpreted by Lacan, Lagache and others in much the same way as was Marx's. Both are credited with having discovered the underlying principles of operation, the structure, of observed phenomena. In both cases what was discovered, the mode of production and the unconscious, was not amenable to the senses, and had to be theoretically produced for the scientific understanding of social or psychic life. Much of the reinterpretation of Freud is influenced by structural linguistics.

The essential point is that Freud established the unconscious as an autonomous sphere, irreducible to other levels, and which explained certain observed characteristics obviously issuing from the 'mind' (Freud, 1933, p. 88): ' "Unconscious" is no longer a term for what is temporarily latent: the unconscious is a special realm with its own desires, and modes of expression, and peculiar mental mechanisms not elsewhere operative.' He was adamant that mental processes could not be accounted for in terms of any analogous processes existing in other fields than the mind, and that the unconscious was a real structure. He upheld a realist as opposed to instrumental view of science in *The New Introductory Lectures on Psychoanalysis*, where he stressed that the importance of psychoanalysis lay in the knowledge it offered of the human mind, rather than in its therapeutic use. The search for underlying principles brought with it a widening perspective and showed that dreams, neurosis and psychosis, for instance, previously thought to be manifestations of 'normal' and 'pathological' mental life are expressions of the same thought process operating at different strengths, and all to be seen as withdrawals from the external world. They could be comprehended adequately only when shown to be the same—a feature similar to Lévi-Strauss's analysis of very different phenomena under the same heading. Freud explained these apparently different states by introducing the concept of 'superego'.

Freud's approach to the structure of the mind was highly analytic: he attempted to isolate all the separate levels and elements of which it was composed and show how these interacted. He distinguished at least two series existing in the mind: the id, ego and superego which are regions of the mind, and the unconscious, preconscious and conscious which are qualities rather than mental provinces. Any psychic structure represents a compromise formation between the multitude of conflicts and contradictions existing at the structural level between id, ego and superego fought out over time. The exact nature of the compromises and repressions is discernible only at the level of the consciousness series.

Lacan's novel claim is that the only way to approach the unconscious is through language: the structures of the mind take shape gradually with the acquisition of language. We learn, not through experience but through language: the child learns that fire burns not by touching it but by being told so. The unconscious can be revealed through language, but this realizes only a small number of the combinations possible from its elements. Psychoanalysis explains the breakdown of the psychic structure and attempts a cure through the medium of language.

Barthes

The study of cultural products is another field in which the analysis of 'structures' has recently become a major preoccupation. This is most clearly expressed in Barthes' project for semiology, the science of signs. In *Elements of Semiology* (1967e), he attempts to extract from linguistics a set of adequate analytical concepts for the study of sign-systems. These include the distinction between language and speech, signifier and signified, and syntagm and system which are applied to the Highway Code, food, fashion and cars. In all his work Barthes attempts to reduce the customary distinction between art and art analysis, and he characterizes structuralist activity as creating a representation of the phenomenon under study through a de- and recomposition of its elements (see 1966b, p. 12):

The aim of all structuralist activity, in the fields of both thought and poetry, is to reconstitute an 'object', and, by this process, to make known the rules of functioning, or 'functions', of this object. The structure is therefore effectively a representation (simulacre) of the object, but it is a representation that is both purposeful and relevant, since the object derived by imitation brings out something that remained invisible, or, if you like, unintelligible, in the natural object.

Here again we get the concern with reaching the inner structure of elements by a formal analysis. In this sense, there is no difference between the scholar-analyst and the artist since both work to produce something, whether the primary object to be represented is found in social reality or in the imagination; it is not the nature of the object that defines art but what man supplies in reconstituting it (ibid., p. 12):

> When Troubetzkoi reconstructs the phonetic object in the form of a system of variations, . . . when Propp constructs the form of the folktale from all the Slav tales he has already decomposed, when Claude Lévi-Strauss discerns the homologic functioning of totemic imagination . . . when J-P Richard divides the Mallarmé poem into its distinctive vibrations, they are in fact doing what Mondrian, Boulez or Butor do, when they set up a particular object, to be known precisely as a composition, through the orderly display of certain units and certain associations of these units.

We could examine the use of 'structure' almost *ad infinitum*. Examples from Saussurean linguistics, Russian formalism, Propp's folktale analysis, Piaget's genetic structuralism in psychology, Foucault's work on madness and the history of ideas, Chomsky's study of transformational grammar, Bachelard's and Canguilhem's approach to the philosophy of science—all these utilize the notion of structure in a way similar to Lévi-Strauss and those just examined. However the essential features of this approach are apparent from the work of Marx, Freud, and Barthes and on the basis of these we may attempt to answer the question posed at the outset: are there distinct varieties of structuralism?

Conclusion

The general approach outlined for Lévi-Strauss, Marx, Freud and Barthes reveals striking resemblances despite the variety of subject matter. For all, 'structure' is a basic theoretical concept whether or not explicitly recognized as such, used to isolate principles underlying observed phenomena. It is, in all cases, their basic tool and often rests on an analogy with linguistics and the systematic approach it embodies. They all attempt to delve beyond appearance to structural determinants. Thus 'structure' refers not to observed social relations but to a more abstract level of reality, and is the syntax of transformations which is present only in its manifestations but can never be observed as such in itself. They all analyse social or psychic phenomena into their detailed constituent elements and parts, and aim to establish the type and range of possible relations between two or more series of phenomena. 'Structure' is the relational system latent in an object and so it may be found in very varied objects. This tends to break down interdisciplinary barriers as we have seen.

These features constitute a distinct use and meaning of the term 'structure', which distinguish it from the way it has been used in mainstream anthropology and sociology. For Radcliffe-Brown and most of social anthropology, and for Durkheim, 'structure' was not such a crucial concept. They are not so self-conscious or explicit about its theoretical importance. Structure was a way of formalizing observed social relations and did not refer to a more abstract notion of reality. Nor was such attention paid to the complexity of possible relations between a given number of terms. Based on an analogy with biology, social structure was of the same order of abstraction as the anatomy of the organism.

We may thus conclude that there are two distinct conceptions of 'structure' current in the social sciences, best exemplified by Radcliffe-Brown and Lévi-Strauss. Both use the term 'structure' but denoting different systems of ideas. However, this does not mean that they have nothing in common, nor that some authors are not intermediary between the two. Leach's conception of structure, for example, is in many ways intermediate between the two ideal-type systems of ideas.

All the definitions examined in this chapter have certain features in common. They presuppose that social life has a patterned character; they assume that phenomena are explicable synchronically, and that a structural account is as valid as an historical one. So 'structure' refers to the permanent and non-individual characteristics of society, the arrangement of social relations which as a whole constitutes the skeleton of society, and is the only means by which a specifically sociological approach can be achieved. Lévi-Strauss and Marx however take for granted the analysis of social relations, and try to see if there are more abstract principles governing the organization of social relations. Hence, their 'structure' is of a quite different level. The difference is that between a 'structural' and 'structuralist' approach to the analysis of social reality.

Some of the differences between the two major groups are not surprising: while the former concentrated on analysing particular problems, based on fieldwork, and developing theory in an empirical fashion as they went along or using ideas already developed in other disciplines, the latter have to a greater extent concentrated on drawing out the methodological and epistemological problems associated with the study of social phenomena, and on elaborating a specific method prior to embarking on substantive work.

The 'structural' and 'structuralist' approaches are to be distinguished primarily by their epistemology and methodology. The former is explicitly empiricist, the latter anti-empiricist. However these are very broad categories. Just as there are differences between structural anthropologists, so there are important differences within the 'structuralist' camps, as the comparison of Lévi-Strauss with Althusser will attempt to show.

3 Claude Lévi-Strauss

Introduction

Claude Lévi-Strauss uses studies of kinship structure, primitive classification and myth as the basis for hypotheses about the nature of the human mind, the meaning of history and the philosophy of the social sciences.

In this chapter I shall attempt a critical exposition of the major themes of his work, including a genealogy of the elements of his thought and an examination of the various sources that have influenced him; this will be followed by a discussion of the main themes that guide his research and the problems they raise, in particular the degree to which they imply an 'idealist' or 'psychological reductionist' perspective. Then in chapter six the various levels which comprise Lévi-Strauss's system of ideas will be compared with that of Althusser.

Lévi-Strauss tries to make a reading of his work as difficult for the reader as the deciphering of myth was for himself, yet he does not explain this. He uses a literary, poetic and musical style, full of ambiguities, double meanings and plays on words, which leads the English reader, in particular, to assume that this is merely the idiosyncrasy of an arrogant intellectual trying to confuse rather than clarify issues. Yet, from Lévi-Strauss's point of view there are very good reasons for this style: pursuing his structural approach to its logical conclusion, he applies his method of analysis to his mode of presentation. This means that the reader has to discover the structure of Lévi-Strauss's thought, and since the meaning of his writing does not necessarily reside in the chronological succession of words and chapters, the reader has to undertake what Althusser calls a 'lecture symptomâle', trying to fit together the various threads and themes so as to discover their underlying relationship. What appears in

Mythologiques (1964b, 1966a, 1968a, 1971), for example, to be more or less haphazard layout is in fact a carefully planned scheme which Lévi-Strauss says (1967d) took twenty years to perfect. Lévi-Strauss's training in linguistics and familiarity with poetry such as that of Mallarmé and Char leads him to use words and chains of words which are capable of conveying more than one meaning, each of which is relevant to the object of study. In this connexion, he is obviously influenced by surrealism—a debt he acknowledges (1967e) and particularly by its preoccupation with finding sense 'under the nonsense' and conveying the essential ambiguity of meanings or levels of signification inherent in what is being examined.

Lévi-Strauss makes clear that the literary aspect of his writing is functional rather than decorative, a means of making the method of analysis and mode of presentation compatible with the object of study. The various 'languages' he employs—mathematical, linguistic, poetic—relate to the relative precision of knowledge about what is being studied and the level of formalization that has been achieved. The reader is expected to 'work' at reading his books, since the jigsaw nature of the writing is in fact a carefully thought-out strategy for particular intellectual purposes.

The nature of Lévi-Strauss's writing, the variety of sources on which his theories are based, and the far-reaching philosophical implications of his research make his work of interest generally, not just to anthropologists. Leach (1970, pp. 19–20) distinguishes between the anthropologist as celebrity and as 'scholar-analyst', epitomized by Malinowski and Lévi-Strauss respectively. Yet, Lévi-Strauss seems to encompass both roles, or at least is treated as if he did. During the 1960s he steadily achieved a certain celebrity among the French intelligentsia as the 'founder' of structuralism, which itself has become fashionable, and vast numbers of journals and literary newspapers devoted issues to him. In fact, this fame has more to do with the way thought and ideas become objects of consumption in France, in a way quite unknown in Britain, than with any behaviour on his part. The way Lévi-Strauss's ideas have been received into French intellectual and Anglo-American academic life could be the subject of a thesis in itself. British anthropologists tend to think of him somewhat as a *bête noir*, and as a celebrity rather than conforming to their conception of an anthropologist; yet much of his untranslated work takes the form of straightforward reports or evaluations of fieldwork, accounts of developments in dating techniques or other anthropological methods, interventions at conferences on detailed empirical questions, and so on. In fact, as Leach says, he has always confined himself to being a 'scholar-analyst', and any account of the impact of his ideas would have to distinguish between Lévi-Strauss, professor at the Collège de

France, respected, but not always accepted, by his colleagues, and Lévi-Strauss fulfilling the role of object of consumption by the French avant-garde, much as Sartre and the existentialists did for a previous generation. This celebrity is rather paradoxical in view of his style of work and the lack of prestige and resources generally accorded to social anthropology. Just as the function he fulfils has much to do with the history and structure of French intellectual life, so also the passions aroused by his work among his colleagues and philosophers such as Goldmann and Sartre are often more interesting for what they reveal about the authors themselves than for what they tell us about Lévi-Strauss.

Genealogy

It would be possible to take almost any of Lévi-Strauss's theories or principles of method—such as the concept of structure, the necessity of demystifying apparent reality, social interaction as communication—and trace it back to the ideas of some previous thinker, Gestalt psychology, Marx, linguistics. The sources of his thought are many and varied, ranging from geology and linguistics to psychoanalysis and information theory, but the use made of these is anything but eclectic. They fuse to a synthetic unity to which Lévi-Strauss himself has contributed the major part. I shall return to this point at the end of the section.

Lévi-Strauss has had contact with several disciplines other than anthropology. He studied law and philosophy, but early on rejected these in the search for a subject which would take the 'whole human experience' as its field, not just a few forms of thought. His interest in psychology and linguistics also dates from his student days. He spent most of the Second World War in New York at the New School for Social Research where he became acquainted not only with American anthropology (he mentions particularly Lowie, Kroeber and Boas), but also with information theory and with Prague linguistics under the influence of Roman Jakobson.[1]

Anthropology, history, etc.

In the last chapter, I examined Lévi-Strauss's debt to his anthropological predecessors; from Radcliffe-Brown, he inherited a concern with social structure and discovering the skeleton of a society and its principles of operation, which could be analysed independently from functions and history. This entailed a much greater attention to ethnological data than was customary in French anthropology, and Lévi-Strauss's own experience of field work, meagre though it is, represents a major concession to the Anglo-American approach.

Morgan is credited with being the first to analyse kinship terminology as a systematic cultural product. The notion of structure as used by Lévi-Strauss already existed in an undeveloped form in the work of the Année Sociologique school, especially Mauss. Lévi-Strauss rejects Durkheim's evolutionism and social reductionism: whereas for Durkheim society was primarily a moral universe and individual life meaningful only in relation to society as a whole, for Lévi-Strauss 'society' in this sense is an abstraction or residue—his interest being in the specific mechanisms by which goods, women and words are exchanged in particular societies and with general modes of conceptualization. It is the 'structures' of kinship rules or classification which are 'coercive' in Durkheim's sense, and not society as such.

However, the major foci of Lévi-Strauss's anthropology are taken from the French school; for example the interest in the relationship between individual and society, but Lévi-Strauss, following Mauss, pays most attention to the intermediary levels. He inherits the concern of Durkheim, Lévy-Bruhl and others with primitive classification and modes of conceptualization, but with a different orientation; whereas Durkheim tended to reduce the categories of time, space and so on to reflections of the geographical layout of the village or to the division of the year into seasons in accordance with the occurrence of religious festivals, Lévi-Strauss is more interested to discover universal features of abstract thought which are common to all men. Like Durkheim and Mauss, Lévi-Strauss is suspicious of facts as self-explanatory, and is never satisfied with an explanation unless it integrate particular empirical findings into wider categories which are not confined to any one social group.

From the 1920s, the relationship between thought and language, particularly in ancient or primitive societies, and the structural similarity between different religions have occupied French historians outside the Année Sociologique school. Given the fluid boundaries between academic disciplines, it is not surprising that Lévi-Strauss has transferred some of these themes to the field of anthropology proper. Marcel Granet (1920), for example, attempted a reconstruction of the basic concepts of ancient Chinese thought on the basis of some hitherto untranslated texts. These texts turned out to be songs sung at feasts, which became meaningless as customs changed, and were later thought to be wise sayings. He concluded from an analysis of the vocabulary that Chinese concepts were concrete and expressed particular synthetic images and that written words were phonetic rather than graphic. His hypothesis that speech and writing reflected pictorial images almost exactly was confirmed by the peculiar syntax which lacked anything corresponding to verbs, subjects or predicates, and did not differentiate between active and passive mood. He concluded that syntax never developed more than a purely rhythmical function since each word was tied to an ideogram. The Chinese language was essentially a means of pictorial expression and this prevented the enrichment of both its grammar and vocabulary. This sort of approach, with its interest in the parallel structure of thought and language, is a clear forerunner of Lévi-Strauss's interest in categorization, systems of naming and multiplicity of linguistic structures.

The work of Georges Dumézil has a more direct thematic relevance. Dumézil is a classicist and historian, and a professor of comparative religion whose works centre on isolating the common 'ideological structure' of much Indo-European thought, and, by comparative analysis, demonstrating its importance on the mythological, ritual, cosmological and social planes. For him, all religion is 'system' and he argues that there are great similarities between the gods, cults, myths and ritual observances of various parts of the ancient world, particularly Indian and Roman, but also German and Scandinavian. His study of Latin and Vedic texts suggests that in both cases it was the gods' role to ensure the performance of three functions: magical and judicial sovereignty, physical prowess, and fertility. Comparative analysis thus reveals an underlying structure common to the most ancient forms of these religions. The distinction between these three functions is to be found also in the social structure and in rites, Indian society being divided ideally into castes on this basis, and the oldest evidence of Greek and Roman society also indicates the division of society into priests, warriors, and farmers and artisans.

The method Dumézil uses in *Déesses latines et mythes védiques* (1956) to compare the Latin and Vedic 'svouetaurilia' and 'santramani', and 'Forcidia' and sacrifice of 'astapadi' is quasi Lévi-Straussian. He starts by showing that philological and archaeological evidence are insufficient to explain a Roman or Latin god. Then he turns to a better documented god or homologous mythical structure in Vedic India, and realizing that the divine function of a person is extremely rare, and mathematically 'improbable', develops the hypothesis of an Indo-European prototype to explain both cases. Dumézil thus starts from the conviction that the characters and functions attributed to divine beings cannot be understood as isolated cases, and ends up by postulating a prototype which does not exist empirically but relates all known cases to each other. This is very similar to Propp's analysis of Russian folk tales, or Lévi-Strauss's dissection of the various Oedipus myths. In all cases, the question of structural similarity precedes that of origins and of empirical historical relationship between the various examples.

E

He insists that only a group of facts or 'structure' has meaning, and that there are similarities of conceptual thought and social structure throughout the ancient world. Before a structure can be isolated, it is necessary to prove the homologous functioning of the five sectors of the religious system: concepts, myths, rites, social divisions, and priests. Lévi-Strauss takes this a step further in seeking relations between social and conceptual systems based on relations more complex than homology: inversion and various other forms of transformation. For Dumézil 'structure' really means 'structural elements' since there is little attempt to integrate the sectors into a whole, and it is this orientation that Lévi-Strauss takes over from him. Dumézil, like Lévi-Strauss, conceives of the human mind as organizing, conceptual and systematic having an active force on civilizations throughout history.

'Mes trois maîtresses'

In *Tristes Tropiques*, Lévi-Strauss describes geology, psychoanalysis and Marxism as his 'three mistresses', making clear that his debt to them is primarily methodological since they all discover fundamental properties and show that 'true' reality is not necessarily the most apparent. His early fascination with geology seems to have remained a constant inspiration whenever it is a question of coming to terms with the relationship between very ancient or primitive, and contemporary societies. He describes a landscape where very old and quite recent rocks may be found superimposed on each other (1961, p. 61):

> Sometimes . . . on one side and the other of a hidden crevice we find two green plants of different species. Each has chosen the soil which suits it: and we realize that within the rock are two ammonites, one of which has involutions less complex than the other's. We glimpse that is to say a difference of many thousands of years: time and space suddenly commingle; the living diversity of that moment juxtaposes one age and the other and perpetuates them.

The theories of Freud became known in France in the 1920s at the time Lévi-Strauss was rejecting the static antinomies of academic philosophy, and its overriding interest in the rational and non-rational. Psychoanalysis seemed to him more fruitful as it showed that there was meaning beyond the rational and irrational, and like linguistics it concerned itself with signification and meaning. Psychoanalysis seemed to apply the methods of geology to the individual (Lévi-Strauss, 1955, p. 49): 'In contrast to historians' history, geological history, like psychoanalysis, attempts to follow through time . . . certain fundamental properties of the physical or psychic universe'. There was nothing arbitrary or contingent in the order Freud brought to a seemingly incoherent collection of facts, and methodologically the use of 'structure' as an organizing and explanatory concept for Lévi-Strauss has much in common with Freud's use of the unconscious. At another level, Lévi-Strauss's approach is immensely influenced by Freud's discovery of the unconscious dimension of reality—with his constant seeking for the unconscious structure underlying conscious reality.

As Lévi-Strauss conceives it, his debt to Marx is primarily methodological: Marx realized that science was no more based on events than physics is on sense perceptions, and attempted to construct and test conceptual models. In fact all three 'mistresses' seemed to proceed in the same way (ibid., p. 61):

> All three showed that understanding consists in the reduction
> of one type of reality to another; that true reality is never the
> most objective of realities, and that its nature is already apparent
> in the care which it takes to evade our detection. In all cases the
> problem is the same: the relation, that is to say, between reason
> and sense-perception; and the goal we are looking for is also
> the same: a sort of super-rationalism in which sense-
> perceptions will be integrated into reasoning and yet lose none
> of their properties.

However, there is more to Lévi-Strauss's relation to Marxism than this. Indeed it is significant that at a time when most Western European intellectuals were drawing attention to the humanistic aspects of the early Marx, Lévi-Strauss was struck by the rigorous and scientific characteristics of his later work,[2] where there is little trace of idealism or Hegelianism, and where Marx argues that, within limits, the various superstructures of the social formation possess a relative autonomy. Lévi-Strauss considers his own work complementary to that of Marx by providing the theory of superstructures which Marx did not have time to develop, and showing the convergences and divergencies between infrastructure and superstructure. He describes himself as a superstructuralist in relation to Marx as a structuralist (1966b, p. 130):

> Without questioning the undoubted supremacy of infrastructures,
> I believe there is always a mediator between praxis and practices,
> namely the conceptual system by the operation of which matter
> and form, neither with any independent existence, are realized
> as structures, that is as entities that are both empirical and
> intelligible.

Marx's scientific approach, the distinction between infrastructure and superstructure and the complex and varying relations between them, are to be found in a modified form throughout the writings of Lévi-Strauss. What Lévi-Strauss inherits from Marx is a concern with structure as an entity and as a whole, rather than with its reduction to component elements.[3]

Some commentators argue that Lévi-Strauss's use of the 'dialectical method' is Hegelian rather than Marxist,[4] particularly his analysis of myth. This seems to have been prompted by his use of terms such as contradiction, negation, and dialectic rather than on a consideration of what Hegelianism would mean in the context of anthropology. It is true that his work does bear some relation to the central problems in dialectics, particularly the resolution of contradictions between unity and multiplicity, nature and culture, freedom and necessity, subject and object, but this does not mean that his thought is Hegelian.

In this connexion, it is important to distinguish between two uses made of the 'dialectical method': as a basic framework for the analysis of social reality which recognizes its complex and dynamic nature, the existence of internal contradictions and the masking of the true level of reality by ideology; and on the other hand, as a preconstituted view of the structure of the social totality assuming the existence of one central contradiction, and the determination of all the other levels of society by this. It is in the former sense only that Lévi-Strauss is Hegelian; the use of this framework does not determine his specific analyses. He is not influenced by the essence of Hegelianism which views society and history as the emanations of one central idea, and dissolves all the other parts of the social formation into an undifferentiated unity. Lévi-Strauss's emphasis on the relative autonomy of structures is the exact opposite of this. In fact it would appear that there is no direct relation between the thought of Hegel and Lévi-Strauss, except that mediated by the Marxist critique of Hegel. He rarely mentions Hegel, and whenever concepts are used which may be Hegelian in origin these are always integrated into his structural problematic, which has nothing of the monocausality or emphasis on history with which Hegel is imbued. Certainly Lévi-Strauss's analysis of myth, particularly in *Mythologiques* (1964b, 1966a, 1968a, 1971), does utilize the notions of contradiction, transformation, opposition and others but these are inherent properties of the myths, and not the application of the Hegelian dialectic. The presentation of the findings attempts to mirror the complex developments of the myths but there is nothing essentially Hegelian in this.

Rousseau

Lévi-Strauss (1955, 1962b, 1962c, 1967e) never misses an opportunity to express his philosophical debt to Rousseau. Certain aspects of this heritage are apparent from his general approach: an anti-evolutionism which treats all forms of society and thought, however 'primitive' or 'advanced', as equally valid; respect towards the 'noble savage' with the hint that he is perhaps more 'authentic' than industrial man; the interest in the boundary between nature and culture and the crucial importance of language in the constitution of society. But Rousseau's influence on Lévi-Strauss goes further: it affects his whole attitude towards the occupation of the anthropologist and also suggest answers to particular ethnographic problems. One of these, for example, is the interpretation of totemism. Lévi-Strauss (1964b, pp. 101–2) credits Rousseau with having been the first to enable an internal understanding of totemism since he realized that metaphor, on which it depends, is an original part of language and not a later embellishment. In an essay commemorating Rousseau's bicentenary, Lévi-Strauss characterizes him as the founder of social science in general, and ethnology in particular: in the *Discours sur l'inégalité* (1955 edn), Rousseau had conceived the project of studying the customs of other societies at a time when travellers were usually interested only in exotica and savages, and had distinguished ethnography from historical and moralistic interests. Lévi-Strauss's aim to study the whole of the human experience reveals certain echoes of Rousseau:[5] for both, study of one's own society can only yield information about men, whereas study of more distant cultures can tell us about man. It must be stressed that the nineteenth century association between evolution and progress was not yet present in Rousseau, and is abandoned by Lévi-Strauss. For both of them evolution is a value-free term, denoting only the mechanism of change with no implication about the direction of the change. Lévi-Strauss returns to Rousseau's conception precisely for this reason.

In the *Discours* Rousseau argued that society produces a triple transition from nature to culture, feelings to knowledge and animality to humanity, and in the *Essai sur l'origine des langues* (1970 edn), language was singled out as the most important factor of this transition. This orientation imbues Lévi-Strauss's work, notably his equation of culture with intellect. Derrida goes as far as to call Lévi-Strauss a 'militant Rousseauist' who reintroduces the belief in the original violence of writing (since its emergence is tied up with the exercise of power and the development of social stratification), and who sees the 'natural society' and 'natural goodness' in primitive man. It is doubtful whether *Tristes Tropiques* is amenable to a 'lecture symptomâle' such as Derrida undertakes, since Lévi-Strauss himself describes it as the incoherent 'songeries' of an ethnologist in the field. But he is correct in drawing attention to one important effect of Rousseau on Lévi-Strauss: a concern with the subjective attitude of the anthropologist, both towards himself, his own society and the societies he chooses to study, and the self-doubt that this engenders. For both of them, the ethnographic experience is also a philosophical one and is personally disturbing. Whenever Lévi-Strauss refers to the physical discomfort of the ethnographer, when he wonders why people choose to leave their own society and travel half way across the earth to study others, it is invariably Rousseau that he turns to for comfort and inspiration, since for him the greatness of Rousseau is due to his respect for and identification with others as men, his humility, and his recognition that the understanding of other cultures would lead one to question the worth of one's own (1962c, p. 245):

> Rousseau's thought is based on a double principle: identification with the other, and the refusal to identify with himself, accept himself. These two attitudes complement each other: I am not 'me', but the weakest and most humble of 'others'. This is the discovery of the *Confessions*.

For Lévi-Strauss, an important part of the work of the anthropologist consists in his 'confessions', a conception of the anthropological ethos far removed from anything to be found in Malinowski or Radcliffe-Brown.

Lévi-Strauss (1961, p. 391) sees himself as continuing Rousseau's search for 'what in the present nature of man is original, and what is artificial', rather than for the 'natural society' since natural man does not predate society.

The essay on Rousseau ends with a final tribute, in which Lévi-Strauss credits his ethnography with overcoming the barriers that politicians and philosophers have attempted to erect for over two hundred years between men, between societies, between nature and culture, experiential and rational, and humanity and life.

Vladimir Propp

The influence of Russian formalism on Lévi-Strauss, both as regards linguistics and the analysis of literature, has been lasting, yet never acritical; he has attempted to transform their formal approach into a structural one which would avoid reducing what is studied to a formal archetype, denuded of content, and which would re-synthesize the myth or poem after the analysis. Lévi-Strauss takes his point of departure from Vladimir Propp's 'Morphology of the Folktale' (1958), a classic of the Russian formalist school.

Propp started from a critique of the then contemporary approach to the study of folklore, in particular the unprincipled selection of criteria of classification, and the study of history and origins before structure. For instance, folk tales were commonly divided into fairy tales, tales of everyday life and animal tales, and the plot was described by randomly selecting some 'striking' part of the tale and adding the preposition 'about'. Propp rejected this as unscientific both because the classification into types was not mutually exclusive and because he maintained that it was not the themes that were decomposable into motifs but that the sentences could be further decomposed into many elements. He tried to establish a classification of folktales from an analysis of their structure. Russian folktales were described in terms of their 'functions': what the dramatis personae do, independent of who they are and how the functions are realized. The functions were enumerated and classified according to their significance and position in the course of the narrative. Propp found a great recurrence of functions in different folktales though their means of realization varied greatly. In fact, functions served as the basic components and stable elements of the tale; the number of separate functions was limited to thirty-one and their sequence was always identical; authentic Russian peasant folktales all belonged to one and the same type. The fact that tales with identical functions belong to the same type enabled the construction of an index of types according to exact structural features rather than a vague plot. Tales of a given type could be compared and variations between them shown to be different realizations of the same functions and therefore structurally identical; or as related in different ways by inversion or some other form of transformation. The particular elements of the individual folktale and different means of realization of the functions added by the storyteller were shown to be related to the social setting and geographical area where the tale was found. Once the functions and their sub-types had been labelled, it was possible to transcribe an individual folktale into an algebraic schema in terms of its structural components, to compare a large number of tales in tabular form according to their functions. This permitted an investigation of possible but non-existent permutations.

The distinctive feature of the formalist approach thus consisted in reducing the object of study to its component parts in an objective way; then, depending on its generality, comparing all its variants as transformations of each other, and constructing on this basis a tabular representation of the structure or family of structures and their interrelationship, which drew attention to structurally possible but empirically non-existent variants. Propp, like Dumézil and Jakobson, is important as a forerunner to Lévi-Strauss for his attention to structural elements and method of analysis which seeks the component parts of phenomena.

Propp believed that his purely morphological method would not apply to myth since he thought, erroneously, that myths were the origin of folktales and therefore required a historical explanation. Lévi-Strauss (1960c) has taken the opposite point of view: myths are more susceptible of morphological analysis than folk tales because they are constituted by stronger oppositions which refer to cosmology, nature or metaphysics, and are not so much constrained by local variations in morality. Also they are more subject to logical coherence and reach us in a less adulterated form—the permutations are less arbitrary than in folk tales and the storyteller has less freedom to add literary embellishments.

Lévi-Strauss's earlier analyses of myth follow Propp's procedure almost exactly—for example, the myth of Oedipus (1968b)—except that a linguistic terminology is used and Lévi-Strauss is concerned not only with the structure but also with the meaning of the myth to society. He starts from the hypothesis that myths are constructed from 'gross constituent units' or 'mythèmes' and that the manifest events of the myth can be reduced to several 'bundles of relationships'. In this case the mythèmes are four: the overrating and the underrating of blood relationships, the slaying of monsters and the autochthonous (aboriginal) origin of man. Each significant event such as Oedipus killing Laius, or his marriage to Jocasta, is assigned to one of these 'bundles' which are similar to Propp's 'functions'. In Lévi-Strauss's view the myth attempts to solve the contradiction between the cultural belief that mankind is aboriginal and the fact that humans are born out of the union of man and woman.

Elsewhere, Lévi-Strauss (1960b) postulates a relation of inversion between the Oedipus myth and North American myths about a girl visited at night by a man she believes to be her brother. In both cases the elaborate precautions taken to avoid incest make it inevitable; the mother-son incest is analogous to the brother-sister incest; the double identity of Oedipus, thought to be dead but in fact living, is a permutation of the personality of the hero-brother who has a double; the sphinx episode in the Oedipus myth is replaced by an episode involving an owl in the Iroquois myth, and is related in both cases to riddles. Lévi-Strauss then looks for other permutations of this 'bundle of relationships': the riddle is a question to which there is no answer; an inversion of this, an answer which has no question, is to be found in the myths of the Holy Grail in which the action depends on the timidity of the hero, and the story of the death of Buddha made inevitable because a disciple failed to ask the required questions.

Lévi-Strauss argues that these myths form a system though they are culturally unrelated—the internal relations between the various elements is one of internal reason rather than contingent or external fact. The characteristic elements of one group can be seen as inversions of the other: in one case the hero misuses sexual intercourse by committing incest, in the other he is chaste; in one group there is a shrewd person who knows all the answers, in the other an innocent one who is unaware even of the need to ask questions. Lévi-Strauss contends, on the basis of a structural analysis of the myths in question, that there is an Oedipal 'type' of myth which assimilates the discovery of incest to the solution of a living puzzle, and that this may be found in any cultural context.

This analysis is formally similar to Propp's, yet it is not based on the antinomies between form and content, and between abstract and concrete which permeate Propp's work, and make it formalistic. Propp thought his formalism was due to his neglect of historical data, whereas it was in fact lacking in context: the formalists considered the form the essential feature of a poem or tale since it permitted morphological analysis, and consequently content was seen as separate from form, arbitrary and of only secondary importance. Form alone was intelligible and content was a residue with no signifying value.

For Lévi-Strauss's structuralism this opposition does not exist: form and content are of the same nature and to be analysed by the same method. Content gets its reality from the structure and the form is a 'mise en structure' of local structures of which the content consists. His problems are of a different order, concerning primarily the relationship between myth and its social context. Propp did not raise the question of the orgin or determinacy of folktales and thus avoided this problem.

The second major limitation of formalism is that the form tends to become so abstract that it signifies very little. The richness and the diversity of the folktale are reduced to a formal archetype, and there is no means of looking at the diversity between tales nor of returning from the abstract to the concrete. Propp discarded the variations between the tales as unamenable to analysis. But for Lévi-Strauss the 'proof of the analysis is in the synthesis'. This means that the extent of variation in the content is to be exhaustively analysed since this level may also manifest a system which expresses fundamental contrasts and oppositions. For instance, his analyses of North American myth reveal that different animals often fulfil the same functions, and he tries to find examples of all the possible permutations to arrive at the logical system which underlies them; if pushed far enough, the study of content will also reveal meaningful relationships: for instance, the connotation of apple tree with strength and of plum tree with fertility is common to much American myth. It may thus be possible to find constancy behind the apparent diversity and arbitrariness of the details of the content.

Myth analysis on the lines envisaged by Lévi-Strauss rests on the assumption that all aspects of the myth are motivated and may thus be analysed structurally, whereas for Propp only syntax has this privilege. For Lévi-Strauss all is syntax in this sense, but simultaneously all is vocabulary since the differential elements of the myths are words. The relationship between puzzle and incest is one of internal logic and all the other elements of the myth are internally motivated. However, an appreciation of Lévi-Strauss's approach to myth cannot be complete without taking into account the influence of linguistics proper.

Linguistics

In the last chapter, I looked briefly at Lévi-Strauss's use of the concept of communication, and the extent and validity of his linguistic analogy will be assessed below. The aim here is to show the direct impact of some of the key concepts of linguistic theory on Lévi-Strauss's themes and methods, in particular those of Saussure and Jakobson.

Saussure's linguistics was based on a critique of the atomism of the nineteenth-century approach which saw language as the mechanical sum of units used in speaking and aimed to trace the evolution of the separate elements of a given language. This did not recognize the reality of language as a system of signs, and the interdependency of the parts which function and acquire value through their relationship to the whole. Saussure on the contrary defined language as a system of signs, a sign being the union of signified ('signifié') and signifier ('signifiant') and which is arbitrary as there is no essential relation between a sound-cluster and the idea it denotes. The fact that a particular sound-cluster is linked to a particular idea derives from their status as a sign within an integrated sign-system which constitutes a particular language. A sign gains its significance negatively—in being distinct from other signs. The radical originality of Saussurean linguistics and the central importance of the concept of system or structure within it can easily be seen: the reality of language is to be grasped not by an atomistic or historical analysis which slices through it vertically, but through a synchronic analysis, a horizontal slicing which comprehends the whole system. Words are significative in terms of their relationship in the total linguistic system which has a synchronic existence. Yet this recasting of the task of linguistics does not deny the importance of history as Saussure's crucial distinction between langue and parole makes clear. Language (langue) denotes the total system of linguistic apparatus: word conventions, syntax and so on, all of which are given from the point of view of the individual speaker. But language is realized only in and through speech (parole), by which the individual makes utterances by selecting certain words and conventions from the total fund. However, speech derives its meaning solely from the language which it actualizes. For Saussure the proper field of the study of linguistics was the synchronic and social aspects of language; the syntax of linguistic signs rather than the history of individual languages or individual speech. This holistic approach contrasts with the somewhat atomistic method of Propp, Dumézil and Jakobson.

Saussure's conception drew linguistics closer to sociology, since it would also be possible to treat social conventions such as forms of etiquette and exchange as systems of signs. The collaboration between linguistics and sociology dates from the time of Saussure and Durkheim, and indeed there are close theoretical parallels between the two; for example, Saussure's langue/parole distinction and Durkheim's view of society as external to the individual and coercive, and individual social action being entirely predetermined by the society.

Lévi-Strauss (1967c) has taken Saussure's project for a general semiology much further than his predecessors, conceiving anthropology as 'that area of semiology which linguistics has not claimed as its own'. Man, for Lévi-Strauss, is basically a signifying creature, and the aim of his anthropology is to study the processes by which meaning is attributed to things. Thus in *Mythologiques* (1964b, 1966a, 1968a, 1971) he examines the cooking procedures of Brazilian Indians as based on an internally coherent system of meanings, and cooking in general as a semiological system in its own right. Language is recognized as an essential factor in the construction of reality: to name a thing is to put it in a system of articulation, which, by differentiating it from what surrounds it in a chain, gives it meaning. Much of the analysis of naming and categorization in his *The Savage Mind* (1966b) is to be seen in this light.

Lévi-Strauss takes over much from Saussure: the whole idea of semiology, the crucial distinctions between signifier and signified, diachrony and synchrony, and langue and parole, and applies them in his analyses, particularly those of myth. However the criticisms which were made of Propp's formalism also apply to certain aspects of Saussure's theory: for Lévi-Strauss the nature of the sign is not as arbitrary as it was in Saussure and hence the distinction between signifier and signified is not so rigid, and is transformed to that between code and message. Several other crucial concepts of structural linguistics are also to be found in Lévi-Strauss's work, but these are adopted from the Prague school, particularly Jakobson.

One of the distinctions which Lévi-Strauss uses to characterize the symbolization of primitive classification and myth is that between metaphor (paradigm) and metonymy (syntagm). Metaphor relies on the recognition of similarity or substitutive character of one word for or concept for another; metonymy on the recognition of contiguity in a syntagmatic chain.[6] For Lévi-Strauss, totemism for example is based on the former since it uses birds, animals or fish variously to represent another world of supernatural beings, which are supposed to be 'like' men. In the other form of symbolization, when the individual knows how a particular syntagm is formed from the elements of a code he can reconstruct the whole when shown only a part.

Jakobson is best known for his analysis of the phoneme as the fundamental element of language (phonetic rather than semantic) and of the finite distinctive features from which it is constructed (Jakobson and Halle, 1956). Each language can be broken down into letters or combinations of letters which are its irreducible sound units, and which, like building blocks, are put together to produce speech and meaning. In themselves these phonemes are meaningless but when they are combined in words they create a system of differences which differentiates between various meanings. Jakobson claims that in all known languages, the apparent complexity and variety of phonemes is no more than the elaboration of a more simple system common to all of them, which consists of twelve oppositions between such features as vocalic and non-vocalic, consonantal and non-consonantal, voiced and voiceless, tense and lax and so on. The same system of twelve basic discriminations is said to underlie all languages, and Jacobson attempts to demonstrate this and to show how children acquire them. They are assumed to be universal and hence in some sense 'natural'. Jakobson is interested in the atoms of any language rather than with the structure of any particular language in which these are combined.

A passage from Jakobson's analysis of distinctive features may make this somewhat clearer:

'Did you say pig or fig?' said the cat. 'I said pig,' replied Alice. In this particular utterance the feline addressee attempts to recapture a linguistic choice made by the addresser. In the common code of the cat and Alice, i.e. in spoken English, the difference between a stop and a continuant, other things being equal, may change the meaning of the message. Alice had used the distinctive feature stop versus continuant, rejecting the latter and choosing the former of the two opposites; and in the same act of speech she combined this solution with certain other simultaneous features using the gravity and tenseness of /p/ in contra-distinction to the acuteness of /t/ and laxness of /b/. Thus all these attributes have been combined into a bundle of distinctive features, the so-called phoneme. The phoneme /p/ was then followed by the phonemes /i/ and /g/, themselves bundles of simultaneously produced distinctive features. Hence the concurrence of simultaneous entities and concatenation of successive entities are the two ways in which we speakers combine linguistic constituents (ibid., pp. 58–9).

Lévi-Strauss's analysis of modes of preparing food (1965b, 1966c) is an exemplary case of the application of Jakobson's method to anthropology, as he maintains that cooking, like language, is also based on an underlying system of distinctive features and signifying oppositions, and he places different cooking procedures and types of end product on the two intersecting axes of nature versus culture and normal versus transformed to arrive at his 'culinary triangle', which is analogous to Jakobson's triangle of phonemes.

Conclusion

There are several other influences on Lévi-Strauss which I shall not examine, such as Gestalt psychology, information theory and surrealism. It would be superfluous to go on charting the impact of each, and only too easy to overestimate the significance of other theories in determining Lévi-Strauss's work. The reason for this is that, as we have seen, he tends to look for similar methods and theories among all the sources to whom he acknowledges a debt, to select from them characteristics that they have in common, in accordance with his own prior interests. For example, he always draws attention to highly analytical approaches and attempts at formalization of sociological subject matter in terms of other, more neutral, codes; he highlights methods which distinguish between empirical observations and the structures which underlie them (psychoanalysis, the French sociological school, linguistics), or which examine similarities between unrelated cultural phenomena (Propp, Dumézil), or which attempt a synchronic explanation as opposed to a historical or purely functional one (Radcliffe-Brown, Marxism, structural linguistics), or which are concerned with complex inter-relationships and feedback between different elements which require a rigorous and systematic approach (information theory, use of mathematics, Hegel), and a philosophical outlook which is willing to see the 'other' (whether primitive or mad) as similar to 'us' (Rousseau, Freud). Each of Lévi-Strauss's ideas could be traced back individually to one or more sources, and in this sense, they are 'overdetermined': each element has several raisons d'être and inter-links with all the others. Yet the relationship between them is not to be found in any of the sources, all of which were concerned exclusively with their own field of specialization. Lévi-Strauss himself had provided the synthesis by internalizing and processing them, ironing out the most blatant contradictions, so that they can be re-produced as a system of ideas in which they are relevant at one or more levels (method, theory, metaphorically, literally, etc.). This is not to say that the system is entirely self-consistent or without contradictions as we shall see in the next section.

From some of the sources Lévi-Strauss has inherited a concern with isolating elements, fundamental attributes and reducing phenomena to their skeleton (particularly from Jakobson); from others an interest in the structure or social formation as a whole. He adopts both an analytic and holistic approach. These two are combined in the theories of both Saussure and Marx, but Lévi-Strauss's references to all of the sources always highlight one of these perspectives, never the two together. It remains to be seen how well he succeeds in integrating them, and combining an analysis of structural elements with an examination of the structure as a whole, and to what extent he overcomes the atomism of Jakobson and structural linguistics.

It is likely that Lévi-Strauss's main foci of interest were formed very early on in his intellectual career, and that he selected whatever suited him from the theories that were at his disposal, much as the bricoleur, according to a prior theoretical framework, rather than that his theories were developed gradually from the contact with Marxism, linguistics, Freud and others. This is not to deny the undoubted interaction and development between his own ideas and those he came into contact with, but it does certainly appear that his selection from, say, Freud and Marx is very selective, and always biased in the same direction. Like myth-makers he chooses from amongst the intellectual 'débris' at his disposal to clarify his own ideas and express them in as many different codes as possible.

Critical analysis

Lévi-Strauss's work is thus premissed on a number of methods and theories drawn from anthropology and elsewhere. We turn now to see how these are recombined within his framework, and the problems this raises. The most important questions to be kept in mind are the following:

(1) Lévi-Strauss characterizes structuralism as a method of analysis when referring to its origins. Is this all, or does it assume the status of a theory in his work, which, unlike a neutral method, makes assumptions about the way human society is organized? If so, how valid is this, and how are method and theory related?

(2) For Lévi-Strauss, the 'structures' he discovers are 'real'. But in what does their reality consist? Do they have an ontological existence? Is their basis material or ideal? Are all the structures to which he refers of the same type?

(3) Lévi-Strauss is sometimes interpreted as an idealist, either Kantian or Hegelian, or as a psychological reductionist. Are his empirical findings in fact explained as emanations of the human mind, and if so, is this a necessary explanation? Would this philosophical position invalidate his findings?

(4) Does structuralism imply that all societies throughout time are but different combinations of the same elements? Does this deny the efficacy of history?

(5) What is the relationship between atomism and holism in Lévi-Strauss's work? In other words, how successful is he in integrating the structural elements that he isolates into a structural whole? Does he privilege structure or structural elements at the expense of the other?

These questions will be approached from an examination of some of the substantive issues which fashion Lévi-Strauss's framework: the nature/culture distinction, the relevance of the linguistic analogy and the structural analysis of myth.

Nature and culture

The transition from pre-social to social life has long intrigued social theorists. Lévi-Strauss's interest centres on the transition from nature to culture rather than to society: men are both natural (animal) and cultural (creative) and the problem is how this antinomy is mediated. He focuses on the intellect and forms of thought rather than political and social organization, and on the different ways in which the distinction between nature and culture has been perceived. His analysis lacks a historical dimension—he is not interested in discovering pre-social 'natural' society (like Rousseau he does not believe in this), but in the ways both 'primitive' and 'modern' men have coped with the problem. His earlier studies are primarily concerned with the mechanisms man has employed to make himself cultural and distinct from animals; this implied that the distinction between the realms of nature and culture is a real and absolute one; but since 1960 his treatment of the subject has been increasingly oriented to the way the distinction has been conceptualized, the distinction itself being seen as a culturally created one.

Lévi-Strauss takes his cue from Rousseau in postulating that the transition from animality to humanity is also a shift from affectivity to reason, marked by the emergence of language: 'Whoever says man, says language, and whoever says language, says society' (quoted in Lévi-Strauss, 1961, p. 421). For both Rousseau and Lévi-Strauss (1962b), man can become self-conscious, and aware of himself as belonging to a particular social group, only when he is capable of using metaphor as a means of contrast and comparison, and this is one of the mental operations made possible by language. This belief justifies Lévi-Strauss's study of the categorization of the natural world, and the different means adopted to create an orderly universe, all of which are seen as equally legitimate rather than being placed on an evolutionary scale. This is why totemism disappears as such in Lévi-Strauss's theory and becomes just one specialized variety of a universal human activity, the classification of social phenomena by means of categories derived from the non-social environment. Lévi-Strauss develops Radcliffe-Brown's argument by suggesting that a major characteristic of totemic systems is that verbal classifications which impose order on the natural environment are also used to impose order on human societies by means of establishing meta-phorical relations between human groups and animal series.

Verbal categorization and language are universal means of mediation between nature and culture. But Lévi-Strauss draws attention to certain other phenomena which share this characteristic: the incest taboo, the preparation of food, the principle of reciprocity. All these are universal features of human life yet they take different forms in different societies, and along with communication, con-stitute the basic means by which man distinguishes himself from animal life.

The accuracy of some of the arguments used to establish this may be somewhat dubious. For example, incest prohibition may not be as universal as Lévi-Strauss would like to think, and although marriage may be forbidden between certain kin, the prohibition may not apply so stringently to sexual relations *per se*. It is true that Lévi-Strauss does not distinguish between these two, but for his purposes the distinction is relatively immaterial, since his point is that kin are categorized into separate groups: those with whom marriage is permitted or prescribed, and those with whom it is prohibited. The classification is a social and intellectual device, since the division into groups is not necessarily based on biological affinity, and so while marriage with close matrilateral kin may be prohibited, marriage with the person occupying an equivalent kin position on the patrilateral side will be prescribed. The incest taboo thus operates as an artificial categorization which ensures that men will marry outside a defined group, that women will be exchanged between social groups, and ultimately that social solidarity will be maintained through the system of alliances set in motion by these exchanges in marriage.

In the conflict between nature and culture it is always culture that 'wins'. But the very simplicity of Lévi-Strauss's argument conceals the problems it raises. Lévi-Strauss is a fervent anti-naturalist in the sense that he believes that no social or cultural phenomena are to be explained by reference to a biological base. Yet he argues that some of the cultural means at the disposal of men are universal. What then is the difference between 'natural' and 'culturally universal'? What unifies the various cultural attributes? Lévi-Strauss solves the problem to his own satisfaction by referring to principles of operation which underlie these manifestations as attributes of the human mind. The principle of reciprocity really underlies all communication, verbal or material, and ultimately social interaction as such, and the logical and intellectual faculty of the brain accounts for language and mental operations based on it. Thus he returns deviously to the position he starts out by rejecting, in positing innate cultural universals which exist at a psychological level, much like Jakobson's phonemes. Biology is taboo for Lévi-Strauss yet psychology apparently is not. What Lévi-Strauss dislikes about naturalism is its evolutionist overtones and its assumption that certain social arrangements, especially kinship, are 'natural' in the sense that they are determined by biology or some indeterminate 'human nature', and apply to different stages of social development. It also tends to explanations based on the individual and individual affective preferences. For Lévi-Strauss the diversity of social forms is also limited, but this determination is posited at the much more abstract level of structural compatibilities and incompatibilities which constrain human activity within certain limits. Thus he respects the uniqueness of particular social arrangements, and sees them as manifestations of a universal logic, but many steps intervene between the logic and the resultant social form.

The distinction between these positions is clearest in relation to the study of kinship structure. In *Marriage, Authority and Final Causes* (1955), Homans and Schneider take a naturalistic position in arguing that cross-cousin marriage, for example, is due to individual psychological predispositions and emotional preferences. While personal preferences may be important in establishing marriage in industrial society, this is not the case in many other societies, and Lévi-Strauss tries to show in *The Elementary Structures of Kinship* (1969a) that in many primitive societies cross-cousin and other types of marriage are to be seen as particular instances of an ongoing and institutionalized structure of exchanges between social groups which have nothing to do with the emotional preferences of the individuals concerned. He examines different types of exchange in terms of the degree to which they set in motion narrower or wider cycles of reciprocal exchanges, and isolates two basic types of exchange to which many of the elaborate arrangements can be reduced—direct or restricted exchange and generalized exchange. In all cases the choice of partners is structurally determined. Unfortunately Lévi-Strauss has never produced the complement to this study, which would deal with the 'complex' structures of kinship where demographic and sociological factors override the strict determination of marriage partners, and individual choice has an important role.[7] In *Elementary Structures*, he does not maintain that kinship structure is directly based on universal psychological characteristics, or only by implication, since the reason for exchange via marriage is the innate tendency to reciprocity of which the incest taboo is a prime example. But as we have seen, Lévi-Strauss confuses incest prohibition with exogamy and it is really the latter that he is talking about. In any given situation these are interrelated as the prohibition on sex between primary kin usually predisposes the individual to marry outside the primary kin group, yet they remain analytically distinct, and sometimes are distinct in practice too (see, Fox, 1967). Lévi-Strauss does provide a plausible account of exogamy but this does not explain the universality of the incest taboo as he believes. To do this he would have to take into consideration the variety of types of incest, the varying degrees of harshness with which incest is met, and the fact that the prohibition is not necessarily universal, and that incest is avoided rather than being actively prevented.

Does it invalidate Lévi-Strauss's argument about the structural determination of kinship organization that he does not provide an explanation of the incest taboo? I think not, since for him the main point is that reciprocity as a universal cultural trait is at the basis of social life, and is the root cause of exogamy. But in this case as in many others where it is a question of dealing with technical problems of anthropology, Lévi-Strauss oversimplifies the problem, fails to make essential distinctions, and uses the anthropological evidence in a rather manipulative way. Nevertheless it remains that the universal truth he is trying to prove by the use of anthropological arguments, although not based strictly on evidence, does say something revealing about social life and helps us see the similarity between different types of society without relying either on an evolutionist or 'human nature' perspective.

A further problem relating to the universal means of acculturation is that the operations on which they are based exist in the unconscious, yet Lévi-Strauss never tells us clearly what he means by 'unconscious'. It seems to predispose men to certain social relationships and certain mental acts, and thus to have an active role in relation to social organization. But Lévi-Strauss deals with it only at the individual level, or at a very general level, that of the primitive mind as such. He bypasses the societal level and never examines the workings out of unconscious structure in social interaction. He argues convincingly in the case of Bororo society, that the real structure of social relationships is not clear to the social actors and in fact is masked by an opposed view of the workings of society. The same may be the case in very many other societies, but it is illegitimate to conclude from these empirical cases and as a general principle that there is always an unconscious social structure at variance from the apparent one or that social relationships are necessarily mystified. Whether or not Lévi-Strauss would be led to postulate the existence of a 'group mind' or 'collective unconscious' one can only conjecture, but as social anthropologists are primarily interested in the behaviour that is characteristic of individuals acting in the context of their cultural situation, a discussion of the societal dimension of the unconscious structures is a basic omission on Lévi-Strauss's part. He rejects the concept of 'collective conscience' as it appears in Durkheim's work, yet seems to return to it in treating the human brain in general as a conscious and creative entity and in asserting that the pure individual has no existence independent from the structural determinants of society.

In his more recent writings (1964b, 1966a, 1968a, 1969a, 1971), the problems of the transition from culture to nature have been transformed to a consideration of the way the distinction between the two realms is conceptualized, and to some extent this avoids the above problems, particularly that of the universality of the incest taboo. Lévi-Strauss even goes as far as to question the validity of the distinction (1967d, p. 4): 'The opposition is not an objective one; men need to invent it. Perhaps it is a precondition for the birth of culture'. The change of view comes as the result of developments in the last twenty years that have shown that animals can communicate, and that they use tools. The distinction is thus less valid because more of culture is in nature, and cultural models such as genetic codes, and information theory can be used to explain natural phenomena (Lévi-Strauss, 1969a, pp. xxix–xxx):

> The contrast of nature and culture would be neither a primaeval fact, nor a concrete aspect of universal order. Rather it should be seen as an artificial creation, a protective rampart thrown up around it . . . ultimately we shall perhaps discover that the interrelationship between nature and culture does not favour culture to the extent of being hierarchically superimposed on nature and irreducible to it. Rather it takes the form of synthetic duplication of mechanisms already in existence but which the animal kingdom shows only in a disjointed form.

The analysis of logic, classification and myth, which will be examined in subsequent sections, is still concerned with the relation between nature and culture, but with the ways in which it has been variously conceived and used for intellectual purposes.

The linguistic analogy

I have looked at the way Lévi-Strauss utilizes the notion of communication in the study of social and cultural life, and certain key linguistic concepts he uses have been traced to their origins in Saussure and Jakobson. The adoption of a rigorous method like that of linguistics, and an interest in communication, both literal and metaphorical, are the ways in which Lévi-Strauss has been influenced by linguistics. However it is often thought that his method consists in the wholesale application of linguistics to social anthropology. Is this the case, and, if so what effect would it have on his anthropology?

Lévi-Strauss refers to linguistics most frequently in connexion with methodology. He argues that the revolutionary changes brought about by the methods of structural linguistics will play the same renovating role for the social sciences that nuclear physics played for the physical sciences: the method does not apply to language alone, but would provide the basis for a scientific approach to the study of all social life. The essence of the method as adopted by Lévi-Strauss was formulated in terms of four basic operations in N. Troubetzkoi's *Principes de phonologie* (1949):

First, structural linguistics shifts from the study of conscious linguistic phenomena to their unconscious infrastructure; second, it does not treat terms as independent entities, taking instead as the basis of analysis the relations between terms; third, it introduces the concept of system—'modern phonemics does not merely proclaim that phonemes are always part of a system: it shows concrete phonemic systems and elucidates their structure'; finally, structural linguistics aims at discovering general laws, either by induction—'or . . . by logical deduction, which would give them an absolute character' (Lévi-Strauss, 1968b, p. 33).

Leaving aside for the moment the first point, the other three certainly describe, at a programmatic level, what a scientific approach to social and cultural phenomena requires: the examination of empirical data with a view to isolating their units or elements and to discerning interrelations between the phenomena under consideration, and the search for systematic principles of organization within and between them. Lévi-Strauss's study of totemism follows this programme almost exactly.

However, Lévi-Strauss recognizes that some of the specific features of language make it especially susceptible of scientific analysis—most linguistic behaviour lies at the level of unconscious thought since one is not aware, in speaking, of using syntactic or morphological constructions, nor of the phonemes used to convey different meanings. Hence language may be mathematically treated, and as writing has a long historical existence, long runs of relationships may be statistically studied especially at the phonemic level.

Language consists of several linked systems which exist in the unconscious of each speaker. Their structure was discovered by a linguistic method which stresses synchrony, necessary relationships, and systems. The unconscious location of linguistic structures is argued *a posteriori*: the existence of a system is discovered, which is used by all speakers but not consciously. Since it is obviously internalized in the mind, and since linguistic malfunctioning accompanies certain psychological disorders, it is argued that language exists in the unconscious.

Whether this argument can be extrapolated to the data studied by anthropology is another question, and one that Lévi-Strauss does not consider at any length. He seems to assume that the unconscious logical faculty of the mind organizes individual and collective life, albeit indirectly, and this leads him to trace all the relationships he discovers between, for example, the different modes of preparing food in different societies, back to the workings of the unconscious mind, whose efficacy is taken as given. While, in the case of language, mediation by the social environment is important only at the time of its internalization and does not generally mediate between unconscious linguistic structure and the enunciation of speech, the same is not necessarily the case for kinship classification, cooking and other activities all of which occur within an ongoing social context. Lévi-Strauss does pay some attention to the way these phenomena are affected by their context, and this is a problem of which he is aware. But it remains that the mediating effect of the social environment on individual behaviour is rarely touched on, and this is a recurrent omission in his work. Perhaps this criticism is not so crucial since most of the areas which he is concerned with focus on behaviour which is neither individual nor social, and he cannot be criticized for not studying what he has chosen not to study: since 1960 or earlier he has been exclusively concerned with myth and we shall deal with the question of the social context of myth in the next section.

To summarize, the importance of linguistics to anthropology is due to the fact that it provides a scientific model since it has defined constituent units, studied their interrelations and isolated constraints: as both language and culture are built of oppositions, correlations and logical relations, language may be treated as a conceptual model for the other aspects of culture; these aspects can also be regarded as systems of communication.

Language has also a substantive relevance: Lévi-Strauss often refers to social interaction as embodying a language, or to myth as a language. But the terms language, syntax, vocabulary are usually used metaphorically as in the following passage (1967e, p. 3):

Mythology constitutes a 'language'. Ritual, social institutions, technical-economic procedures, and art are also discrete 'languages'. Thus, if for one of these, we have correctly isolated the syntax which forms its latent structure, this syntax should be transformable into the syntax of the other languages.

What Lévi-Strauss means is that society is decomposable into several distinct levels, each of which possesses an internal organization or principles of operation—and each should be studied separately. Together they add up to the whole social formation and there may be parallels between their internal structures.

However, when it comes to the analysis of some specific data, the analogy may be a more literal one, as is the case, for example, with kinship terminology (Lévi-Strauss, 1968b, p. 34):

In the study of kinship problems, the anthropologist finds himself in a situation which formally resembles that of the structural linguist. Like phonemes, kinship terms are elements of meaning; like phonemes they acquire meaning only if they are integrated into systems. 'Kinship systems' like 'phonemic systems', are built by the mind on the level of unconscious thought. Finally the recurrence of kinship patterns, marriage rules, similarly prescribed attitudes between certain types of relations, and so forth, in scattered regions of the globe and in fundamentally different societies, leads us to believe, that in the case of kinship as well as language, the observable phenomena result from the action of laws which are general but implicit.

Here the analogy is so close that kinship structure is held to derive from the mind. But how and from whose mind is unclear.

The *Structures élémentaires* (1949) deals with the different types of communication system implicit in marriage rules, but is little influenced by linguistics and makes no reference to it.[8] However, several later essays from the 1950s argue the substantive similarity between language and kinship behaviour, and draw attention to certain parallels of structure. 'Structural Analysis in Linguistics and Anthropology' (in 1968b) deals with the nature of the relationship between kinship terminology and prescribed attitudes towards kin, and shows, for a variety of societies, the systematic relation between four attitudes within the same basic unit; that is, the correlations, oppositions, and possible combinations between them, and also sheds new light on the avunculate. Lévi-Strauss's conclusions were summarized in chapter 2. In 'Language and the Analysis of Social Laws' (in 1968b), Lévi-Strauss compares the structural properties of a variety of kinship systems in various geographical areas with features of the languages found in the same area, and argues that, if homologies between preferential marriage rules and linguistic structures could be established, we would be closer to an understanding of the unconscious structuring of social life. The substantive analogy is taken furthest here: he suggests for instance that in Indo–European cultures the kinship system is based on generalized reciprocity with only a few negative prescriptions, and relative freedom and randomness characterize the unions that result. Indo-European languages similarly possess simple structures but a multiplicity of elements. In the Sino–Tibetan sphere, however, both kinship and linguistic structure are complex although the elements from which they are constituted are few: marriage with the mother's brother's daughter ensures social cohesion simply and may be indefinitely extended so as to include any number of participants. However the results of this investigation are inconclusive and have never been followed up.

The earlier attempts at the analysis of myth also start from the assumption of its fundamental similarity with language: the content of myth appears contingent yet throughout the world myths manifest basic similarities. Linguistics could develop only when it was realized that there is no inherent relationship between meaning and sound, but that clusters of sound become associated in a given context with particular meanings, although the same sounds occur elsewhere, but in different combinations. The same applies to the elements of myth, and the analysis of myth can be rigorous only when this is taken into account.

Cooking, face painting and primitive sculpture are also treated as languages, but more specifically as semiological systems in which they provide the signifiers for a rather imprecise ensemble of signifieds.[9] However, in the essay on the 'culinary triangle' Lévi-Strauss does argue that concepts used in structural linguistics, to refer to systems of oppositions between phonemes, such as 'minimum vocalism' and 'minimum consonantism', may be transposable to cooking (1966c, p. 937):

> I will start from the hypothesis that this activity (cooking)
> supposes a system which is located according to very different
> modalities in the functioning of the particular cultures one
> wants to consider—within a triangular semantic field whose
> three points correspond to the categories of the raw, the cooked
> and the rotted. It is clear that in respect to cooking the raw
> constitutes the unmarked pole, while the other two poles are
> strongly marked, but in different directions: indeed the cooked
> is a cultural transformation of the raw, whereas the rotted is a
> natural transformation. Underlying our original triangle, there
> is hence a double opposition between elaborated and

73

unelaborated on the one hand, and culture and nature on the other.

The culinary triangle is exactly analogous to Jakobson's triangle of primary phoneme distinctions (see Figures 1 and 2):

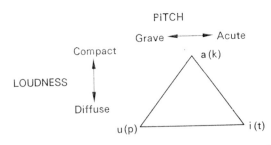

FIGURE 1   *Jakobson's primary vowel-consonant triangles*

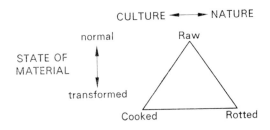

FIGURE 2   *Lévi-Strauss's culinary triangle (primary form)*

Figure 3 summarizes Lévi-Strauss's argument that the principal modes of cooking form another structured set which is the converse of the other (Figure 2). Roasting brings meat into direct contact with fire, the agent of conversion, without the mediation of cultural apparatus; boiling reduces the food to a pulp, like rotting, but requires the cultural mediation of both fire and water, whereas smoking requires air only. Roasting and smoking are natural processes as regards the means of cooking and boiling is a cultural one, but as regards the end-product, smoking belongs to culture and the other two to nature. The universality of this schema and its correctness are less important to Lévi-Strauss than the fact that it is possible to demonstrate that all humans make a cultural activity out of eating, and that the various procedures have different significations. Jakobson's method is thus secondary to Lévi-Strauss's main concern.

Lévi-Strauss always stresses the provisional nature of the analogy between language and society, a point that his opponents do not like to concede.[10] In 'The Structural Study of Myth' (Leach ed., 1967) the differences between myth and language are clearly discussed, as well as their similarities. Myth belongs both to reversible and non-reversible time (it refers to past events yet their specific pattern is timeless and this gives the myth an operational value). It retains its

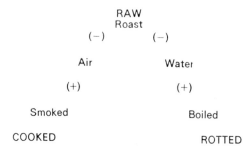

FIGURE 3   *Lévi-Strauss's culinary triangle (developed form)*

meaning even through the worst translation, and is still felt to be a myth by all readers everywhere. These characteristics distinguish myth from language: it operates on a particularly high level of meaning, where the style and syntax are subject to the story. Myth uses language and is part of language, and creates its own meta-language—but it is not structurally the same as language.

Already in 1952 at the Conference of Anthropologists and Linguists, Lévi-Strauss had found the methods of Jakobson insufficient and partly irrelevant and he asked, for example apropos of his own work on kinship (1952a).

Are such formalizations able to be transposed onto the linguistic level? I do not see in which form they could be. It is clear however that in this case, the anthropologist is using a method that is closely allied to the linguist. Both are concerned to organize constituent unities into systems. But it would be vain to push this parallel further.

Lévi-Strauss's relationship to linguistics is complex and varies both according to the level of abstraction at which he is talking, and to the development of his theories. He believes first, that the structural method of linguistics which isolates structural elements and attempts to integrate them within structured wholes, is a scientific one and of general validity, yet he never manages to combine these two aspects successfully. Second, he speaks of anthropological phenomena in terms of languages and codes because he believes he has discovered a logical system which is internal to them, and not imposed by reference to an artificial linguistic schematism. Third, some of the concepts of linguistics are explicitly rejected, in particular the arbitrary nature of the sign, and the antinomy between form and content. However, problems arise wherever he takes over linguistic terms and applies them in an unmodified way to sociological data. This is the case, for example, with binary discrimination, derived from Jakobson's distinctive feature analysis but applied quite indiscriminately. Lévi-Strauss contends that much of primitive culture consists in dividing all things into X and not-X, and repeating this same operation on each of the elements, as the precondition for complex categorizations. It produces the 'science of the concrete' which *Totemism* (1964c) and *The Savage Mind* (1966b) explore. In the eyes of some commentators such as Leach and Lane binary discrimination is the principal concept of structuralism, or at least the Lévi-Straussian variety. However, in Lévi-Strauss's earlier work, the concept had a pragmatic and empirical importance rather than being rooted in theory, and he attempted to show that it is not the only mental operation on which primitive culture relies. His conclusions to the *Mythologiques*, though, do confirm some of their objections. Here he asserts (1971, p. 617) not that binary discrimination is the basis of thought, but that it is universal in the plant, animal and human worlds, because it is a basic component of any communication process.

Myth attempts to relate categories systematically in a much more abstract way than does totemic classification, and in this it is the precursor of science. Yet the fact remains that he does not stress sufficiently that there are probably a host of other mental operations which he has not isolated, nor does he attempt to show in any detail how binary discrimination manifests itself in modern thought.[11]

Binary discrimination certainly seems to be a major characteristic of Lévi-Strauss's own mental faculties. His discussion (1964a) of problems of method, for example, divides all possibilities into dichotomies. The differences between sociology, history, ethnology and ethnography are presented in terms of the position they occupy on one side or the other of a binary discrimination: statistical or mechanical model, observation or experimentation, mechanical or reversible time, structure or measure, conscious or unconscious and so on. It is always an either-or question and Lévi-Strauss does not consider the possibility that the relationship between some of the methods may be continuous or that there are intermediary positions. This engenders a rigid, mechanical outlook which characterizes all of Lévi-Strauss's discussion of questions not directly related to anthropological data, for instance his conception of the merits and otherwise of the historical method.[12]

The phoneme as a concept relating to structural elements is again taken over, in unmodified form, from Jakobson, and is the basis of Lévi-Strauss's views on, for example, the 'atom of kinship': the basic unit on which kinship structure is based is that of husband, wife, wife's brother and son, and marriage regulations can only be understood in terms of this. While the argument may hold for the areas in which Lévi-Strauss 'discovers' it, it does beg certain questions by assuming that the incest taboo is the ultimate determinant of exogamy, and that marriage is always initiated by men. The argument that marriage provides the basis for alliances between social groups, and that kinship structure is to be explained solely in terms of alliance is at variance for example with British descent theorists, but Lévi-Strauss never tests his case in their areas of specialization.

The same goes for his use of 'homology' and 'inversion'. Both are of obvious relevance to the description of myth and social organization but their use is loose and pragmatic, and not based on a prior discussion of their relevance to the material.

On the whole, the inspiration Lévi-Strauss has drawn from linguistics is both to the point and useful. He never says that the content of language and culture are the same, only that they both embody semiological systems which may be treated in a similar way. There are two main problems arising out of the association between linguistics and anthropology: the lack of attention paid to the question of the social integration of cultural structures, and the assumption that the systems isolated derive from the unconscious. Whereas for language this is empirically demonstrable, and a legitimate assumption anyway, this is not so with social and cultural structure. Lévi-Strauss takes as a principle of explanation something which must be proved. Because of the different nature of language these are not problems for linguistics, and are not raised by the analogy with language in itself. What seems to attract Lévi-Strauss to language is precisely that it is an unconscious and structured system, and he is attracted to linguistics because it has enlarged the relevance of Freud's discoveries. He would like to do the same for the rest of culture and social life. But the validity of this and arguments based on it, is quite separate from the use of the linguistic analogy.

The structural analysis of myth

Lévi-Strauss takes his examination of the abstract logic underlying primitive thought a stage further with the analysis of myth. According to Lévi-Strauss messages are communicated through the structured relations between the elements of myth, combined in a narrative of events. However, the message transcends the narrative and may be expressed by a number of different arrangements between its elements. The sequence is thus secondary to the structure. The same structure may be found in myths from unrelated contexts: they transform into each other to produce a set in which the basic structure remains constant, like a hard core. This implies that myth has a relative independence from its social context, and should be studied as a phenomenon *sui generis*. Lévi-Strauss believes that myth is intelligible because it constitutes a system; that individual myths have meaning only by virtue of their position *vis-à-vis* the whole set; that the narrative cannot be reduced to the social context; that fundamental attributes of myth can be understood only by minute dissection; that what it tells us about the workings of the mind is a good deal more interesting than what it reveals of the social structure; and finally, that it functions to mediate felt contradictions and to exercise the intellectual, and particularly the logical, faculties of men. Myth is of intellectual rather than social significance since it emanates from a mental logic which is natural and unconscious.

The method devised by Lévi-Strauss to argue these points consists in taking all the variants of a particular myth, regardless of origin, isolating their basic elements, the 'mythèmes', and charting their interrelationship within each myth and between the whole set. They may be related in a number of complex ways such as homology or inversion. From this it becomes possible first, to construct a proto-type to which all the variants tend but which has no empirical existence; second, to suggest the meaning of the message and to demonstrate the variety of codes used to transmit it, and third, to relate differences between the variants (such as differing degrees of markedness between its oppositions, the presence or absence of certain elements, and the minute details of content) to the culture and society in which they are embedded.

This, in outline, constitutes Lévi-Strauss's approach to myth. His very definition of the project raises certain questions: whether structural analysis entails a strict distinction between form and content, and between internal structural analysis and external sociological analysis. We shall return to these problems. His approach has developed considerably over the past fifteen years, and the discussion of it will distinguish between two broad periods: that prior to 1962 and to the publication of *Le Cru et le cuit* (1964b), and that subsequent to it.

Lévi-Strauss's orientation differs from other theories of myth, but is not incompatible with some of them, as long as we acknowledge that they deal with different aspects of myth and are relevant at different levels. The alternative approaches are broadly symbolic or functional. In the last century Frazer and Tylor considered myth to be a literal explanation of the phenomena dealt with. They recognized the intellectual capabilities of primitive men but failed to account for the social and symbolic character of myth. A later position taken by Cassirer is that there is a 'mythopaeic' form of thought, rooted in the 'perception of expression' which is essentially fantasy and does not comprehend real objects. The sociological theories of Durkheim and Malinowski are more sophisticated than these. For Durkheim myth was a verbal analogue of ritual and part of a religious system, functioning to maintain and express social solidarity. He realized that myths provided the means for categorizing the world and were the basis of science and philosophy. Malinowski's theory was more exclusively functional since he held that myths serve to legitimate rules by referring to unreal events and imaginary people so as to distance their origin from any social reality. The psychological theories differ from these in paying attention to the symbolic characteristics of myth. In Freudian theory, for example, it is assimilated to day-dreams: it makes use of the symbolism and some of the mechanisms of dreams (condensation, displacement), and expresses unconscious wishes and desires; but the conscious element is stronger than in dreams and the manifest content has an importance of its own rather than being a mere vehicle for the unconscious. In psychoanalytic theory myths deal with universal concerns such as sex, aggression and incest (see Cohen, 1969).

All these theories consider only one aspect of myth and represent a partial explanation. They ignore either the social context or the symbolic nature of myth, or fail to explain why this particular means of expression has been chosen. However in combination they go some way to explaining certain of the attributes of mythical thought and are complementary to Lévi-Strauss's attempt at the exhaustive internal analysis of myth.

The earlier, more tentative, period up to 1962, concentrated on developing a theory and method to do justice to the specific character-istics of myth. The influence of Propp, Dumézil and linguistics is very clear in Lévi-Strauss's overriding concern to isolate structural elements rather than reconstitute their system, and this is the case in the analysis of myths like that of Oedipus and Asdiwal. The latter is a most detailed examination of this type, as Lévi-Strauss (1967b) looks at a single complex of myths located in a particular cultural region. The study aims to isolate and compare the various levels on which the myth evolves, each being seen as a transformation of an underlying logical structure common to all, and to compare different versions from the same cultural area and examine the reason for their discrepancies. The relationship between the myth and empirical fact is a dialectical one so that, for instance, institutions in the myth are the reverse of those found in society: in the myth there is patrilineal inheritance and matrilocal residence which is the opposite of the real life of the Tsimshian Indians. All the events and beliefs are taken from real life but are modified in some way, so that the myth is of little use as a documentary source although a knowledge of social organization and cultural beliefs is a prerequisite for an understanding of the myth. Candlefish and salmon do make an annual east–west journey but their operative value derives from the fact that the Indians imagine themselves in the place of the fish.

The myth as a whole is less a representation of society than a contemplation of the unsatisfactory compromises on which it rests. All the antinomies are assimilated to the contradiction implicit in patrilocal matrilateral cross-cousin marriage which the Tsimshian practise. They do not benefit from the equilibrium this arrangement could provide in the form of a fixed hierarchy of wife-givers and receivers since they revise the whole system of ranking at each potlatch and marriage, thus engendering a deep-seated disequilibrium. 'All the paradoxes . . . geographical, economic, sociological and even cosmological . . . assimilated to that less obvious yet so real paradox which marriage with the matrilateral cousin attempts but fails to solve' (Lévi-Strauss, 1967b, pp. 27–8).

The comings and goings in the myth express the tensions between lineages connected by marriage, and the successive marriages of Asdiwal amount to speculations about types of residence which are latent potentials in the society. The myth seeks to justify the shortcomings of reality by imagining extreme solutions and showing them to be untenable. It is to be understood as a negative comment on social reality though this is never explicit in the narrative. It reconciles the Tsimshian to the compromise they have reached by 'showing' that any other solution is equally beset with difficulty.

Differences between variants of the myth found in neighbouring communities are referred to differences in economic organization. The Nass river version has much weaker oppositions, a fact which Lévi-Strauss refers to the fact that they are not so dependent on fishing expeditions for their food and hence not so subject to famine. In this case, the economic and alimentary code cannot be used so successfully to convey oppositions which have a social basis.

The orientation of *Mythologiques* (1964b, 1966a, 1968a, 1971) differs from the earlier studies. The aim is to examine myth as a system of logic in its own right rather than as an attempted intellectual solution to social problems. The data of the first volume consists of a whole set of myths from the Bororo and neighbouring tribes of Brazil and the later volumes draw on other South and North American sources. All the segments of the myths are exhaustively analysed and related to homologous episodes in other myths, the analysis moving like a spiral between themes. The study has no definite conclusion since there are always further layers of the logic which could be discovered by a more thorough examination.

The Raw and the Cooked (1969b) shows how empirical categories like raw and cooked can be treated as conceptual tools to form abstract ideas which may then be interconnected in logical propositions. Lévi-Strauss contends that if a logic underlies myth, then all the other aspects of human activity must also be structured and determined by logic. South American mythology provides a test case since the myths are relatively pure and also extremely complex (Lévi-Strauss, 1967d, p. 1): 'Myth is often thought to be based on fantasy and hence completely arbitrary. But if it can be shown to rest on internal laws then we can assume that laws underlie other, perhaps all, areas of life'. Choosing the most difficult case will also be a test of the validity of the structural method (ibid.): 'If my method is valid for mythology, it ought also to be applicable to other activities of the human mind, such as poetry, music and painting.' He gives the full text of one Bororo myth (M1) and places it in ethnographic context. This draws attention to some aspects of its content which cannot be interpreted sociologically and so he turns to an examination of its internal structure. He tries to show for each sequence the group of transformations within the same myth to which it is related and the isomorphic sequences from other myths. The beginning and end of the analysis are relatively arbitrary; it is immaterial at which point the system of logic is entered. The same problems are attacked from several different perspectives, and the development, which attempts to mirror that of the logic of the myth, is circular rather than linear.

Lévi-Strauss demonstrates that the 187 myths examined do not vary haphazardly but rest on an internal coherence. Unintelligible elements become clear when contrasted with homologous segments of other myths from the same area. For example he shows that the incest myth of Geriguiguitugo is 'about' the origin of cooking though this motif does not appear in the text. The latent structural level can be grasped only by working through a very large corpus of myth. In an effort to explain every detail of the reference myth he examines others which deal with the origin of pigs, women, jaguars, tobacco, the senses, the seasons and the constellations.

Some unifying concepts are provided to link the myths: the 'armature' comprises those elements that remain constant in a number of myths, the 'code' denotes the interrelationship between the elements, and the 'message' is the content of the elements. Thus it is possible to explain some myths as transformations of one or more of these aspects, and to approach the complexity of the relations more systematically seeing them as isomorphic, symmetrical, inverse or equivalent. For example, there is an inverse symmetry between the Bororo myth about the origin of rain and a Sherente myth about the origin of fire. Lévi-Strauss tries to find the reverse of this to validate the structure of oppositions postulated.

Lévi-Strauss keeps to the very high standard of rigour he set himself. Since there are no accidents in mythology, everything must be explained (1964b, p. 170): 'When a contradiction appears, it proves that the analysis has not been taken far enough.' Each element has meaning only as one link of a chain, and is quite unintelligible when examined in isolation. It is the relations between the elements that are significant, and by studying the effect on the themes of substitutions of code, Lévi-Strauss is able to define the invariant traits which characterize groups of myths or isomorphic sequences, and hence the rules of transformation. The same theme may be encountered in several different codes: the opposition between continuity and discontinuity can be expressed by astronomic, kinship or zoological codes. Analysis of these schemes leads to the logical problematic of myth. Cooking serves as a code to contemplate many aspects of human nature not just the transition of nature to culture.

The meaning implicit in myth is unconscious. For this reason Lévi-Strauss says (ibid., p. 20) that 'Myths think themselves, and without mans' knowledge'. Their translatability gives them meaning, rather than an already existing meaning making them capable of translation. The system of relations to which the analyst reduces a myth is not a fabrication, since these are 'immanent to mythology itself' (ibid.), and as Lévi-Strauss notes (1967d, p. 5): 'I have not preconceived the analysis: the myths reconstruct themselves and I am their intermediary. I am only the place through which the myths pass.'

In *The Raw and the Cooked*, myth is not seen as an attempted solution to social problems. Rather it provides an ensemble of alternative answers to all manners of questions. The relation between myth and society is neither causal nor functional, but (see Pouillon, 1966a, p. 102):

> Their reciprocal relationship has more to do with the logic of the myth than with the social condition of the questioners. Myths do rationalize the internal needs and disequilibria of society. But the source of these justifications is to be found in the formal relations between the terms of the myth, rather than in the explicit story or images.

Lévi-Strauss examines whether the symbolic systems found in South American mythology are universal since they are based on universal experiences like food and sex. In the Bororo myth noise was associated with reprehensible unions and silence with proper ones. Domestic fire, which unites earth and sun, also demands respect and silence, but eclipses are met with noise. These associations are paralleled in the European tradition of the charivari which was undertaken on the remarriage of widows and when pregnant women married in white; in other words, noise was called for whenever the expected order of events was interrupted or reversed.

In *The Raw and the Cooked*, Lévi-Strauss establishes a rigorous logic of alimentary and sensible qualities, like raw and cooked, fresh and rotten, and wet and dry. This does not exhaust the fund of native categories, and the second volume postulates a more fundamental logic of forms, expressed in the opposition between, for example, open and closed, full and empty, and inside and outside. It examines the opposition, constant throughout South American mythology, between tobacco and honey: honey is 'less than raw' since it is naturally produced and ferments naturally. It connotes purity, sweetness and value. Tobacco, on the other hand, is 'more than cooked', 'worthless and bad.' It connotes violence and disorder. These connotations are universal but more marked in Brazil where they are important in the economic life of the Indians: honey is the main food of the nomadic season, and symbolizes a return to nature. Tobacco is an intoxicant held to permit communication with supernatural forces. Whereas raw and cooked had static meaning, the descent to nature and ascent to the supernatural introduce a dynamic disequilibrium into the logical system. Lévi-Strauss is led from here to an examination of the time categories by which disequilibrium, periodicity and the oppositions between high and low and sky and earth are conceived.

The third volume turns to myths about good manners to show how Indian thought thematizes continuities and discontinuities in time, and the final volume establishes equivalences between North and South American mythology and examines variations as the result of 'infrastructural' differences.

This highly ambitious approach to myth is not without problems or faults. Most of these derive from the fact that Lévi-Strauss's main interest is almost exclusively the logic of myth, and the unconscious mental structures on which it depends. This accounts for the pattern or structure of myth, but not for its content. Nor does he pay much attention to the purpose of myth, which must have a social as well as an intellectual dimension. His study of myth is analogous to Freud's interpretation of dreams, but whereas Freud was successful in integrating the mechanisms of the dreamwork with a study of the derivation of its content so as to be able to 'explain' both the content and structure of the particular dream of a

G

particular patient, Lévi-Strauss is not so successful. His can only be a partial account of myth. This omission is less apparent in *Mythologiques* where Lévi-Strauss integrates form, structure and content by showing how different codes function to express logical propositions. But he must also examine why particular codes are chosen, and their relation to social practice.

Most of the criticisms made of Lévi-Strauss are related to this central issue. He has been criticized for neglecting the emotional and expressive content of myth and its social context (Ricoeur, Mary Douglas), of choosing a set of myths to which his approach is relevant although it does not apply elsewhere; of manipulating the data to fit his categories (Leach, Douglas), of being unsystematic and overschematic so that it is unclear whether the oppositions are in the myth or in Lévi-Strauss's mind; of being unclear whether there is one or more logics of myth throughout the world (which he admits himself).

Douglas accuses him of using a 'lemon squeezer' analysis which forces myth through a computer to produce a 'timeless synchronic form'. This argument mistakes exhaustive analysis for reductionism and neglects that unlike the formalists, Lévi-Strauss is able to move between abstract and concrete, and code and message, and still preserve the richness of a particular myth.

Particular relationships that Lévi-Strauss isolates appear relatively arbitrary and, as he gives no reason why he privileges one aspect rather than another, it would be possible to reorganize the data in another way. On the other hand, it is true that it would be almost impossible to disprove any of the asserted relationships; the total dissection of a myth into schemas and structures of oppositions is extremely convincing and each opposition can be grasped only in terms of the structure as a whole. He tends to turn apparently contradictory evidence into proof of his case, by means of 'secondary dimensions'. In *Mythologiques III* (1968a) he refers to a Choco myth which uses wild honey as a metaphor for sperm, while the philosophy of honey established in the previous volumes is based on the analogy of honey with menstrual blood (see Leach, 1970, p. 118). According to Lévi-Strauss this is an inversion which, far from contradicting his interpretation, enriches it with a supplementary dimension. Here, as elsewhere, his manipulation of the data makes it difficult to judge his main theory in any critical way.

His use of technical terms is equally unsatisfactory. He is unsystematic in the use of terms such as homology and inversion, and fits the data into these formal categories in a rather mechanical way. He is overkeen to discover discontinuities and oppositions, and neglects even the possibility of continuous or complementary relationships.

The two substantial problems raised by the structural analysis of myth are the role of the historical dimension and of the social context. Ricoeur (1963), for example, argues that Lévi-Strauss's claims are too general for his method and that he has deliberately chosen examples from the cultural areas where, in myth, structure takes precedence over the manifest events. This, he argues, is not the case elsewhere and he refers specifically to the Old Testament stories, where form and content cannot be separated, nor structure and event, but the sequence of events and expressive content play an important role. He suggests an alternative 'hermeneutic' approach to myth which would emphasize semantic elements and provide a structural explanation only to supplement the symbolic interpretation of the themes.

Cohen and Leach, among other commentators, have also drawn attention to the fact that the meaning of Bible stories resides in the specific succession and repetition of events in the narrative. In a sense, this is less an objection to Lévi-Strauss than an admission that myth is not a homogeneous category but shades into legend, folktale and prophecy; there may also be different kinds of myth which vary as to which aspect takes precedence in different contexts. We cannot expect the same theory to explain all these phenomena— the aim should be to distinguish between the various types of myth and to produce a method flexible enough to adapt to the specific characteristics of each without the *a priori* assumption that structure or history must be the main element in all.

Lévi-Strauss does not claim exclusivity for his theory of myth and such a flexibility is implicit in much of what he says. For instance, he criticizes Leach's analysis of Genesis on the grounds that Bible stories are only quasi-myths since they have been edited for an end different from the original one. They are closely related to their social context and the history of Israel but the information about this is sparse and not independent from the stories themselves. Again, the distinction Lévi-Strauss makes between societies which are 'warmer' or 'cooler' historically (see Charbonnier, 1969) is very pertinent here although he never applies it to myth. From this point of view, Bororo society is much cooler and more static than Israel and the historical dimension would have little relevance, unlike Israel where the establishment and dissolution of states and dynasties, and political and territorial conflicts, implied a more cumulative history where past events would be significant as stages in the succession from the beginning of time to the present. Social change and temporality are experienced differently in different contexts, and will come to be perceived differently and have an appropriate cultural expression. Here as in other areas, Lévi-Strauss's approach permits the flexibility for such necessary variation of focus, but he does not draw out its implications. An important question which he does not ask is whether myth, folktale and related phenomena are all based on the same logic and mental constraints or whether they are completely independent.

The problem of the social context of myth has two aspects: the function fulfilled by its content and constant repetition, and the social origins which are responsible for its content. It is true that Lévi-Strauss does not pay sufficient attention to the social functions of myth. In the earlier studies they are interpreted as an imaginary contemplation and solution to universal intellectual problems or particular problems of social organization. The later analysis of South American mythology is more concerned with the intrinsic logic of myth and does not imply such a clear function. This bias is a function of Lévi-Strauss's style of work which permits him to dissociate the social and intellectual life of the peoples he is studying. His study of myth is based not on fieldwork, but on second-hand collections of myth. However an explanation in more functional terms would not be incompatible with his outlook, and part of the value of his approach is that it attempts an exhaustive account of one aspect of myth. This must be complemented by analyses of all the other aspects: sociological, symbolic and psychological, if a 'total' explanation is to be achieved.

The other aspect of the criticism refers to Lévi-Strauss's lack of attention to the social context. He does attempt to refer all the episodes in the myth of Asdiwal to their ethnographic context and show how the events of real life are transformed in the course of mythologization. But he always upholds the relative autonomy of myth and cultural products in general, and establishes this methodologically by seeking the internal structure of each. Certain of his critics, and notably Lucien Goldmann, imply that cultural products are completely determined by social structure and are mere reflections of it. This attitude can lead to social reductionism, which by 'explaining' everything as a reflection of social structure neglects to ask why culture takes the form it does and implicitly denies any intrinsic value to philosophy, culture or thought in general. The purely synchronic explanation such as Lévi-Strauss provides is inadequate, but the purely sociological on the other hand is likely to be very partial and must be complemented by structural, symbolic and aesthetic evaluations which take account of some of the other dimensions.

Lévi-Strauss demonstrates that cultural products are not free-floating but constrained by internal limits, and that they have a relative autonomy from their social context; he provides a method which rigorously examines myth from the inside, preserving its unique characteristics yet relating it to cultural beliefs and social structure. Particular propositions may be doubtful but Lévi-Strauss's overall contribution to anthropology is indubitable.

But how far does he succeed in his self-set task? 'All the tasks I have set myself consist in trying to find out how the human spirit works.' (1967d, p. 1.) The whole project is undertaken from this problematic—the assumption that mental constraints limit the freedom of cultural production and orientate it in a specific direction. Taken collectively the myths refer to the 'human spirit'. This is evident throughout the volumes (1969b, p. 341):

> And if it is now asked to what final meaning these mutually significative meanings are referring—since in the last resort and in their totality they must refer to something—the only reply to emerge from this study is that myths signify the mind that evolves them by making use of the world of which it itself is a part. Thus there is simultaneous production of myths themselves, by the mind that generates them and, by the myths, of an image of the world which is already inherent in the structure of the mind.

But mental constraints and 'l'esprit humain' are not necessarily the same, and Lévi-Strauss does not define the latter. This has led to many confusions. Ricoeur, for instance, describes Lévi-Strauss's position as a 'Kantism without a transcendental subject', a formula which Lévi-Strauss accepts. Since myths are collective representations no particular mind is responsible for them, and the categories which are discovered to have an objective existence in the myth do not correspond to those of any individual mind.

Leach (1965a) readily interprets the 'human spirit' as a Hegelian 'objektive Geist' and concludes his review of *Le Cru et le cuit* by saying that Lévi-Strauss is really not interested in the meaning or social background to which the myths relate, only in their metaphysical existence ruled by Hegel's 'Geist'.[13]

But is this so? Lévi-Strauss says that myth constitutes an autonomous system like mathematics and this is why they 'think themselves'. In both, the intelligibility is internal and depends neither on events nor on consciousness. He proves that thought does not reign free but is constantly channelled into particular patterns. This is very far from idealism, whether Hegelian or Kantian, in which ideas are determinant and free-floating. It is clear that the 'human spirit', so far as myth is concerned, is a rather decorative name for what might be called the logical faculty of the brain. This is determinist, but in a psychological or physiological direction. What determines the logic of myth is the psychological structure of the brain. Lévi-Strauss would maintain that there exists a logic which men obey at all times and everywhere (see Pouillon, 1966a, p. 105):

If myths furnish an image of the world, it is not because free and conscious thought grasps the world through them; rather it is because they manifest the 'natural' functioning of a constrained and unconscious thought which is itself part of the world.

Lévi-Strauss argues that mythical thought is based on a logic that may be natural and universal. It is possible to accept this and to defend him against charges of psychological reductionism and idealism. He has shown why primitive men use myth—an economic way of storing knowledge which categorization provides in the absence of writing, and which can be used for producing images of the social world as well.

What does not follow is that this logical faculty is synonymous with the human mind, rather than being one of the many faculties which are all determined. Nor does it follow that the constraints apply to all aspects of cultural, and more important, social life.[14] We return thus to the major problems of Lévi-Strauss's outlook.

Conclusion

We are now in a position to tie together the various criticisms made of Lévi-Strauss in this chapter, and the contradictions and paradoxes in his work.

His implicit psychological reductionism is responsible for most of these paradoxes. For example, his avowed anti-naturalism (noted in his attitude towards the theoretical origins of structuralism) conflicts with the quite blatant naturalism—albeit of another variety—of the study of myth, namely the notion that its logic and structure is rooted in a psychology common to all men. But what is the difference between biological and psychological naturalism? Lévi-Strauss rejects the former because it implies that social organization is the direct result of biologically innate characteristics, unmediated by the human mind. His position credits men with the capability of inventing cultural items and creating social organization in accordance with intellectual and utilitarian aims, but the sort of inventions that are made is determined by the logical faculty of the brain. In the last analysis the difference between the two naturalisms is negligible and they are equally determinist.

A second paradox is related to this first one: Lévi-Strauss credits men, and more important, primitive men, with intellectual creativity: the neolithic revolution was the result of centuries of careful experimentation; like the bricoleur primitive man invents complex items from left-over bits and pieces; totemism is based on highly complex biological classifications. In fact the whole cultural life of primitive man is evidence of his intellectual prowess. This argument is found throughout Lévi-Strauss's works, but against it he also argues that this prowess is only the result of the physiological structure of the brain. He explains structural similarities between historically and geographically unrelated societies and cultures as resulting from different combinations of elements pre-existing in the human mind. In this connexion he states categorically that man is not absolutely inventive and can only rediscover already existing possibilities (Lévi-Strauss, 1961, p. 160):

> Human societies, like individual human beings never create absolutely: all they can do is to choose certain combinations from a repertory of ideas which it should be possible to reconstitute.

Elsewhere he says that liberty (to create) is an illusion. The arguments are two sides of the same coin, and the contradiction between them illustrates Lévi-Strauss's inability to strike a balance in acknowledging the difference between societies and their structural similarities. He considers (1967d) that 'ethnology is psychology', and conceives the future task of the social sciences as the isolation of other mental and psychological constraints which shape social action. This will be a means both to integrate the various disciplines of the social sciences and to utilize the discoveries of linguistics and psychoanalysis.

However, Lévi-Strauss is ill at ease with this psychologistic structuralism, and occasionally gives alternative explanations of structural relationships: either they are contingent, and each society discovers, more or less by chance, a particular set of structural constraints (*The Savage Mind* (1966b)), or he argues that similarities are neither psychological nor contingent but are real relationships based on historical and demographic movements of the peoples concerned in the remote past (*Race and History* (1958b), *Tristes Tropiques* (1955)). So far as cultural products are concerned all three explanations are feasible, and Lévi-Strauss has demonstrated adequately that mental constraints are an important factor in shaping the logical framework of myth.

But he goes too far. First, he implies that the 'logical' faculty which he has isolated is the only one. This is patently too great a claim and his faculty will have to be seen in relation to all the other—cognitive, linguistic and others—before a complete picture of the mental constraints on social action is possible. Lévi-Strauss's work complements the attempts of Chomsky and others to discover the missing pieces of the jigsaw puzzle of the brain.

In addition, he is not content with limiting his argument to culture but extrapolates erroneously to society, with serious philosophical consequences. His attempt to demonstrate the limited number of structural possibilities of social organization, and particularly kinship organization, is admirable. But to go on to imply that these are due to an unconscious psychological structure which men unwittingly realize is a step backward. It provides an explanation where none is needed since it is at this level that social organization can be autonomous.

Lévi-Strauss does not deal with the implications of this position even from his own point of view: he does not examine in any satisfactory way the interaction between conscious behaviour and unconscious structure, but assumes as a matter of course that the one lies beneath the other. This is the case in the essay on 'dual organization' which claims to demonstrate the real and unconscious triadic structure behind the conscious dual view of social organization, and the ways in which the latter masks the former. While this may be the case in Bororo society, it cannot be concluded that in all societies everywhere and at all times there exists a mystified conception of society, and that there is always a real unconscious structure behind the apparent one. In this view, society cannot therefore be acted upon purposefully since the social actors can never have a correct account of its workings. This is a regrettable position: theoretically it is no more than an assumption, based on pre-existing psychological reductionism, and politically it highlights only the obstacles to social change and so contradicts Lévi-Strauss's professed Marxism. For any Marxist, philosophy must be based on the premiss that man makes history and is able to discover the laws of history and society, which may then be acted upon by conscious political action. Lévi-Strauss's psychologism is a mystification from this point of view.

The tendency to psychological reductionism is certainly the most important problem for Lévi-Strauss; it is not only unfounded but also entails unwarranted implications and contradictions which he is unable to solve within his problematic. It is all the more regrettable since the structural analysis of myth could be conducted within a materialist framework linking their structure and content to the internal structure and exigencies of subsistence economies dominated by kinship at the political, ideological and even economic levels, but without reducing them to 'expressions' or 'reflections' of internal necessity between the political-economic structure of such societies, the absence of writing and of history, and their analogical or metaphorical mode of thought, which holds for totemism and classification of the natural and social world as well as for myth.[15] But by refusing this approach, and making a theory out of his structuralist method, Lévi-Strauss is prevented from distinguishing between different forms of thought except in terms of the content to which they are applied, and from relating knowledge to the social formation in which it is found. His problematic leads him automatically to postulate an original mythical form of thought, found in bastardized versions elsewhere, and to erect thinking man as natural and universal, and savage thought as a pure category.

The supposition that there exist natural categories of thought, of which savage thought is the best example, confuses Lévi-Strauss's own epistemology. As his work progresses, he becomes increasingly convinced of the mythical nature of his work and believes that his mind works in the same way as the myths do. In this way, he confuses his theory with the object it is theorizing, which, at the beginning of his project, were kept separate. It requires a science of myth to disclose the science which is myth, and the former must be of a higher order of knowledge than its object, and yet by the end of the *Mythologiques*, he affirms no distinction between the two. In order to do the kind of analysis that Lévi-Strauss undertakes naturally requires instruments not available to myth-makers: notions of homology, inversion and transformation, conceived abstractly which rely heavily on modern mathematics. To reveal the unconscious structure of myth patently necessitates more than a myth-science. In so far as his knowledge is not identical to the knowledge of myth, there is a blatant contradiction, and an about turn as regards his initial epistemological starting point and explicit critique of positivism.

Of course, primitive men do think in as complex ways as modern man and it is to Lévi-Strauss's credit to have stressed this. But there is no need to see them as more intellectual, nor their forms of thought as natural. Lévi-Strauss gets himself into a vicious circle by resorting to innate and essential categories of thought: if there is one universal human mind, then there can be no difference between the scientificity of myth and other forms of science. And if thought is independent of social reality, there is no need to specify the relationship between different thought systems and the reality they articulate. He ends up, inevitably, by asserting that the internal structure of the mind by which all knowledge is produced must be the precondition for any relation with reality.

How successful is Lévi-Strauss as a structuralist? I have already implied that he takes the method too far and creates a theory out of it. He isolates structural elements and then attempts to explain these in their own terms without recourse to any other order of reality— but a structuralist analysis need not be as anti-reductionist as this, nor need it resort to the psyche and physiology as the only possible explanatory criteria. This answers the questions posed at the beginning of the last section, but how well does he adhere to the programme for structural analysis as set out in chapter 2? The aim was to select the correct level of abstraction for analysis—an item, whether social or cultural, which could be found in different manifestations, in unrelated societies. The basic common elements were to be isolated, and the types of possible interrelation between them demonstrated so as to reach an exhaustive inventory of the structural wholes composable from the same elements.

Except in a few instances, Lévi-Strauss fails to do justice to his own schema. It is best followed through in the study of totemism, but elsewhere he tends to omit one or other of the levels of analysis, the elements or the wholes. The elements he isolates are not abstract and contentless but psychologically predetermined. He does not reduce the data to necessary elements common to several societies but differently realized, but to the psyche which makes possible both the skeleton of society and its particular content. He rarely attempts to reconstruct the wholes from the elements and thus fails to show how elements can be variously combined. His structural elements are really psychological universals and for this reason the wholes cannot be approached sociologically in a satisfactory manner. Part of the difficulty is due to the lack of definition of the unconscious in the first place, so that it becomes a depository for all the structured aspects of social and cultural life.

Lévi-Strauss is not a very good structuralist in another sense. The types of formal relationship of which he conceives (homology, inversion, etc.) are limited to a very small number, largely drawn from the analogy with linguistics, and are applied in a somewhat mechanical way as I argued in the section on myth. As with his psychological reductionism his approach is much more valid in the analysis of myth than in the study of social organization in general. But even so, it is an arbitrary method, in so far as it cannot be learned and applied to other data, including myths. To analyse myths as Lévi-Strauss does must require a good deal of individual flair and genius—but he is so individualistic that practically no one else would be able to learn the method.

A final point on Lévi-Strauss and Marxism. Most of Lévi-Strauss's substantive propositions about primitive societies not only do not complement Marx's theory of the infrastructure,[16] but are profoundly anti-Marxist and anti-materialist. Both myth and kinship structure derive from the unconscious structure of the brain—man cannot create social structure, nor change history, and he must always be mystified by his own understanding of society. At a superficial level, Lévi-Strauss adopts certain of Marx's methodological precepts and he counters theoretical ethnocentrism and evolutionism, which represent some of the worst incursions of an imperialist attitude into anthropology. But he respects the bourgeois division of disciplines in the social sciences, and his theory has no counterpart in practice; he ignores the productive nature of man, replacing it with an unchanging homo sapiens. The autonomy of the superstructures is so great that there is no need even for investigation of the relationship between the social formation and its cultural products.[17]

4 Louis Althusser

Introduction

The project of Althusser and his collaborators in *For Marx* (1969a) and *Reading Capital* (1970) is to establish a Marxist epistemology as the basis for a scientific theory of society and history, or historical materialism. Most of their work takes the form of a 'symptomatic' reading of Marx's work, in particular *Capital*, which attempts to show that the basis for this epistemology exists in the mature works of Marx, albeit in a latent, silent and untheorized form. The concepts are present but terms adequate to describe them are missing. They are concerned to demonstrate on the one hand the epistemological break between Marx's early humanist writings, influenced by Feuerbachian philosophy, and his later scientific works which reject both humanism and historicism, a break which signals the absolute difference between Marxism and Hegelian philosophy; on the other hand they attempt to define the specificity of the object studied in *Capital* and the method used to study it in contrast to that of the classical political economists.

Althusser was trained as a philosopher[1] and emphasizes that his reading of Marx is a philosophical one. But 'philosophy' has particular connotations for him. His reading is in no way an academic philosophical one, but is crucially influenced by his political position, and is that of a committed Communist philosopher.[2] His broad aim is to strengthen Marxism from within by providing the necessary concepts and rigour for a scientific theory of social formations and their transformation. His work occurs within a specific political and theoretical conjuncture and is related to the particular circumstances of French Marxism in the post-war decade. One of these was the denunciation of the personality cult and of Stalinist dogmatism at the twentieth Party Congress in Moscow in

1956 which was experienced by Communist intellectuals in the west as a 'liberation', and gave rise to what Althusser (1969a, p. 10) calls 'a profound ideological reaction', in which the philosophical themes of alienation, freedom and man were 'rediscovered' as Marxist and justified by a reading of Marx's early works. Althusser's avowed aim is to prove that Marxism is not contained in Marx's early work, that Marxism is not a humanism and that the scientific basis of Marxism is to be found only in Marx's later work. He views humanism as an ideology and a threat to scientific knowledge (1969a, p. 12), and discusses at length the reason for this and for his basic distinction between ideology and science.

The ideology of humanism was the immediate stimulus for Althusser's re-reading of Marx but it is clear that this 'deviation' was possible only because of the historical conditions under which French Communism developed, and this constitutes the conjuncture in which Althusser's work is relevant in a more general sense. In the introduction to *For Marx*, he examines the lack of a theoretical tradition in French Communism as being due to specific historical conditions under which the revolutionary bourgeoisie was able to assimilate intellectuals to its revolution and retain their support after the consolidation of bourgeois power in 1789, 1830 and 1848. French intellectuals accepted this situation and felt no need to rally to the emergent working class; even when they did, their theory was imbued with bourgeois ideology in the form of idealism, reformism and positivism. The particular form of bourgeois domination in France thus deprived the workers' movement of the intellectuals indispensable to the formation of an authentic theoretical tradition in a way that was not the case in other European countries (Althusser mentions Germany, Russia, Italy and Poland). An additional factor contributing to the theoretical vacuum was the close link between French philosophy and religion, and the academicism of French philosophy in general. When French intellectuals began to join the Communist party in large numbers, in the Popular Front and immediate post-war period, they came for political reasons and integrated themselves as activists rather than as intellectuals. Althusser (1969a, p. 27) criticizes them for failing to realize the legitimate role of philosophy as opposed to economic and political theory and for 'paying their debt to the working class in pure activism', when they could have contributed much more in the form of theory as intellectuals. Given the precarious nature of Marxist philosophy as such, there was little resistance to the reinterpretation of Marxism as humanism which was stimulated outside the Communist movement, and Althusser sees his own work as fulfilling to some extent the urgent need for French Communism to reverse the circumstances which made this possible.

95

One of Althusser's epistemological propositions is that science is not socially determined, but 'relatively autonomous' and irreducible to other practices. He maintains that each science has its own raw material and means of transformation of the raw material with which it produces knowledge. Both the content and method of the science are internally given: their proof and validation are internally guaranteed and do not depend on external guarantees in the real world. Given this, Althusser's insistence on the conjunctural nature of his work, which he claims as scientific, is either contradictory or superfluous. The conjunctural reasons are either relevant or they are not. Althusser claims that they are at the outset but the implication of his later substantive theses is that they are unimportant, as theory is autonomous.

Althusser's assertions about the nature of philosophy and himself as a philosopher are also confusing since what he means by philosophy is quite different in *For Marx* and *Reading Capital* from what he means by it in *Lenin and Philosophy*. In the earlier work (1969a, pp. 168–9), philosophy is identified with dialectical materialism as 'the theory of practice in general'; it functions to integrate the knowledge established by historical materialism in the specific fields of economics, politics and ideology and justifies it by reference to a theory of theory. In this view science appears to have an existence as such, independent of particular sciences, and exists in the form of canons of method applicable to all sciences and practices. However in the later work, a quite different picture emerges: scientificity is seen as an internal property of particular sciences, with no general existence, and philosophy is reinterpreted as political intervention. Does this change of perspective alter Althusser's conception of his own work in any radical way? If philosophy is a form of political intervention, what does it mean to undertake a philosophical reading of Marx? And if philosophy is not science, what is scientific about Althusser's own work? His aim at the outset is to establish an epistemology for historical materialism, but if his later position is that science as such does not exist in general, then this must apply to epistemology as well. He cannot logically maintain that there is no such thing as science but that there is epistemology, but this seems to be what he does by introducing epistemological concepts which are implied to be of general correctness, that is, apart from the particular sciences in which they are contained. He certainly retains a view of the procedure of scientific practice as production and transformation of raw material into knowledge, and argues that this applies to all sciences, natural and social, and indeed to all forms of production. But the *raison d'être* of this meta-science is unclear. Thus we are presented with an apparent internal contradiction in Althusser's own theses on science and scientific proof which must throw doubt on his status as epistemologist and meta-theorist.

This contradiction is only one of many which occur in Althusser's work, and they will be examined more fully in later sections. The aim here is merely to indicate the existence of an ambiguity at the outset which must guide our reading of Althusser.

The intention in this chapter is to examine the contribution of Althusser to Marxism and to epistemology, and to discuss the problems contained both in his general outlook and in particular propositions.

Genealogy

The last chapter included a genealogy of the intellectual influences on Lévi-Strauss, and the same will be done for Althusser. The main influences on him are within the Marxist tradition, mainly Marx himself, but also Lenin and Mao, and these do not need to be dealt with separately from Althusser's contribution to Marxism. A second influence derives indirectly from the political conjuncture of contemporary French Communism which has already been mentioned, and has a negative character: Althusser's work is a critique of Hegel, Feuerbach and all humanist, historicist and idealist reinterpretations of Marxism from Gramsci and Lukaès to Sartre and Goldmann. In fact there are no influences on Althusser in the same sense as there were for Lévi-Strauss, whose general outlook was shaped by many different theories in diverse academic disciplines. The difference is largely due to the different nature of their work: Althusser's work consists in an original re-reading and exposition of Marx, and the theoretical innovations he makes depend on this reading rather than on the work of others. Where he is influenced by others it is in a highly specific way: he borrows particular concepts and terms to describe concepts that are already present in some form in Marx. The most important theorists whose influence he acknowledges are Bachelard, the French philosopher of science, Freud and Spinoza.

Bachelard

The most obvious borrowing from Bachelard is the concept of the 'epistemological break' which marks the transition from ideology to science within a theoretical problematic. The concept was introduced in Bachelard's *La Formation de l'esprit scientifique* (1967), and has been subsequently used in studies in the history of ideas by Canguilhem and Foucault, whom Althusser also acknowledges. It describes the rupture between the prescientific and scientific world

97

of ideas which involves a break with the existing pattern and frame of reference and the construction of a new pattern or problematic. Althusser applies it to Marx's rejection of the Feuerbachian ideology of his youth and construction of the basic concepts of historical and dialectical materialism in his later works, and to his break with the concepts of classical political economy.[3]

Althusser's conviction that the production of scientific knowledge proceeds by ruptures with previous modes of thought rather than by a cumulative process derives from Bachelard. His outlook on the scientific process as a whole is influenced by Bachelard in a more general way than he admits. For Bachelard, science is founded on a break with all theoretical elaborations of social and practical experience in the real world. The orders of perception and knowledge must be kept distinct since the elaboration of abstract concepts based on observation is an 'epistemological obstacle' to be overcome by science. Scientific knowledge is the product of a 'rational materialist' practice which produces knowledge through the reflection of scientific concepts on their theoretical object. In this way, Bachelard maintains the autonomy of science and the independence of its concepts from those based on observation. Much of his work takes the form of a 'psychoanalysis' of thought in the natural sciences from the seventeenth century, and he draws attention to the errors introduced by two major obstacles: not going beyond the first experience and premature generalization which often followed chronologically. In his view, science is not given directly; its problems and methods must be specific and must be produced, so the first experience is inevitably dangerous in preceding these prerequisites. For instance, until Coulomb electricity was thought easy to explain an explanation centred on its amusing aspects (tricks that could be performed with it), while at the same time scientists were concerned to discover empirical contradictions that would testify to the unknowable mystery of nature. In alchemy too, the orientation was not towards abstract theorems that could explain empirical observations, but to a moral evaluation of the different minerals and of the experimenter, so that the failure of an experiment or differences in experimental results were interpreted as being due to the personal inadequacies of the experimenter.

According to Bachelard, this 'false' science, fixated at the first experience and on external appearances, satisfied curiosity and produced admiration and images rather than knowledge and ideas. The first experience is too easy and gives the illusion of understanding, and science can be established only by a complete break with this necessary first outlook. Overconcentration on perception as the basis of knowledge leads to the faulty substantialization of abstract properties which are assumed to constitute the essence of phenomena. For example, for a long time the concept of coagulation, seen as a process that occurred in one type of matter, was used to explain the transformation from liquid to solid, and between different solid states in all others (sap becoming wood, wood becoming stone) so that all solid beings including men were thought to be the result of a process of coagulation.[4]

A second epistemological obstacle discussed by Bachelard is that of analogy and metaphor which demonstrate inadequate scientific terminology. He gives the example of the sponge which was, at one time, used analogously to explain many phenomena which were in fact quite unrelated. Réamur saw air as a sponge because it could be easily compressed; water was also conceived as a sponge and 'spongeosity' came to explain how any matter was filled by another. In this way, an image based on external traits and on very general and undefined notions was hypostatized as a process of property with a real existence, and thus inhibited the accumulation of genuine knowledge (Bachelard, 1967, p. 81): 'The danger to science of the most immediate metaphors is that rather than being passing images, they tend to become autonomous.'

As we shall see, Althusser's epistemology is very largely based on the ideas of Bachelard. He retains the crucial distinction between science and ideology, and maintains that science develops through theoretical production, and that scientific concepts are developed theoretically and not by abstraction from observation. Both argue that science develops through a critique of previous ideological thought; that is, it works on already existing concepts rather than facts and objects, and that the guarantees of the scientific nature of a science are internal to the science. Many of these points are presented by Althusser as assertions with very little explanation. Where he does refer them back it is usually to Marx's methodological *Introduction to the Critique of Political Economy*, but they are in fact argued in a more extensive way in the work of Bachelard.

Freud

Freud is relevant to Althusserian theory in two ways. First, Althusser credits Freud with having founded a science by defining the specific object of study of psychoanalysis, which was the unconscious, and he finds confirmation of his analysis of the latent epistemology in Marx in Lacan's re-reading of Freud and reinterpretation of the scientific basis of his work, which is similar to his own reading of Marx (Althusser and Balibar, 1970, p. 157): 'Freud's object is a radically new object with respect to the "object" of the psychological or philosophical ideologies of his predecessors. Freud's object is the

H

99

unconscious.' More specifically, Althusser borrows certain notions and concepts from Freud as of relevance to political economy: the notion of 'symptomatic' reading, the concepts of displacement, condensation, overdetermination and finally ideas on historical time.

The notion of a 'symptomatic' reading is based on the model of the Freudian analyst's reading of his patient's utterances. Althusser maintains that the problems of any theory can be solved only by learning to read the texts correctly. Neither a superficial reading which takes what is written as the total text, nor a Hegelian reading which deduces the essence of a work by extracting the 'true kernel from the mystical shell' are sufficient. Only a 'symptomatic' reading will do and this involves constructing the problematic and bringing out what remains latent or silent in the text. The reading considers the absence of problems and concepts within a problematic as much as their presence. Thus Althusser argues that there may be an unconscious in theory as in the mind, and to comprehend it a particular approach is needed. It was Freud who first realized this for psychology (Althusser and Balibar, 1970, p. 16):

> Only since Freud have we come to suspect what listening, and
> hence what speaking (and keeping silent) means (*veut dire*);
> that this 'meaning' (*vouloir dire*) of speaking and listening
> reveals beneath the innocence of speech and hearing the
> culpable depth of a second, quite different discourse, the
> discourse of the unconscious.

Althusser uses certain terms introduced in Freud's *Interpretation of Dreams* (1954) to describe the internal structure of the Marxist totality. The most important of these structural concepts are condensation, displacement and overdetermination. The first two are applied to the analysis of contradictions. Freud used them to indicate the two ways in which dream thoughts are represented in the dream work, by the condensation of a number of dream thoughts into one image, or by transferring psychical intensity from one image to another. Althusser uses them analogously to denote the overdetermination of contradictions in the Marxist theory of history. For example, in stable periods the essential contradictions of the social formation are neutralized by displacement: the determinant role may be displaced from the economy to other instances of the social formation. However, in a revolutionary situation, they may fuse into a revolutionary rupture through a process of condensation.

Overdetermination is a central concept in the Althusserian notion of structural causality (see below p. 147). Freud used the term to describe the representation of the dream thoughts in images through the condensation or displacement of several dream thoughts.

Althusser uses it to describe the relationship between the parts of a social formation and the whole, and to describe the effects of the contradictions in each level of the social formation on the social formation as a whole. This in turn reacts back on each level and each contradiction so defining the pattern of dominance and subordination between the various parts of a social formation at any given moment in time. For Althusser, contradictions are never simple, but always overdetermined. In his use of this term, Althusser is careful to point out that it is not borrowed by arbitrary analogy but because it is of relevance both to the science of history and of the unconscious because of their common need to conceptualize the determination of an element by a structure (Althusser and Balibar, 1970, p. 188):

> As one might suppose, this transfer of an analytical concept to Marxist theory was not an arbitrary borrowing but a necessary one, for the same theoretical problem is at stake in both cases: with what concept are we to think the determination of either an element or a structure by a structure?

In *Reading Capital* (1970), both Althusser and Balibar acknowledge their debt to Freud's thoughts on time and the form in which phenomena are related to each other in time and history. In their view, each element in a mode of production has its own history, developmental trajectory and independent time-scale. Because of this, the history of such element needs to be constructed separately, and the resultant totality has to be viewed as a conjunctural fusion of elements which may develop independently rather than the evolution of elements on the same time base. They claim that Freud was one of the first to realize that time is not a simple concept: he recognized that the time of the unconscious must not be confused with biographical time and that the concept of unconscious time must be constructed. Just as historical materialism is concerned with the replacement of one mode of production by another, where the relation between the old and new is one of displacement rather than evolution, so Freud's analysis of the history of the libido in *Three Essays on Theory of Sexuality* (1962) rejects the idea of evolution in favour of a theory of stages of development and reorganizations.

The relevance of all these notions drawn from Freud and their extensive use in Althusserian Marxism will become clearer in the following sections of this chapter and the next.

Spinoza

Spinoza has a similar role in Althusser's theory to Freud but less

101

important. Althusser credits him (Althusser and Balibar, 1970, p. 31) with philosophical insights of great importance to science but which have been largely ignored and in many cases suppressed. In *For Marx* (1969a, p. 210), Althusser congratulates Spinoza for having realized the need for the production of theory, and for having 'laboured' as a theoretician himself in much the same way as Galileo and Marx. More important, he developed a theory of the 'opacity of the immediate' based on the realization that the manifest does not present the latent, and this is an additional influence shaping Althusser's conception of 'symptomatic' reading. Spinoza also anticipated much later philosophy by distinguishing the object and knowledge of the object as distinct orders, a distinction of profound importance in Althusser's epistemology. He emphasized that the object of knowledge was absolutely distinct from the real object and that the two should not be confused: 'the idea of the circle, which is the object of knowledge, must not be confused with the circle, which is the real object' (quoted in Althusser and Balibar, 1970, p. 40). This distinction between real and knowledge of the real was taken up by Marx in the *Introduction to the Critique of Political Economy* (1904), and is greatly elaborated in Althusser's essay 'From Capital to Marx's Philosophy'.

Althusser (Althusser and Balibar, 1970, pp. 187, 189) implies that the idea of 'metonymic causality' is prefigured in Spinoza's essentially synchronic approach to reality. Whereas the Hegelian totality is an essentialist one where one instance determines all the others, Spinoza posed the problem of the determination of the elements by the structure of the whole, and thus saw cause as immanent in its effect and hence the possibility of synchronic explanation. For both Spinoza and Althusser, explanation has a synchronic dimension where knowledge of the relations of articulation and dependence of the various parts make the whole intelligible as an organized system. In this way, Althusser claims Spinoza as a predecessor to Marx's conception of cause, rather than Hegel.

Like Bachelard, Spinoza saw the development of knowledge as discontinuous rather than cumulative, and in this respect again Marx's position seems to owe more to Spinoza than to Hegel. For Hegel developments in knowledge were cumulative and present knowledge preserved all past knowledge through a process of supersession (*Aufhebung*). Spinoza on the other hand, emphasized radical discontinuities rather than the growth of knowledge, and distinguished different systems of thought on the basis of the different questions they asked (Althusser 1969a, p. 78).

Bachelard, Freud and Spinoza all provide terms or concepts which Althusser finds indispensable for historical materialism, and which he integrates into his notions of structure and history.

Althusser and Marxism

The bulk of the work of Althusser and his collaborators consists of a symptomatic reading of Marx to demonstrate the theoretical rupture between his early and later works. This reading is premissed on the assumption that beneath the visible text lies another which is not amenable to an 'innocent' reading. This second text is 'the presence of a necessary absence in the first' and considers the silences and what is not said to be as significant as the visible text. The implication is that the existing formulation of a text does not necessarily express what the author wants to say, or that, in the case of *Capital*, Marx did not possess the theoretical concepts in which to conceptualize the rupture that he had made with previous ideological forms of knowledge including the works of his youth. Althusser's symptomatic reading is thus crucial to his central argument that Marx's work is characterized by an epistemological break in 1845, after which he worked within a completely different problematic.

On the basis of textual analysis, Althusser and his collaborators postulate the stages through which Marx's thought passes. They attempt to show the specificity and distinctiveness of Marx's concepts of structure, totality, and history and by implication provide a critique of past and contemporary variants of Marxism which are influenced by empiricism, historicism and idealism. Finally, Althusser and Balibar extrapolate from what they find in Marx to elaborate concepts referring to the internal structure of the Marxist totality and the periodization of structures through time. These have important implications for Marxist theory as a whole since for them the notions of consciousness, class, and the role of the economy have a very much more limited role than in other variants, and they present an alternative framework for the analysis of social formations. The present section will be devoted to a brief exposition of their most important propositions, and the problems raised by them will be discussed in a following section.

Stages of Marx's thought

Althusser divides the stages of development of Marx's thought as follows:

(1) 1840–2. This was the period of the *Rheinische Zeitung*, dominated by a rational liberalism closer to Kant and Fichte than Hegel.[5] Politically, Marx was leading the struggle against censorship and criticizing Prussian absolutism and the feudal laws of the Rhineland as irrational, and this depended on a philosophical conception of man's essence as liberty and reason: man was destined for

103

liberty by his very nature. Marx counterposed the non-rational system of privileges of German absolutism to the modern French state which to him exemplified liberty in the form of law, and he demanded that the Prussian state become that of human nature.

(2) The years between 1842 and 1845 were dominated by Feuerbachian humanism. Marx rejected his previous rationalism when the Prussian state failed to reform itself, and came to see its abuses no longer as deviations from its essence (Reason) but as due to the contradiction between its existence and essence, or unreason and reason. This conflict was the basis of Feuerbach's philosophy where history was the production of reason in unreason, of the true man in the alienated man. Man was at present realizing his essence through the alienated products of his labour but would ultimately reappropriate his essence to become the subject of history once more. Marx no longer appealed to the state since this too was a product of alienation, but to an alliance between philosophy which affirmed man in theory and the proletariat as the negation of history and human nature. Philosophy would give the proletariat the theory of what it was and the proletariat would provide armed force for a 'Communist' revolution.

(3) The period of 1845 and after was that of the epistemological break from a theory based on the concept of human essence. This rupture included a critique of the theoretical pretensions of all philosophical humanism and a definition of humanism as ideology, but more important, it founded a theory of history and politics on entirely new concepts: social formation, productive forces, relations of production, superstructures, ideologies, determination by the economy, relative autonomy, and others. According to Althusser, this rupture with anthropological humanism is inseparable from the birth of historical materialism as a science: these concepts could not have been 'thought' in the old problematic. The old problematic had assumed that there is a universal human nature which constitutes the essence of man and that this is an attribute of each individual man, and rested philosophically on an empiricism of the subject and idealism of the essence.[6] In rejecting this, Marx also rejected a whole set of postulates in political economy, history and philosophy, and the foundation of his scientific theory of society or historical materialism was correspondingly accompanied by a new philosophy whose main characteristic was the replacement of the subject/essence couple by a dialectical materialism of practice; that is, a theory of the different specific levels of human practice: economic, political, theoretical and ideological.

Althusser argues that this break occurred in 1845, and that Marx's work was of a transitional nature between 1845 and 1857.

The mature Marx appeared in 1857. The works of the rupture are the *Theses on Feuerbach* and *The German Ideology*. The period of maturation includes works prior to *Capital* such as *The Communist Manifesto, Poverty of Philosophy* and *Wages, Price and Profit*.[7]

Althusser's periodization contrasts with other conceptions of the development of Marx's thought in several ways. For one thing, Althusser maintains that Marx was constantly moving away from Hegel, even in his very early works, and that he never worked within a Hegelian problematic except in the *1844 Manuscripts*. At first he criticized Hegel from a Feuerbachian standpoint and later from a materialist point of view. This view of Marx conflicts with that of most humanist Marxists from Lukaès to Marcuse who see a substantial continuity between Marx's early and later work with the concepts of alienation, praxis and negation as central to Marx's entire œuvre. How these different views of Marx's development and particularly his relation to Hegel affect the notions of structure and history will soon become clear. The only other philosophical interpretation of Marx which also sees a rupture between Hegel and Marx and Feuerbach and Marx is that of the Italians Della Volpe and Colletti but they locate it in 1843 in the 'Critique of Hegel's Philosophy of Right.'

The periodization is specific in another way: it exemplifies Althusser's view that science develops by rupture with an ideological past, whereas Marxist historicists following Hegel see the development of knowledge as cumulative, with past ideology being preserved in a superseded form in the present. This difference explains the abruptness of the break Althusser attributes to Marx in 1845.

Certainly concepts derived from Hegel and Feuerbach continue to be used in Marx's later work (fetishism, alienation, dialectic) but Althusser does not find this a problem. Rather than being evidence of the continuity of Marx's thought, the survival of these notions is due to a lack of terminology available to Marx to describe his new concepts. The terms may be borrowed but the problematic is quite different, and so where Hegelian terminology continues to be used its denotation is no longer Hegelian.

Given that Althusser's periodization is a particular one the question arises as to whether it is a correct interpretation and whether Althusser's Marx is the 'real' Marx. However this will not concern us very much here since we are more concerned with Althusser than with Marx. What interests us especially is the implication of this periodization for Althusser's conception of Marxist history and philosophy, rather than the problem of validating his interpretation of Marx, although this will be relevant to a general evaluation of Althusser's contribution to Marxism.

The Marxist totality: structure and history

The touchstone of the structuralist interpretation of Marx resides in the interrelated concepts of structure and history after 1845. Though Hegel and Marx both used the terms totality and contradiction what was meant by them was quite different in the two cases. In Hegel's totality there is a kind of circular unity of equivalent elements whose mode of articulation is determined by their interiorization in the Idea. Social realities are phenomena or exteriorizations of the self-development of the Idea and there is no possibility of these having an autonomous or dominant role. As a result there is one major contradiction in Hegel's totality, between essence and phenomena, or Idea and civil society, and any secondary contradictions are not mere phenomena of the ongoing central contradiction but have their own autonomous influence on the system as a whole. The Marxist totality is not constructed from essence and phenomena but is a complex unity of separate and specific levels which may be relatively autonomous of each other within a given historical social formation. The totality is asymmetrical and may be dominated by one of its elements. This Althusser calls a 'structure in domination' (structure à dominate). The autonomy and interdependence of the various contradictions is expressed in terms of 'overdetermination' and a key distinction is made between determination by the economy in the last instance and the dominant role of any level in a social formation. The essential point is that the Marxist totality is not to be understood as a simple dialectic of essence (the economic base) versus the phenomena (the superstructure) where the latter is reducible to the former, but as a complex internally structured totality of various layers and levels interrelated in all sorts of relations of determination. The internal construction of the structure is not given in advance of a particular social formation, as it is in the Hegelian conception.

The specific differences between the Marxist and Hegelian concepts of totality and contradiction are discussed in Althusser's essay 'Contradiction and Overdetermination' (1969a). He argues that it is an illusion to believe that the characteristics of Marx's totality derive from a simple inversion of the Hegelian schema. If Marx had merely 'turned Hegel on his head' he would have maintained that civil society (or the economic base) constitutes the essence and determines the realm of ideas in a total way, and that the relationship between them was that of essence and epiphenomena. But Althusser argues that this was not the case on two counts. First, where Marx used the same terms as Hegel they referred to different concepts: 'civil society' in Marx's terms was not equivalent to individual economic behaviour, but all economic phenomena were conceived as the result of a more fundamental and concrete reality, the mode of production of a determinate society, so where individual economic behaviour is examined it is always referred to its conditions of existence. Similarly the state is not conceived in individual terms, but related to the ruling class and ultimately to the relations of production of a particular mode of production.

The second reason for the discrepancy between the Marxist and Hegelian totalities is that they posit a different relation between the parts. For Marx there is not one simple single contradiction between essence and phenomena but the possibility of secondary and autonomous contradictions is admitted. Society is determined 'in the last instance' by the economy but the economy is never active in a pure state and the last instance may never come. Thus at any given time, the social formation may be dominated by another of its levels: political, ideological or other, rather than the economy. So whereas Hegel's totality is an 'expressive' one where the phenomena merely 'express' the essence and have no independence, Marx's contradictions overdetermined and in the structure in domination there is the possibility of a hierarchy of levels and contradictions which may be relatively autonomous, dominant in the short run or determinant in the long run. The task of theory is to reveal the internal articulation of the structure and the hierarchies of efficacy of its various elements.

In this way the relationship between base and superstructure does not replicate that between essence and phenomena, and it is clear that the interpretation of Marxism as economic determinism relies on a Hegelian view of Marx. The relationship between base and superstructure is at the same time more complex and less predetermined because of the relative autonomy of all the levels, including those of the superstructure, and the fact that they can also have an effect on the economy which is itself only determinant in the last instance.

Althusser draws support for this formulation from Marx's analysis of concrete historical revolutionary situations in France which deal specifically with ideology and politics, and from Engels, Lenin and Mao. Engels was aware that the distinction between base and superstructure could be interpreted in a Hegelian and economic determinist fashion, and many letters that he wrote after the death of Marx attempted to defend historical materialism for this interpretation. For example, in his letter to J. Bloch in 1890 (Marx and Engels, 1951 edn, vol II, p. 443) he wrote:

> The ultimately determining element in history is the production and reproduction of real life. More than this neither Marx nor I have ever asserted. Hence if somebody twists this into saying

that the economic element is the only determining one, he transforms that proposition into a meaningless, senseless phrase. The economic situation is the basis, but the various elements of the superstructure: political forms of the class struggle and its results, to wit, constitutions, established by the victorious class after a successful battle, etc.; juridical forms, and then even the reflexes of all these actual struggles in the brains of the participants, political, juristic, philosophical theories, religious views and their further development into systems of dogmas, also exercise their influence upon the course of the historical struggles and in many cases preponderate in determining their form.

Lenin's theory of the weak link and of the accumulation of contradictions necessary for a revolution provides additional evidence of the complexity of the Marxist totality, though his formulation was based on actual revolutionary experience and analysis of the historical conditions of pre-revolutionary Russia. Rather than being due to a simple contradiction between the forces and relations of production, the revolutionary situation in Russia depended on the accumulation of a number of contradictions and the fact that Russia was simultaneously a century behind the imperialist world and at the highest point of its feudal development. This contradiction could not be solved by the ruling class and Lenin saw in it the objective conditions for a revolution. In this way, political experience shows that, of itself, the contradiction between the forces and relations of production cannot provoke a revolutionary situation (Althusser, 1969a, p. 99): 'If this contradiction is to become "active" ... to become a ruptural principle, there must be an accumulation of circumstances and currents so that whatever their origin and sense, they fuse into a ruptural unity'. Thus for Lenin it was incorrect to speak of the sole power of a general contradiction since others also have an independent efficacy. The contradiction is inseparable from the total structure of the social body in which it is found, and it is affected even by the levels it dominates. As Althusser puts it (1969a, p. 101) the contradiction is 'determining and determined in one and the same movement by the various levels and instances of the social formation it animates; it might be called in principle overdetermined'.

Mao's writings similarly contain a distinctively unHegelian conception of contradiction. He distinguishes between principal and secondary contradiction, principal and secondary aspects of the contradiction, antagonistic and non-antagonistic contradictions, and discusses the uneven development of contradictions.[8]

So for Marx, Engels, Lenin and Mao the contradictions of

capitalism and imperialism are never simple, but always specified by historically concrete circumstances including the superstructure, the national past, and the international context. Their concept of totality and contradiction is anti-economist and anti-essentialist, and Althusser's reassertion of this is an attempt to combat such deviations which derive basically from a misconception of the relation between Marx and Hegel. The belief that the content of the Hegelian contradiction was only inverted results in economism, and essentialism results from retaining the same relation between the parts of the whole as existed in Hegel.

This conception of the Marxist totality is the basis for Althusser's rejection of historicism. The structure is not reducible to a unitary essence; it becomes intelligible through an examination of the mode of articulation of its levels, rather than the origin of its elements. Marx's conception of history is again quite different from Hegel's since in both cases the concepts of structure and history are interrelated. For Hegel history is the homogeneous continuity of time and is always contemporary. The characteristic of homogeneous continuity is a reflection of the continuous development of the Idea, so history becomes the task of periodizing moments of the Idea. The homogeneity of time legitimates the second aspect, the present as history, since it is possible at every moment to uncover the ensemble of elements constituting the original whole which permits periodization. As all the elements of the whole coexist always and simultaneously, the structure of history permits any essential section (*coupe d'essence*) of history to exhibit all the elements. The contemporaneity is directly related to the concept of unity which excludes the possibility of the domination by one of the elements. In Althusser's view the concept of history can be given content only be defining historical time as a specific form of existence of a social totality with structural levels of different temporalities in relations of correspondence, noncorrespondence and so on. Different levels of the totality are thus considered to have their own time-scale related to their relative autonomy which may be related to each other in different ways at different moments. The relationship between one social formation and the one that follows it is to be understood in terms of displacement rather than the gradual unfolding of an innate developmental potential. Each element has its own history and time scale and the resultant structure must be viewed as a more or less conjunctural unity of different and separate histories. There is no general time base or general conception of time which can comprehend this structural history.

Marx's conception of history becomes clear from his criticisms of the classical economists. He criticized their analysis of primitive accumulation for attributing to men of an earlier epoch, characteristics which were appropriate only to capitalist society. By seeing accumulation as the result of thrift on the part of proto-capitalists, they treated as universal, characteristics applicable only to one type of society, and hence denied the historical diversity of different social formations.

But Marx did not merely historicize political economy. Balibar maintains that his notion of complex 'structures in domination' is realized in the analysis of modes of production as specific combinations of different elements necessary to all production. Each element of the combination has its own history. For example, the transformation between feudalism and capitalism required two elements: the free worker and capital. These have different histories and their relationship can be studied only retrospectively from the point of view of the capitalist system where they are combined. So rather than focusing on the gradual unfolding from one system to another through a series of contradictions, or on origins, it is argued that Marx's analysis centres on a genealogy of the different elements. In this way, history represents the discontinuous succession of modes of production.[9]

Balibar's central argument is that a close reading of *Capital*, *Precapitalist Economic Formations*, and *Grundrisse* reveals that Marx thought five elements were necessary to any mode of production:

(1) The worker or direct producer—labour power
(2) The means of production: objects and instruments
(3) The non-worker, appropriating the surplus labour

These are combined by two relations

(4) Property connexion—refers to the relations of production
(5) Real or material appropriation connexion—refers to the productive forces.[10]

Each mode of production is the result of a different combination of these elements, and the content of each varies according to the particular mode, so the worker may be individual or collective depending on whether the mode of production is capitalistic or feudal. The elements are not 'invariable atoms of history' but comparative analysis defines each mode of production by a specific combination of them, and the combination in turn influences their content. Balibar gives the example of the capitalist and feudal modes where the elements are the same, though their content differs: in feudal societies there is the relation between serf and lord, and in capitalist ones between the worker and capitalist. However, the relations between the elements differ: labour power and the means (instruments) of labour are unified in feudalism since the serfs own their tools (this is relation 5 above) and the worker is not separate from the means of production, whereas in capitalism the worker is formally 'free' and labour power is separate from the means of production. In feudalism, necessary and surplus labour can be distinguished in time and space and surplus labour is provided only after the intervention of non-economic, primarily political factors. The opposite is the case under capitalism: the work process and process of production of surplus value coincide, necessary and surplus work are indistinguishable, surplus value goes automatically to the ruling class so there is no need for the intervention of non-economic factors in the labour process.

Another example is Marx's analysis of primitive accumulation which studies the genealogy of elements constituting the structure of the capitalist mode of production. This is based on two concepts: the pre-conditions of the capitalist mode and the historical conditions in which these are fulfilled. The history of different modes is not the history of their succession but a historical analysis of the different routes by which the separation of the worker from the means of production, and the constitution of disposable capital, are accomplished. By envisaging the formation of the 'free' worker and capital separately the analysis of primitive accumulation does not coincide with the history of anterior modes of production. Marx recognized that these two elements were inextricably associated only in capitalist societies and so avoided projecting a contemporary structure on to the past. Transformation is examined at the level of elements rather than the structure as a whole. The same presuppositions apply to a series of historical conditions. Each mode of production is constituted by 'finding' several already formed elements which its structure combines. The analysis of the dissolution of a social formation takes a similar form.

Clearly this approach has nothing to do with history as evolution nor as linear causality through time. The concept of structure determines the way in which the temporal dimension is relevant. Where the structure is one of relatively autonomous elements it must be recognized that each has its own development and trajectory.[11]

Marxist anti-humanism

Althusser's readings of Marx reveals the profoundly anti-humanist implications of Marxism: it lacks any notions of human essence or nature and its unit of analysis is the social formation as a whole rather than the individual.

One root of this is the key role of production in Althusser's theory. He claims that all production is of the same kind, though he establishes this only by analogy. There are four kinds of production: material, political, theoretical and ideological. Each of these is also a practice and is specific so that for example, the practice of theory occurs entirely within the process of thought and results in the production of knowledge. So for Althusser, Marx's *Capital* is a theoretical production and cannot be verified or compared with everyday experience in social reality. It is because the theory is correct that it has been applied successfully; it is not because it has been applied with success that it is correct. Thus later historical practice cannot give the knowledge that Marx produced its status as knowledge (Althusser and Balibar, 1970, p. 59). 'The criterion of the "truth" of the knowledges produced by Marx's theoretical practice is provided by his theoretical practice itself.' Theory is not part of the superstructure but science produced by transforming a raw material, ideology or pre-scientific ideas into knowledge by a particular means of transformation. This process of transformation of a raw material into a product with the aid of particular means or instruments characterizes all productions, which thus have an analogous character. The notion of praxis used in certain variants of Marxism to characterize meaningful action, or the dialectical unity of theory and practice, has no role in Althusser's schema. It is replaced by those of production and practice, where theory is one among other instances, and each production rests on practice.

The mode of production is presented as a 'combinaison articulée' of five elements (see above, p. 110) which coexist and define each other reciprocally. It is defined by the various modes of articulation between these elements. Althusser describes this as an 'immense machine', or 'play without an author' or 'presence of an absence', since the internal articulation of the social formation does not rest on the activity of men, as individuals or groups. It is anti-humanist: the lived relations between particular men are not of interest to science, they are only one part of a specific combination of agents and objects in a specific structure of relations, places and functions. In this conception, men do not consciously create structures, and it is more pertinent to think in terms of an absent cause or 'the existence of a structure through its effects.'[12] History here is not based on man as in humanist Marxism which relies on the concepts of the early Marx. Men do not constitute a unit of analysis, only relations of production. So for Althusser (ibid., p. 66), what Marx is studying in *Capital* is the mechanism which makes the result of history's production exist as a society, so focussing his theoretical attention on the mechanism 'producing the society-effect peculiar to the capitalist mode of production'. The subjects of history are social formations and these include three main instances: the economy, polity and ideology, each of which have a relatively autonomous existence and practices specific to them. Ideology here has the meaning of the lived relations between men and their world, and is a necessary part of all societies including post-revolutionary ones.

This anti-humanism is one of the most distinctive aspects of Althusserian Marxism, and has many similarities with Lévi-Strauss's anti-subjectivism. For both of them, relations and structures are the unit for analysis, rather than man's lived and subjective experience, and these are to be explained by impersonal structural forces (play without an author) (see below p. 149). It is on the basis of this that Althusser criticizes and rejects theories and philosophies based on concepts of alienation, human nature or praxis, which all tend to be based ultimately on the individual and to conceive of theory as superstructural; that is, as being an expression of class consciousness and thus directly tied to a social base, rather than having a scientific truth independent of its social determination. Both of these, he would argue, derive from a Hegelian and essentialist philosophy and are incapable of viewing social formations as complex unities of levels and instances with their own specific practices and productions.

To summarize this section, in the structuralist interpretation of Marx, historical materialism is a theory of structures based on certain fundamental concepts: forces of production, relations of production, economic base, and political and ideological level which are related by metonymic causality where the economy is determinant in the last instance but where the other instances have their own autonomous development within limits. Other crucial concepts include determination, dominance, the specificity of practices, overdetermination and production.

History is the development of structures and their transformation. The theory of *Capital* is the theory of the development of the capitalist mode of production conceived as a structure and set of relations rather than a particular society or ideal-type. This conception differs radically from both humanist, historicist and economic determinist interpretations of Marx, and Althusser's philosophy and epistemology are anti-empiricist and anti-idealist.

Though Althusser's approach is negative in making a damning critique of other contemporary variants of Marxism, it is also positive in providing a clear set of alternative concepts. These have many implications which have not been spelt out here and raise many questions and problems, the most important of which will be examined in a later section.

Althusser and epistemology

Althusser's analysis of Marx includes many epistemological propositions about the nature of theoretical activity, its status *vis-à-vis* science, ideology and other activities, and he proposes a 'theory of theoretical activity' and of the production of knowledge.[13] Several of his most important particular propositions have already been mentioned, specifically the notions of symptomatic reading, the epistemological break and the problematic. By problematic, Althusser means a defined theoretical structure or specific conceptual framework which determines the forms of posing all questions and what is seen as relevant to the questions; the problematic includes particular theories, concepts and methods, and places internal limits on what is studied since objects and phenomena which do not have necessary links with its field are excluded (above, pp. 3–6). The notion of epistemological break is related to that of problematic: all problematics are distinct and specific, and Althusser makes a special distinction between ideology and science in this connexion; the transition from one problematic to another either at the point of establishment of a science or within an already established science can occur only by a break with the framework of the old problematic. A symptomatic reading is thought to be necessary for a complete understanding of theoretical works since authors are often not aware of the conceptual innovations or discoveries that they make and use terms appropriate to old concepts which they have in fact depassed—the symptomatic reading makes explicit these new concepts which are only latent in the text.

Chapter 5 will deal with the epistemological approach common to Lévi-Strauss, Althusser and the other structuralists, and will examine their ideas on conceptualization, the relation between description, explanation and types of causation, and on synchrony and metonymic causality as the most appropriate approach to understanding causality in the realm of social and historical reality. These ideas are all discussed explicitly by Althusser, but they will not be examined here. The intention in this section is to give an overview of the general framework of Althusser's epistemology, and the fundamental concepts which are the basis of his particular propositions, so as to show how his substantive points about the Marxist totality are linked to his epistemology, and so provide the basis for a critique which can include these two aspects of his work.

Certain of Althusser's fundamental ideas about why scientific procedure has to operate in a certain way have already been touched on by implication. For example, the idea that reality exists at the level of structural relations between parts of the social formation rather than at the level of individual human beings has consequences for methodology since individuals do not, in Althusser's view, constitute a correct unit of study. The structure of the mode of production or social formation has a real existence which is not invalidated by the fact that it cannot be perceived by observation nor studied at the individual level. However it is concrete and can be made intelligible by theoretical work, so that there is a one-to-one correspondence between the theory and reality.

At an epistemological level this means that Althusser rejects the common distinction drawn between the 'real' conceived as concrete, and science or knowledge conceived as abstract. To Althusser, any view of science as abstraction from the concrete observable rests on an empiricism of the object, that is, the idea that the correct object can be empirically perceived (which may not be so in all cases), and on an idealism of the essence or the belief that the empirical object contains its own truth or knowledge of itself which can be extracted by abstraction. Althusser on the other hand sees knowledge as concrete, and science as proceeding from abstract to concrete rather than the reverse. This is because, for him, theory works not on empirical objects and phenomena but on already existing general concepts which it transforms or refines. For example, he argues that Marx took as his basis for the study of capital not empirical facts about capitalist society but general concepts such as production, work and exchange which had been used by the classical economists and which he transformed. In this way, theory proceeds by a critique of past knowledge, and there is an absolute distinction between reality and the scientific description of reality, or the orders of reality and thought.

In this respect, Althusser is diametrically opposed to Lévi-Strauss. In Lévi-Strauss's most recent works, myth-science and the science of myth are confounded by the one-to-one relations he maintains between the structural elements of his theory and the reality they are intended to conceptualize. But for Althusser, there is a basic distinction between theory and the object of theory, or the 'concrete real' and 'concrete in thought'. Theory is about a theoretical object, and this latter is already at several removes from empirical reality. Neither the relationship between the theoretical object and the raw data, nor between the theory of the theoretical object and the raw data, are made very clear. This basic difference will be further discussed in chapter 5.

The most distinctive feature of Althusser's epistemology is his view of science and theoretical activity as production and as forming one of the levels of the social formation with its own internal organization and relative independence from all other levels. He maintains both that theoretical practice is a specific one and that its products or results and their validity are independent of their embeddedness in the social structure, and that theory is a form of production. All his other propositions about science and scientific method hinge on this. His discussions do not distinguish between science and theory (one assumes they are identical since he makes the distinction between science and ideology and between theory and ideology)—they both produce knowledge by theoretical practice which is one of the four levels or practices of the social formation (the others being economic, political, and ideological practice). Each practice has its own specific forms of combination of productive means, labour and material. The complex totality of all four practices comprises social practice.

Theoretical practice is distinguished from political and economic practice by its raw material: it works in the realm of ideas to produce knowledge, and differs from ideological practice because of its epistemological formation: it is counterposed to all forms of empiricism and idealism. Yet all ideas are produced, including 'ideological' ones, and there is a similar procedure of production in all four practices.

In his theory of production in general and of theoretical production, in particular, Althusser distinguishes between raw material, means of production and resultant product, and he calls these Generalities I, II and III. Generality I represents the first matter which science transforms into specific concepts and concrete knowledge, viz. Generality III. Science thus operates in transforming Generality I into Generality III by means of Generality II which is the means of production of this transformation. Althusser does not write much of Generality II except to say that it is the most crucial, but it is clear that his particular propositions about method and procedure are supposed to form part of the means of production of knowledge. This view is in strict contrast to what Althusser dubs as the 'empiricist' approach which assumes that science works from something given whose 'essence' constitutes knowledge and is reached by abstraction. For him, the real distinction between abstract and concrete is that between Generality I and Generality III rather than between concrete real and abstract science. Thus in Marxist or any scientific theoretical practice it is Generality II that predominates and the transformational characteristic of science is its most distinctive trait. Excessive reliance on Generality I results in empiricism where knowledge is believed to flow from the raw material and speculation is the necessary concomitant of reliance on Generality III.

Althusser is adamant that knowledge must be produced, through rigorous theoretical activity, like all other productions. Science, both natural and social, proceeds through critique and seeks concepts which correspond in thought to the constituent elements of objective reality. Once established, science has a certain permanence, in that new developments build on present knowledge and incorporate rather than reject it, though there is always the danger that science may relapse into ideology. In addition, the non-correspondence of actual events to the theory need not invalidate the theory, which functions not as a heuristic device to predict variables, but as a conceptualization of structure, of which some elements were perhaps neglected, or perhaps some have developed or changed since the formulation of the theory, so the theory must be modified to include these. The latter may be seen as the case with the non-occurrence of the consequences postulated by Marx's analysis of the interplay of the elements of the capitalist social formation. Discussing these points, Althusser claims that Einsteinian physics incorporates Newtonian physics: rather than rejecting the old conceptualization, the field was found to be wider than previously thought. This widening of the field and of the problematic does not contradict Althusser's assertions about the break separating ideology from science nor his criticism of the cumulative theory of knowledge. Within a given problematic, knowledge and discoveries may be cumulative when the same basic conceptual apparatus is used throughout, but the knowledge produced in different problematics is necessarily inconsistent and cannot therefore be cumulative.

So theoretical practice is a process which works by determinate means (an apparatus of theoretical concepts) on selected raw material (including the pre-existing products of theoretical practice and ideology rather than the 'real-concrete') to produce theoretical knowledge (the 'concrete in thought'). Theoretical and ideological practice differ, and they do not fuse even in a revolutionary situation: their relationship remains external throughout. The relation between theory and political practice is also a complex one: theory neither derives from political practice, nor leads it or fuses with it; rather, political practice is 'guided' by theory and the political conjuncture and the history of the class struggle have an important effect on theoretical practice; the two practices are interrelated but remain independent since they are relatively autonomous practices.

The implied relation between the theorist and his field contributes both to the durability of science and to the interaction between politics and theory. Once the structure of the social formation has been elaborated and the consequences of the interplay of its various levels and forces spelt out, it is possible for the theorist to add his own force to those already operating so as to change the structure in a desired direction. He can attempt to impose his own project or that of the party to which he belongs on the structure both practically and theoretically, by including his plan, that is, the plan of the revolutionary party, in the analysis of the total structure. This embodies a particular view of the relationship between theory and practice: the theorist is not passive in relation to his field of study even though his knowledge of the field is objective and scientific,

117

so objectivity does not require passivity or a purely external view of the field. He is active in two ways, first since theoretical practice is in itself active and productive and changes the state of knowledge, and second, because theory can guide political practice by revealing the structure of forces of a given social formation which political practice is trying to transform. In this way revolutionary theory and politics are linked but are not subordinated to each other. Althusser argues that Leninist theory in particular has been the basis which enables the political practice of the proletarian movement to identify the particular relation of forces within a concrete, historical conjuncture and hence to react to it.

The concept of production is thus of paramount importance to Althusser: all sciences have their own specific object, and concepts and methods appropriate to it. Analogies and borrowings between the sciences are thus likely to be incorrect because of the specificity of each object. Thus there is no unity of science at the level of methodology but neither does Althusser see the various regions of knowledge as unrelated. They are brought together through production: produces knowledge through theoretical practice whether this is in the region of mathematics, physics or history, and this production links them with the other practices which constitute the social formation since all production works from a raw material to produce a product. All productions thus have a homologous form though their content differs: they are linked by a general concept of practice rather than any notion of an original production in the past.

In this way the emphasis on relative autonomy that characterizes Althusser's substantive propositions about the Marxist totality also applies to his epistemology. Theory is a relatively autonomous practice: it is independent of other practices occurring in the realm of ideas, and of the social structure in its origins and validation. However, the exact meaning and implications of this relative autonomy are not clearly dealt with, and this problem will be discussed in the following section.

The concepts of production and relative autonomy are connected with a non-empiricist and non-instrumental view of social science and social reality. To summarize: objective knowledge of the social world is possible; it is achieved through adequate conceptualization of the elements of the social formation; science is truth, that is, there is only one correct analysis of reality and it is possible to achieve it, thus the aim of science is correct knowledge, not predictive ability, direct observation of the phenomena of the social world is of limited relevance both to the development of concepts and their validation; science works through the critique of past concepts and knowledge. Many of these ideas are also to be found in Lévi-Strauss, and in structural linguistics and psychoanalysis, and will be elaborated in chapter 5. But the idea of science and theory as productive practices is peculiar to Althusser.

Critical analysis

There are many ways in which a critique of Althusser, or indeed any theorist, could be undertaken, but it would be impossible to incorporate all of them. Given the highly schematic and metatheoretical nature of his writing, it might be thought that any evaluation should be based on an examination of more concrete and applied studies either by Althusser himself or by his collaborators or followers, so as to see whether the utility or correctness of his propositions can be proved by reference to concrete situations. The trouble with this approach is that there would be very little on which to base it: Althusser's recent work has not been any more applied than his original writings and has concentrated on Lenin and on the relationship between philosophy and science, and where his ideas have been used by others they have tended to become even more abstract and theoretical rather than the reverse. Perhaps this is because they have been applied to whole areas of society rather than concrete political conjunctures: Poulantzas for instance has studied the polity and Glucksmann war and politics. This is not to dismiss their works, which are important in themselves, but it is evident that the aim of such a critique would be frustrated by the nature of the material. An additional reason for rejecting such an approach is that, in Althusserian terms, it smacks of empiricism by measuring theory and concepts against concrete empirical situations, which is not what he understands by validation. There is no need for us to accept his view of this, but it is always more valuable to criticize a theory in its own terms and according to its own canons, and any criticism of Althusser's ideas on validation should be made explicitly rather than in this way.

A second approach would be to judge whether his interpretation of Marx is correct since he claims that most of his points are derivations from Marx. This would be of central relevance if the aim here was to situate Althusser within Marxist theory and compare his analysis of Marx with alternative interpretations. However, it is not central to a comparison of Althusser and Lévi-Strauss, nor to an examination of structuralism in general. Given this, we can assume either that Althusser's Marx is Marx and there is no problem of faulty interpretation, or that Marx and Althusser are different and that Althusser has been misattributing concepts to Marx—in either case we shall be concerned only with Althusser and treat what he attributes to Marx as Althusser's. So for the purposes of this analysis the two alternatives reduce to the same thing: we are examining

Althusser regardless of his relationship to Marx, although the truth probably lies somewhere between these two extremes. For the rest of the chapter Althusser's Marx will for the most part be treated as the 'real' Marx. In this connexion it should be borne in mind that Althusser's reading of Marx is a specifically anti-Hegelian one which attempts to rid Marxism of economism, idealism, and therefore differs radically from other interpretations which take Hegel as their starting point. Althusser follows Lenin and Mao in giving a 'hard' and unequivocal basis for correct political practice. He is convinced of the correctness of his own theory and unafraid of what might be interpreted as arrogance or dogma.

The third possibility would be to criticize Althusser by reference to other social theories. But what would be the point of this? As a general principle there seems little to gain by criticizing one theoretical framework from the point of view of another: one is left with an inevitable eclecticism and reductionism, and the problem of validating departure from sociology and his contribution to it will be examined later, but the value of a specifically sociological approach is dubious for the reasons just given.

The final alternative, which will be adopted, is to reveal the internal contradictions within Althusserian theory and the theoretical problems it raises both for itself and for Marxism and the social sciences more generally. This has the advantage of examining a theory in its own terms, avoiding eclecticism, and providing the possibility of combating the enemy (or criticizing a friend) on his own terrain and at his strongest points rather than his weakest. The existence of internal inconsistencies and unsolved problems will necessarily bear on the applicability of the framework to social reality, and more generally on the use and viability of his structural approach. So the rest of this chapter will concentrate on an analysis of the internal problems of Althusser's epistemology and Marxism, incorporating the other critiques where they are relevant.

Theory and practice

There are three separate questions to be looked at here: the relation between science and philosophy, the meaning of theoretical practice, and the relation between theory and practice.

Science and philosophy: historical and dialectical materialism One of the greatest problems of Althusser's epistemology concerns the integration of science and philosophy, or dialectical and historical materialism. If historical materialism is a science, and hence correct and objective, what is dialectical materialism and how does it relate to historical materialism? Althusser upholds an absolute distinction between the two: scientific practice is a specific one and irreducible and hence distinct from philosophy which is defined as the Theory of theoretical activity (1969a, p. 168):

> I shall call Theory (with a capital T), general theory, that is the Theory of practice in general, itself elaborated on the basis of the Theory of existing theoretical practices (of the sciences), which transforms into 'knowledges' (scientific truths) the ideological product of existing 'empirical' practices (the concrete activity of men). This Theory is the materialist dialectic which is none other than dialectical materialism.

But this formulation in fact raises more questions than it solves, in particular the relationship of historical materialism to dialectical materialism on the one hand and to the other practices of the social formation on the other. Given that in Althusser's conception theory is both one of the practices of the social formation and has as its object the other practices (economy, polity, ideology) which are also specific and relatively autonomous, there must be some complex relationship between them, and this is where Althusser's inconsistencies start.

Although they are also practices and apparently equal, economic, political and ideological practice are all subsumed within historical materialism, that is, the theory of these levels is contained within the social formation. But the theory of historical materialism or of science has a different status and is regarded as distinct from the social formation. So although the four practices are all relatively autonomous and specific with no predetermined hierarchy of efficacy, they do seem to be hierarchically related as in Figure 4, where the theory of each level is incorporated at a higher level:

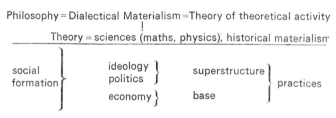

FIGURE 4 *Hierarchy of theories of practices*

In this way a distinction is made between the four practices: three of them exist within the social formation, while the fourth (theoretical practice) is independent of it. While economic, political and ideological practice are carried on within the social formation, the theory of them exists outside it. As Theory of theoretical activity, dialectical materialism or philosophy is also outside the social formation and is a metatheory explaining theory or science. It is the Theory of theory, and stands above it. The rationale of this division and the different degrees of autonomy attributed to each are not adequately explained. The division clearly implies that the theory of science is external to society and that the history of science is independent of the history of society.

Yet this view of science is one that Althusser is attempting to reject: in *Reading Capital* he argues that to see the theory of science as external and independent of particular sciences is to hypostatize it and depends on an idealistic viewpoint which sees the proof of theory as depending on a pregiven logic, an implicit criticism of the philosophy of guarantees. In this way he maintains two contradictory positions of which he is apparently unaware and which are not sorted out until later.

One possible solution to this problem would be precisely to refer to the concept of relative autonomy which deals with the fact that all practices are both determined and independent, and should avoid such problems of hierarchy, externality and internality to the social formation. But Althusser is nowhere very specific about the degrees of relative autonomy and its meaning, and some practices in his schema have more relative autonomy than others, in particular historical materialism since it subsumes the others. The whole discussion is lacking in rigour: obviously it is impossible to determine the limits of autonomy and effectivity of one practice on others independent of the investigation of particular social formations, since there is no predetermined relationship between them except determinance by the economy in the last instance. But Althusser should be able to be more specific about the limits of independence and constraint of theory and philosophy in relation to the other practices.

The other solution is to revise the whole notion of philosophy, and this is what Althusser has attempted in *Lenin and Philosophy* (1971) and his recent articles: while this goes some way towards clarifying the relationship between philosophy and science, the relationship between science *qua* theoretical practice and the other practices remains just as ambiguous. The radical distinction between historical and dialectical materialism is upheld but philosophy is given a completely new meaning. Althusser criticizes his own 'theoreticist tendencies' in which philosophy was defined as the theory of theoretical practice. In the introduction to the English edition of *For Marx* (1969a, p. 15), he writes:

I did not show what it is, as distinct from science, that constitutes philosophy proper: the organic relation between every philosophy as a theoretical discipline and even within its theoretical forms of existence and exigencies, and politics. I did not point out the nature of this relation, which in Marxist philosophy has nothing to do with a pragmatic relation. So I did not show clearly enough what in this respect distinguishes Marxist philosophy from earlier philosophies.

and again, in the foreword to the Italian edition of *Reading Capital* (1970, p. 8):

It is not merely a question of terminological ambiguity, but one of error in the conception itself. To define philosophy in a unilateral way as the Theory of theoretical practice (and in consequence a Theory of the differences between the practices) is a formulation that could not help but induce either 'speculative' or 'positivist' theoretical effects and echoes.

Althusser's subsequent writings contain a thoroughgoing revision in which philosophy is redefined as political intervention, on the basis of a reading of Lenin's *Materialism and Empirio-criticism* (1947). While Marx founded a new science of history, he did not found a new philosophy and it was Lenin who first inaugurated a new practice of philosophy (N.B. not a new philosophy itself but a reinterpretation of the practice of philosophy) and criticized the bases of all previous philosophy. Althusser's new conception starts from the premiss that all philosophy is necessarily partisan and is produced within the theoretical domain by the combined effects of the class

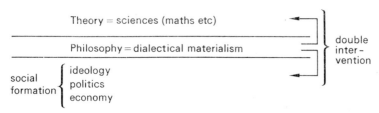

FIGURE 5 *Philosophy as a double intervention*

struggle and scientific practice. Philosophy is not a science, nor a metatheory. It has no object but it is a practice of political intervention carried out in a theoretical form and serves to distinguish between true and false ideas, between science and ideology and defends correct ideas in the realms of science and politics (see Figure 5).

This in itself seems quite clear: philosophy/dialectical materialism is now political intervention, but Althusser does not elaborate on what it means to consider philosophy as a practice. It is not clear whether 'practice' has the same meaning as for theoretical, economic and political practice, in which case it would also be a specific, relatively autonomous level of the social formation, or whether practice just has the ordinary sense of activity. Neither is Althusser specific about the implications of this new position for his formulation of the relationship between historical and dialectical materialism. First, there is no longer any room for a theory of theoretical activity in general or for any metatheories of science separate from specific sciences, since science now contains its own guarantee of scientificity, yet he retains his general theory of production and of the sciences as operating by a homologous process of production. This is highly contradictory: he criticizes all metatheories for providing an external guarantee of the validity of science independent of their own practice which conflicts with his idea of the conditions of existence of knowledge. Metatheory no longer exists, and philosophy is something completely different, yet the theory of the productive nature of theory remains—the scientific and epistemological status of this now requires elaboration since it does not appear to 'belong' anywhere in the new formulation. This is the reason for the ambiguities about the status of Althusser's own work that were mentioned at the beginning of the chapter: if science in general does not exist, this must apply to epistemology as well and in this case what is to become of Althusser's epistemology? He seems to be involved in a highly complex question of relativism and validation here. The other question was that if Althusser is writing as a philosopher and philosophy is not a science, what is scientific about Althusser's own work, does it really have an object, or has this too been redefined as political intervention? In the earlier formulation, his work was both theoretical and philosophical since it attempted to derive a dialectical materialism from historical materialism. But now it must be either political intervention or theoretical practice but not both. Althusser does not face this dilemma or appear even to realize the implications of his new position when applied to himself.

In this way, the relationship between theoretical practice and philosophy is somewhat clarified, but that between theoretical practice and the other practices remains just as problematic. In his later formulation, theoretical practice itself, in possessing its own internal proof and justification, need not be referred to any external theory and so seems to hold an even more privileged position in relation to the other practices. It contains its theory of itself within itself and also the theory of the other practices. But this is to restate the problem that was raised earlier. The question of the position of theoretical practice *vis-à-vis* the rest of the social formation can be examined in a much more concrete way in terms of the social determinacy of knowledge.

Theoretical practice: autonomous or determined? In his recent writings, Althusser is even more adamant than before in maintaining that the production of knowledge occurs entirely within the order of thought, and that this is absolutely free from social determinism and problems of relativism since theory now contains within itself its own methodological and epistemological apparatus. Yet he also maintains exactly the opposite in claiming that theory depends totally on social and historical conditions. For example (1971, p. 8), 'it is only from the point of view of class exploitation that it is possible to see and analyse the mechanisms of a class society and therefore to produce knowledge of it': and in the same place he intimates that the science of history depends on adopting a proletarian class position (p. 8): 'in order to fulfil the conditions that govern the science of history, Marx had to abandon his bourgeois and petty bourgeois class positions and adopt the class positions of the proletariat'. So on the one hand he maintains that science and knowledge are not the property of a class subject whether bourgeois or proletarian, and on the other that science is not independent of the effects of the class struggle. Whether this is because the theory is about the class struggle or class contradictions is not clear. Without postulating a Weberian distinction between value relevance and value freedom, that is, between the necessarily value determined nature of a scientific investigation at its inception, and the value free nature of the results of the investigation, this is contradictory; incidentally even greater problems would arise from the Weberian solution which depends on a subject-object problematic rather than the Marxist theory/practice problematic (see below, pp. 127–8).

This inconsistency is not confined to Althusser's recent work. He recognized the conjunctural nature of his own work in *For Marx* and argues that it is this very characteristic that makes it valuable. But there are important implications for his analysis of Marx: it is Althusser's claim that the epistemological break in 1845 occurred entirely within thought, that is, Marx's critique of humanism and idealism was based on a purely theoretical revolution in the concepts he used rather than on any external political events in the real world. Yet it was at this time that Marx realized in practice the failure of Feuerbachian philosophy as applied to politics and was acquainting himself with French politics. In political terms his critique of Feuerbach led him to distinguish between philosophical and real Communism which involved adherence to a definite political party (Marx, 1965 edn, pp. 55–6): 'It is only possible to achieve real liberation in the real world and by employing real means'. The problems arising from Althusser's contradiction are the following: did the epistemological break affect only Marx's theoretical work or all his work, and in particular what is the status of his political writings? If his politics changed, was this related to the epistemological break, and if not, what areas of thought did the break affect? These are questions about the areas of Marx's thought: does Althusser see them as integrated, independent or relatively autonomous? And how does this compare with Marx's style of work which, in contradistinction to the purely philosophical approach, attempted to integrate theory and practice, and the various areas of theory? The question applies equally to Lenin and Mao and all Marxist theoreticians who were at the same time politically active. Althusser does not answer any of these explicitly and we can only surmise the answers. He refers only on a few occasions to Marx's political works and writings which thus appear to be peripheral to the study of political economy. In this way the epistemological break seems only to affect the science of political economy, history, and philosophy, which can only imply that the political writings do not belong to theoretical practice, but to political practice, and are not scientific. This embodies a very rigidly compartmentalized view of the way in which the minds of individual theorists work, especially since Marx made no radical distinctions between his economic, political, philosophical and other writings.

So while Althusser maintains a complex relationship between theoretical and political practice (pp. 117–18) in which one 'guides' the other, he does not deal with the status of political theory and political programmes, nor with the impact of theoretical ruptures on political practice, though he does maintain that theory depends on the current state of the class struggle. He seems unable to discuss the interaction between these practices in any rigorous or detailed way, and avoids the question by making extremely contradictory assertions to the effect that all theoretical developments are to be explained as internal and autonomous to the thought process, and that Marx needed a proletarian class position. Where it seems inevitable that he will disprove his own theory of the autonomy of thought by revealing its conjunctural nature, in the case of Marx and himself he just switches to say the opposite, that theory is completely determined by the present state of the class struggle. As these imply very different things about the epistemological status of knowledge (whether it is dependent or independent) and also throws into question the whole analysis of Marx it constitutes a very serious problem in the Althusserian schema.

Of course, it is not necessarily inconsistent to say that theory once formulated is independent, but that it cannot exist without preconditions. In this case though, the way in which the conditions affect the resulting theory, the relationship between theory and practice, must be specified.

Theory and practice 'The philosophers have only interpreted the world, the point however is to change it.' Marx's eleventh thesis on Feuerbach sums up the defining feature of the Marxist problematic, the specific relation it maintains between theory and practice. Theory and practice are to form an integrated and interrelated and interdependent whole, where theory is a theorization of past and present social practice and practice validates the use and correctness of theory. Marxist theory is distinct from other theoretical standpoints in the social sciences in that its defining characteristic is its concern with changing the world and this rebounds on its theory, which is transformational and highlights existing contradictions and weak links which may be politically exploited. Thus theory and practice are related in a number of ways: not only does theory have a practical result which can be practically used, but also social structure is understood as the product of human activity and social practice, and its historical development must also be seen in this way, so theories of society and history are those of social practice and its products. In this way practice is theorized, and so Marxism provides a theory of practice, past and present, a theory which is practised, that is, which has practical implications, and the possibility of a theorized revolutionary practice. This integration is upheld throughout Marxist theory from Lenin's 'without revolutionary movement' to Sartre's concept of praxis. Several corollaries emerge from this, the most crucial of which concerns the relationship of the theorist to his field of study: the main relation is between the theory and practice, rather than between theory and its object. The theorist is not required to have a passive or external attitude towards the object of his study, but rather an active and transformative one. Thus Marxism is relatively unconcerned with questions of detachment, objectivity, and value neutrality and freedom since the theorist is not regarded as an external observer of phenomena assumed to be independently given, as his theory of society is allied with a strategy for transforming it. The primary relationship is between theory and practice both as a means of comprehending society and changing it, and the relationship between observer and observed is very secondary. This is not to say that the problems of the social determination of thought and relativism have not been raised in Marxism, but where they have, the solution has been a fairly straightforward one: correct knowledge is that achieved through a proletarian standpoint (Lukàcs, 1971).

The distinctiveness of this feature can be seen best in contrast to other sociological theories for which it would be true to say that the relationship between subject and object, theorist and studied, observer and observed, is the most important and hence the most problematic. This is partly due to the nature of their scientific aims, especially where these derive from positivism or analogies with the natural sciences, the ultimate goal being a description and explanation of society as it is and was, which is objectively true and achieved through detached analysis. The assumption is that the truth of knowledge depends on the externality of the theorist, and his neutrality in relation to the object studied, hence the overriding concern with a correct relation between the theorist and his field which necessitates objectivity, value freedom and an external and detached relationship between them. To say that the social sciences as such assume that only disinterested knowledge can be correct is highly oversimplified, but it is certainly this premiss that underlies most of the methodological discussions on how to achieve such objectivity and detachment or on the methods to overcome the embeddedness of knowledge in a social base. This is of course not to say that non-Marxist social scientists are politically neutral or do not want to change the world, but that they divide up their political from their sociological views, so as to prevent the one affecting the other.

In this way, where the aim of theory is not transformational but to give an account of things as they are, the accent is on the relationship between observer and observed, and so sociology works basically within a subject/object problematic whereas Marxism operates within a theory/practice problematic.

How does Althusser stand in relation to these? He aims both for radical objectivity, where knowledge is of an external variety, and for the strategic importance of theory. In this way he seems to lie somewhere between the two problematics. However, in so far as he has a scientistic view of social science and believes in the possibility of objective knowledge, he does not discuss the problems that this might raise, or rather he does not explain how his 'objectivity' differs from 'detached objectivity', and if it does not differ, he does not deal with any of the problems of the relationship between theorist and phenomena studied. There are really two problems here: first, in so far as he claims radical objectivity and truth, he should explain the meaning of objectivity, and how it is to be achieved once positivism and empiricism have been rejected, and what the scientific indices and guarantees of correctness are. Second, he is unclear about the transformational character of his theory since he does not specify the links between theoretical and political practice.

Integration of the structural totality

The second major criticism of Althusser is that his rigour in the analysis of the mode of integration of the structural totality is more apparent than real. He is particularly unspecific about the relationship between the practices and about the meaning of relative autonomy. This leads to the following ambiguities and problems:

(1) the meaning of the distinction between determinance and dominance, of determination in the last instance by the economy, of materialism and of the distinction between base and superstructure.

(2) the relationship between economy and polity and the problem of political voluntarism.

(3) the role of consciousness in political practice and the relationship between objective structure and subjective consciousness in a revolutionary situation.

(4) the relevance of the concept of class, and the question of contradictions which are not class based.

The distinguishing feature of the Althusserian 'structure in domination' is the distinction between determinance by the economy in the last instance and the dominant role at a given moment in a particular social formation which may be taken by another level than the economy, either politics, religion, kinship, or another. This enables Althusser to retain a materialist approach, even though the last instance may never come, and to attribute relative autonomy to other levels, or more than relative autonomy in the case of the dominant role.

But the status of the economy must be more clearly defined: given that the dominant role can be taken by the economy or by any other level, there is a danger of eclectic pluralism if the dominant role can be displaced indifferently between the different levels. Althusser implies that the distinction between Marxism and pluralism is that Marxism retains the concept of principal contradiction, though this is not necessarily to be found in the economy. But this is not really sufficient: he avoids the problem of how the economy can still be determinant in the last instance without being the principal contradiction, dominant role, or even an aspect of the principal contradiction, by referring to economic determinance in the last instance and the dominant role as two 'aspects' of the contradiction so that the main contradiction is always between the economic and another level rather than between the relations and forces of production. By being unclear about the status of the economy, and admitting the displacement to other spheres of the principal contradiction, he also leaves unresolved the question of the respective spheres of the economy and polity.

The ambiguous status of the economy raises two particular questions: the mode of existence of the economy and the fusion of economics and politics, that is, of the multiplicity of practices and contradictions, in a revolutionary situation.

In so far as it is determinant in the last instance but not necessarily dominant, Althusser implies that the economy is an 'absent presence', and uses psychoanalytic analogies to describe its mode of existence, in particular the concept of the unconscious. The economy can never be observed as such, in itself, and indeed does not exist in this way, but only through its effects in the other levels into which it is displaced. Thus it appears that the economy does not have its own level of existence at all in real processes—but if this is so then all class struggle must be political and the concept of economic struggle loses all meaning. The problem here reduces to that of the relation between the real process and the thought process. As Poulantzas (1966, p. 1978) puts it:

> The fact that scientific theory reveals the existence of economic laws, lived ideologically in the capitalist system, apparently 'absent' and masked, but 'present 'at another level, does not mean that the economy, in the real world, always exists elsewhere and has no autonomous level of existence, and cannot be isolated as playing a 'dominant role'. This would mean, as Althusser implies, that politics is the main 'mode of existence' in the real world, and constitutes men's 'concrete activity.'

If Althusser gave more examples of how economic and political practices are interrelated in concrete social formations these problems might not arise, but as he does not, the scientific status of the economy remains unclear.

In addition, he is not very specific about how in a revolutionary situation, the overdetermined contradiction actually fuses into mass action, and implies that this occurs only through political activity, so revealing the tendency to overpoliticization or voluntarism in his schema. The fusion of the contradiction appears to result in the disappearance of the structure in domination, and Althusser provides no indication of how fusion is effected at the political level and of how the masses and subjective experience and consciousness are interfused with objectively existing contradictions. While Althusser maintains that theoretical and political practice are separate and specific but interrelated, he does not deal with the question of how precisely they do relate in practical political situations. Given that politics seems to be the only level at which active struggle occurs, it might be inferred that he rejects an economic monism for a political monism and 'a political monism runs the danger of oscillating between historicism, and eventually "class consciousness", on the one hand, and a gestaltist mechanism transposed into politics on the other' (Poulantzas, 1966, p. 1981).

This problem of politics is specific to a dehistoricized totality like Althusser's because for many others there is no rupture between theory and politics and hence no problem of their fusion in a revolutionary situation. For Sartre, the fusion is effected through the proletariat-party agent representing the dominant instance, which constitutes a political 'group' rather than a trade union 'series'. However, in his system structure is reduced ultimately to the results of an individual producing agent and so the problem of the intelligibility of structures becomes that of their origin.

Similarly in Lukàcs' conception, theory is class consciousness; that is, a theoretical formulation of the spontaneous activity and views of the proletariat and there is no divorce between theory and political activity. Althusser and Lukàcs can be seen as totally opposed on this issue and hence raise opposite problems: Lukàcs denies any autonomy to theory and hence its strategic importance is unclear. Theory is peripheral to political practice and consciousness is fused with these from the start and there is no problem of their integration. However Althusser sees theoretical and political practice as completely separate and does not deal with the question of the links between them. In this way, Althusser is not too clear about the status of either the economy or of the polity, and because he does not answer the question of fusion at the political level, it results that although he can analyse revolutionary situations, he cannot analyse revolutions themselves.

The other major questions relating to the integration of the structured totality concern class, contradictions and consciousness. Here Althusser's position can be seen best in opposition to the historicism he criticizes and in particular Lukàcs. Very briefly, Lukàcs' historicism is based on the notion that the correctness of Marxism is a function of class position: Marxism expresses proletarian consciousness, and proletarian consciousness is correct because the proletariat is the subject of history, and therefore in a position to grasp theoretically the totality of society just as it grasps it practically and transforms it. In capitalist societies there is only one major contradiction, that between the bourgeoisie and proletariat; Lukàcs assumes the existence of a pure form of capitalism in which the superstructures correspond exactly to the base, including forms of thought so that there can be no 'objective' thought; only through polarization and the disappearance of all secondary contradictions could the proletariat assume its historic role. The concepts of *Capital* are reduced to the 'ideological' categories of the early Marx: alienation, regaining man's essence, and so on. The concept of the 'historical bloc' expresses the unity which embraces structure and ideology and whereby knowledge itself is historicized. In this way, Lukàcs reduces the Marxist totality to a variation of the

Hegelian expressive totality and Marxism is interpreted as the ideology of the time rather than as objective social theory.

Given that Althusser rejects the expressive totality, and the notion of one principal contradiction, this must affect the relevance of the concept of class. Whereas in the historicist conception, the main contradiction is between two classes and all other contradictions are related to this, structuralist Marxism provides the possibility of other contradictions which are not class based and in fact may be unrelated to class, and which are interconnected with each other in a variety of complex ways. They may be mutually reinforcing or they may counterbalance each other. The difference between these two conceptions is best seen diagrammatically in Figures 6 and 7. In the Althusserian conception there may be contradictions internal to

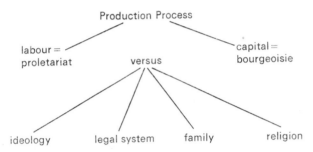

FIGURE 6   *Contradiction in the expressive totality*[14]

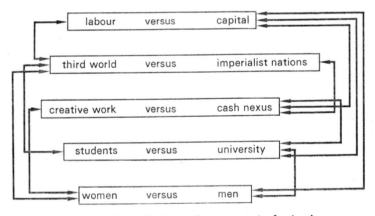

FIGURE 7   *Contradiction in the structure in domination*

Note: These are just examples of possible contradictions.

particular practices or levels of the social formation and contradictions between levels of the social formation. Class contradiction is only one of these and the development of a revolutionary situation depends on the compatibility of all these contradictions and the fact that they work in the same direction.

This is a much more flexible and non-determinist framework for the analysis of social structure than the expressive totality, and much more sociological, but it does raise for Marxism the question of the relevance of class and of consciousness.

In so far as class consciousness is a historicist concept it is rejected by Althusser. But does this imply it is not a real structure and not a legitimate topic for study? Althusser seems to be saying yes and so by-passes major questions in the analysis of class and revolution. He dismisses consciousness but introduces ideology as an objectively real structure distinct from theory and politics. On the one hand, he thus underplays the role of consciousness: theory is the scientifically correct analysis of the social formation but is unrelated to consciousness of class or political oppression. But on the other hand, he reveals a political voluntarism in that the fusion of the contradictions appears to occur totally through conscious political activity. Whereas for Lukačs, consciousness includes both theory and ideology and may be false or correct, subjective or objective, scientific or unscientific and no distinction is made between conceptions of subjectively lived experience and the scientific analysis of the social formation as a whole, Althusser makes a rigid distinction between these two components, which he characterizes as theoretical and ideological practice. The problems of their interrelation have already been discussed. Ideology is understood as the means of conceiving and expressing man's lived relation to the world, and is one of the levels of practice, a necessary one in any social formation, and which is worthy of study in itself. Thus the category of class consciousness is avoided both because it is directly determined by class position and because it confounds theoretical and ideological practice.

So far so good. In the analysis of a social formation it is essential to distinguish subjective experience from objective knowledge, but what happens in political activity? How are subjective and objective knowledge to be integrated? There is no problem for Lukačs because political activity is class consciousness in practice and class conciousness is conversely political action in theory. This is not so however for Althusser: political practice is not an expression of either theoretical or ideological practice but must somehow integrate them with each other and with the objective contradictions. The integration of these levels appears to rest on conscious choice and a kind of voluntarism in which it is implied that consciousness of a certain variety is the major factor in transforming a revolutionary situation into a revolution. Thus we return to the same problem: every thing and all action ultimately seem to occur at the political level, both the fusion of contradictions, and of practices, and in the absence of a more adequate discussion of politics, this engenders an extreme form of voluntarism, since consciousness is not determined by class, and an over-emphasis on the political arena as the sole locus of activity.

In this connexion, there is the problem of the status of class itself. The concept of class is obviously not so important to Althusser as to certain historicists, but as with all problems, Althusser does not deal specifically with it. Class appears to be dissolved into the economy where it exists in a passive state or into the polity/ideology and revolutionary party where it forms part of the political bloc and is one among many social groups, a privileged grouping under capitalism where the economy is determinant in the last instance. But whether this is the conclusion that Althusser would draw himself is not at all evident.

Finally where class and the economy have this ambiguous status, the base/superstructure distinction must come into question. Althusser retains it, but if the notion of relative autonomy is taken to its logical extreme, it should really disappear or be drastically changed in a topological sense, in that the superstructures do not have a necessary base in class. In any other case the simple dichotomous picture of the relationship between the material base and the superstructures must be discarded.

In this way, the problems of the relationship between the economy and polity, and the meaning of class, contradiction and consciousness and the distinction between base and superstructure are all due to insufficient attention on Althusser's part to the relationship between the practices and to the meaning of relative autonomy. Most of the problems could be solved if analysis were done at the theoretical rather than metatheoretical level. However, it should be possible, even at this level, to define relative autonomy more clearly, and to indicate the difference in meaning between specificity and relative autonomy. It is possible that each practice or instance of the social formation has its own specific structure and history, but without being autonomous, relatively or otherwise, of the 'dominant role'. There are many conceivable relationships on the borderline between determined/independent/autonomous/specific which could be elaborated in at least an abstract form. This might make Althusser's discussion of the status of knowledge and science in relation to society less extreme. If, for example, he had talked about the specificity of historical materialism, he could still have had it linked in some relation of determinacy with the social formation. But to deal with it in terms of relative autonomy makes it automatically independent.[15]

The derivation of Althusser's concepts

The last and most important criticism which to a large extent subsumes those of the previous sections concerns the derivation of the concepts that characterize the Althusserian schema.

In a critical article, André Glucksmann discusses the concept of production used by Althusser and its division into three stages, the three Generalities. Given that this concept governs the way in which the social formation is structured and characterizes theory and serves to distinguish science from ideology, it is pertinent to inquire into the basis of the concept, where it comes from and what it means. Althusser is most specific about this in an early section of 'From Capital to Marx's Philosophy': (Althusser and Balibar, 1970, p. 34)

It is therefore a question of producing, in the precise sense of the word, which seems to signify making manifest what is latent, but which really means transforming (in order to give a pre-existing raw material the form of an object adapted to an end) something which in a sense already exists.

But this does not really tell us very much or explain the tripartism of production and Glucksmann concludes (1972, p. 71) that production is merely a word which comes from a dictionary.

The basis for the whole tripartite Althusserian architecture thus arises fully armed from the simple but somewhat forced used of a dictionary. It 'happens' that everything is production, it 'happens' that every production is divided into three. This conceptual empiricism is never questioned in the Althusserian reflection.

It just 'happens' that all practice can be understood in terms of production and it just 'happens' that all production has three parts. The inevitable conclusion from this is that the concept of production is not founded at all but *a priori* and thus Althusser's complex epistemology rests on a very flimsy and elusive base, since its most basic concept has very little substance. It is for this reason that Glucksmann accuses Althusser of conceptual empiricism and calls his system 'a ventriloquist structuralism.'

Now this criticism can be applied to other concepts than production. In fact most of the basic concepts of Althusser's epistemology and Marxism are of this nature: *a priori*, unfounded, and in so far as they are either lacking in substance or justification, they must remain mere words with very limited explanatory value. This is the case in particular with the concepts of epistemological rupture and symptomatic reading. In the former case, it is just presented that there must be epistemological breaks because this is how science works (because Bachelard says so?) and so they are essential for the understanding of the history of science. As for symptomatic reading, this rests on the implicit assumption that there is always an unconscious to theory, but the exact meaning of unconscious is unclear and cannot rest on simple analogy with the mind. As a principle Althusser maintains that there is always something which remains latent in theory and always a distinction between appearance and reality. In this way he juxtaposes two ideas taken from Freud and Spinoza to produce this 'necessary' concept but gives no other justification to the assertion that there is an unconscious in theory, nor does he give any indication of the procedures and methods involved in a symptomatic reading. Philosophically Althusser rejects any distinction between essence and existence as idealism but seems to reintroduce it surreptitiously in his appearance/reality conception of theory.

Why does all production have a homologous form regardless of whether it occurs in theoretical, economic, political or ideological practice? Why are there sometimes four practices and sometimes only three (occasionally Althusser omits theory)? What is the content of the three Generalities, and in particular the crucial Generality II? What is the proof that there are five structural elements and that these are sufficient to analyse any mode of production? In the absence of substantiation of all of these notions, they do certainly appear as *a priori* ideas and assertions without any substantial basis. Perhaps a priorism does not matter, but in so far as all the concepts are interrelated and refer back to each other and ultimately to the ideas of production and relative autonomy, it can be argued that the whole system reduces to nothing because its basic ideas are unfounded and are mere words or assertions that flow only from Althusser's pen. For an anti-empiricist such a conceptual empiricism must constitute a grave contradiction.

Most of the criticisms made in the earlier sections could be rephrased in terms of this one: the relationship between theory and practice, and the integration of the various practices and levels of the social formation, were so problematic because the concepts used to link them were lacking in specificity despite their apparent rigour. Thus Althusser's conceptual rigour falls short of his avowed aim— most of his concepts turn out to be dogmas, words or assertions.

There is another side to this criticism. Althusser lacks specificity also in his discussion of his approach as opposed to other variants of Marxism. He accuses others of idealism, historicism and empiricism with very little definition of these terms. He tends to lump all his opponents together in one undifferentiated category, as for example when he accuses Lukàcs, Korsch, Sartre and Gramsci of historicism. It is true that for all these history has primacy over structure and that the ultimate explanation of the social formation is in terms of its evolution and historical development. But there is an important difference between historicism of this variety and one which assumes that any given states of a social formation are successive totalities of the development of one single autonomous process, whether this is the Idea, economy, technology or growth of consciousness or freedom. This might be called a monistic historicism since it conceives of only one major instance of society, and while it characterizes the theory of Hegel, Lukačs and Korsch the theories of Gramsci and Sartre cannot be understood in these terms. In this way Althusser does not distinguish between varieties of historicism, and blurs over the differences between these theorists, since, for his analysis, their similarities are far more important. But this involves a danger of gross distortion of all theories other than his own, and of the history of Marxist theory.

A final element of arbitrariness concerns Althusser's distinction between ideology and science and his lack of definition of scientificity. It is not really enough to say that the sciences contain their own internal guarantees without specifying what these are. Similarly, Althusser has taken over the basically bourgeois distinction between science and ideology, a distinction which means little more than truth and falsehood, but he gives each a different content. It should be possible for Marxist philosophy to go beyond this distinction and to show the internal relationship between theory and practice between on the one hand the form and content of knowledge and the way it is acquired, and on the other the social formation in which it is found without being completely relativist or seeking eternal truths.

Conclusion

The criticisms made above go a long way towards undermining Althusserian theory as it stands at present: with its internal inconsistencies and inadequacies it reduces to nothing when pushed to its logical limit. But there is nothing to prevent these problems from being overcome by further substantiation of the basic concepts. Nor do they invalidate Althusser's attempt to construct a structuralist framework for the analysis of social formations, nor his view of the construction of reality or of a scientific approach towards it. In a sense, his weakness is also his strength. He realizes many of the most fundamental problems in Marxist theory and tries to overcome them, and that he is not entirely successful in providing alternatives does not mean that he should be rejected. For example he realizes the need for a Theory of theory and of the production of knowledge in historical materialism; his critique of evolutionism and historicism leads him to suggest concepts appropriate to a synchronic analysis, and his rejection of determinism, both economic and idealist, is combined with the beginnings of a much more flexible analysis of the social formation, which conceives of different types of internal relationships between its constituent elements. All the concepts used in this: differential experience of time, separate development of elements, determinance, dominance, levels, instances, relative autonomy, metonymy, weightings, are all of obvious relevance to sociology. From a Marxist point of view, Althusser is to be seen as giving the basis for a philosophical critique of the remaining strands of Hegelianism in Marxism, and of continuing Lenin and Gramsci's critique of academicism, determinism and empiricism and presenting an elaborate understanding of the relationship between theoretical and political practice.

5 Structuralist epistemology

Introduction

In earlier chapters, I dealt with Lévi-Strauss's and Althusser's conception of reality, and their ideas about the sort of knowledge of the social world it is realistic to aspire to. Here, I shall examine the structuralists' conception of scientific procedure. Marx, Saussure and Freud, as well as Lévi-Strauss and Althusser, rejected the methods conventionally used in their fields of study and developed an alternative approach with a distinctive methodology and epistemology, common to all but arrived at independently. They all rejected the crude version of positivism that seeks to establish universal laws on the basis of empirical observation, and a simplistic idealism that denies the possibility of objective knowledge, and their own suggestions are to be seen in relation to this. The following will present, in the theorists' own terms, their implicit ideas and assumptions about the acquisition of knowledge, synchronic causation and the mode of existence of structures. The lack of system and rigour of the structuralists' epistemology will necessarily be reflected in this presentation, and at the end of the chapter, I shall turn to the inadequacies and problems of their approach to science.

The structuralists' view of science is realist as opposed to instrumental: they aim to isolate real structures rather than suggest hypothetical laws. They emphasize that conscious conceptualization on the part of the investigator must intervene between observation and explanation, and their concentration on this stage of research has important repercussions on their ideas about causation and explanation.

The distinction between reality and the scientific description of reality is the key to the structuralist philosophy of science. For the structuralists, observed phenomena are only the raw material from which concepts may be elaborated to describe the real structures of the world. They reject that facts present themselves in their true light, and so perception is not the correct way to acquire knowledge. Knowledge does not filter through the senses but must be produced. A corollary of this is that the units isolated by observation as the object of study do not necessarily correspond to the basic structural elements of phenomena.

Structuralism entails a particular view of the relationship between description and explanation, and of causation, consistent with this general outlook but at variance from both positivism and historicism. The main aim is to demonstrate synchronic causes and real structures, and reveal patterns of structural association and transformation. Thus a radical distinction is drawn between real structures and heuristic models.

I shall attempt to demonstrate these points with reference to Freud and Saussure as well as to Althusser and Lévi-Strauss.

The acquisition of knowledge

How do we acquire knowledge of the world? What mediates between the mind of the scientist and the objects of the world? Do these have an 'objective' existence, which we need only perceive; does the knower constitute what is known? There are two problems here: the relation between the mind and the subject matter in the production of knowledge, and that of the objectivity or the independent existence of the phenomena.

The need for concepts

All structuralists have a similar approach towards reality, which lies within the tradition inaugurated by Hegel's critique of Kant. Kant had held both that we acquire knowledge through sense experience (that the external world has a real existence independent of our mind), and that knowledge filters through categories of understanding which are given and universal and which pre-exist the individual knower; that is, they exist independently of the content to which they are applied. This permitted a *rapprochement* between traditional formal logic and the empiricism of English philosophy, and the claims of the natural sciences to be able to establish laws about the phenomena of the world on the basis of observation. Hegel argued against Kant on both counts:[1] that the subject, the 'universal I', constitutes the objective world and that phenomenal objects are projections of the human mind and have no existence independent of it. Whereas in traditional logic categories were the primary data into which the content had to be fitted, Hegel asserted the unity of form and content: content must be the starting point and theoretical work must produce concepts corresponding to it.

The structuralists uphold the external existence of the world and reject Hegel's subjectivism, but follow him in maintaining that the subject matter alone must be the starting point. They deny the validity of pre-existing categories, and hold that the relative autonomy of the spheres of a social formation demands that a scientific study start by analysing the specific characteristics of each, and by developing concepts to describe them. They uphold the unity of science by arguing that a scientific practice can be established for each area of reality but deny that the relevant categories and methods will be the same for each. Following the views of Bachelard and Canguilhem, they maintain that the concepts are to be irreducible and produced by theory rather than analogy or empirical observation.

The search for appropriate concepts has been one of the major preoccupations of all structuralists in linguistics and psychoanalysis, as well as anthropology and political economy.

Saussure (1959, p. 3), for example, began by criticizing the comparative philology of the mid-nineteenth century on the grounds that it did not 'seek the nature of its object of study'. It was only in the late nineteenth century that scholars sought the principles of language, and even then they saw language as the product of the collective mind of linguistic groups rather than as having an independent existence. Saussure started with the definition of the subject matter of linguistics as 'all manifestations of human speech'. However, language could be seen from so many different points of view that the particular point of view in fact created the object of study. So he determined to use a 'purely linguistic' viewpoint, as opposed to a psychological or physiological one and introduced the concept of 'langue' denoting language as a self-contained whole and a principle of classification, to be used as the norm of all other manifestations of speech. With this, the mass of facts of speech 'fell into order'. Langue was to be conceived as a homogeneous system of signs.

A large part of Saussure's work was concerned with the development of specific concepts to describe linguistic reality and the process of communication. He pioneered the concept of the 'phoneme' as the basic unit of language on the phonological plane as opposed to word or syllable, and the concept of the 'sign' as the organizing principle on the level of communication. These are now basic to the study of language but were the result of conscious theoretical work. Saussure's emphasis was on discovering the principles of operation of linguistic reality, and he thus transcended the atomism of previous analyses of language.

141

Freud named the domain that he discovered the 'unconscious' and maintained that it was irreducible. All the properties of the mind that he isolated possessed, in his view, a real existence (1933, p. 88): 'In postulating the existence of a superego I have been describing a genuine structural entity, and have not merely been personifying an abstraction such as conscience.' His work was carried out in a theoretical vacuum in that no system of concepts existed to express his practical discoveries. He borrowed from physics, biology and political economy but most of the concepts he used were developed specifically to theorize what he had found. In his interpretation of dreams, for example, he continually stressed the need for this (ibid., p. 19): 'The first thing we have to do is to lay the foundation of our new attitude towards the problem of the dream by introducing two new concepts and two new names.' He made clear that mental processes could not be accounted for in terms of analogous processes operating in areas other than the mind. In Freud's view psychoanalysis was a science developed in accordance with the structure of the mind it describes, a scientific theory rather than a pragmatic therapy.

Freud gave a revealing account of the process of conceptualization involved in his description of mental processes, and claimed that he was able to advance theoretically, and to see the structural similarity between unrelated phenomena, only by widening his perspective. The dream, and neurosis and psychosis which were previously thought to be manifestations of 'normal' and 'pathological' mental life, are seen to be expressions of the same thought process when looked at together (though operating at different strengths). Both could be adequately comprehended only when shown to be the same. Freud wrote of dream censorship (1933, p. 26):

So long as we regarded the dream as an isolated phenomenon independent of other psychological formations which are allied to it, we called this force the 'dream censor' . . . this censorship is not a mechanism that is peculiar to dreams. You remember that the conflict of two mental factors, which we—roughly—called the repressed conscious and the conscious, dominates our lives, and that the resistance against the interpretation of dreams, the hall-mark of dream censorship, is none other than the repression-resistance that keeps these two factors apart . . . under certain conditions other psychological formations emerge from the conflict between these two factors, formations which are the result of compromises just as dreams are . . . the dream is a pathological product, the first member of a series which includes the hysterical symptom, the obsession and the delusion among its members; it is differentiated from the others by its transitoriness and by the fact that it occurs under conditions which are part of normal life.

Freud recognized clearly the import of these findings (ibid., p. 29):

> The process of the dreamwork . . . has given us our first glimpse into those processes which go on in our unconscious mental system, and show us that they are quite different from what we know about our conscious thought, and that to this latter they must necessarily appear faulty and preposterous. The importance of this discovery is increased when we realize that the same mechanisms—we hardly dare call them 'thought processes'— are at work in the formation of neurotic symptoms as have turned latent dream thought into the manifest dream.

By widening the perspective, Freud was able to relate two apparently disparate phenomena, dreams and psychosis, and to explain them by the introduction of a concrete concept—the superego—so postulating that the structure of the mental personality, as it is formed in each particular case from the compromise between the id, ego and superego, causes its manifestations. The elaboration of concepts which apply equally to normal and pathological behaviour, was one step in the removal of the barrier between sane and insane. This approach, in addition, permitted Freud to apply an explanation at the descriptive level and to concentrate on the thought mechanisms themselves.

Lévi-Strauss's methodological innovations in social anthropology are of a similar type. He examines the intellect as an irreducible level of reality and attempts to establish the cultural and innovatory aspects of primitive thought. I have already shown that he does not study totemism as a phenomenon *sui generis* but tries to discover the general category of which it is a particular case. The widening of perspective this involves is very similar to that described by Freud. In Lévi-Strauss's view, anthropology requires a reorientation to become scientific: away from the bizarre and exotic (which appear to be peculiar to primitive society) to the universal activities of which these are a manifestation. He writes of the deadlock which the theory of totemism had reached (1964c, p. 46):

> Faced with a situation of this type there are two ways of proceeding . . . to give up all hope of reaching a systematic interpretation rather than start all over again . . . or to broaden one's perspective, seeking a more general point of view which will permit the integration of forms whose regularity has already been established but whose resistance to systematization may perhaps be explained, not by intrinsic characteristics, but by the

fact that they have been ill-defined, incompletely analysed, or viewed in too narrow a fashion.

In *The Elementary Structures of Kinship*, he had already integrated the seemingly unrelated facts of different forms of kinship system and marriage rules in a more general theory of restricted and generalized exchange, and this was done only on condition that he changed the generally held conception of rules of marriage and kinship.

Appearance and reality

The recognition of the need for conceptualization rests on the rejection of first appearances as the only level of reality. Structuralists oppose what Althusser calls 'the empiricism of the object'; that is, the idea that the object of study is immediately present to the senses, can be isolated as such and constitutes the correct unit of study. Freud, for instance, argued that what exists in manifest form is the effects of the unconscious but that the underlying structure of the unconscious is the correct level of study. 'We call "unconscious" any mental process the existence of which we are obliged to assume— because, for instance, we infer it in some way from its effects—but of which we are not directly aware' (Freud, 1933, p. 94). Similarly, for linguists, the word, which appeared to be the basic unit, was rejected in favour of the phoneme, so the focus turned to relationships rather than 'concrete' things. The object of study was regarded as the intersection of several relationships rather than as an object with an ontological existence.

Lévi-Strauss criticized earlier anthropologists on the grounds that their attachment to immediate reality (individual humans or totem poles) prevented them from seeing that relationships and universal thought structures were the correct level of study on which an understanding of these immediate realities depends.

Marx made the same point in his critique of seventeenth century economists in the *Introduction to the Critique of Political Economy* (1904). They took as their point of departure what appeared, incorrectly, to be real concrete aspects. For instance, they started with population, which Marx argued was a meaningless abstraction if it ignored classes, while class was empty without a consideration of the elements on which it was based: wage labour, capital, etc. It was therefore essential to work through existing data and 'knowledge' to reach the structure of elements on which these depended.

In all cases, the structure has to be conceptualized from its effects and these alone are amenable to the senses; but they do not necessarily correspond with the elements of the structure. For positivism, facts and phenomena are 'solid' and have an objective existence; theory depends on the accumulation and interpretation of such facts. The structuralists hold, contrary to this, that facts are socially coloured, that they will not tell us about their nature of themselves and that conceptualization must be simultaneous with, and guide observation. To paraphrase Althusser again, we may scrutinize economic facts (prices, profit, rent) for ever but the economic structure will never be discovered at that level, just as the pre-Newtonian physicist could not see the law of gravity from the observation of falling bodies.

The conceptualization of reality is a theoretical process because reality is not given 'directly' to the senses. Man's conception of his relation to the world is also a specific level of any social formation, which might be termed the 'ideational' level, which has a certain autonomy and mediates between the scientist and his object of study. Our approach to reality is, so to speak, ideologically obscured, and we must go beyond common sense concepts and the first observation of phenomena for a scientific description.

To say this does not imply that the activity of structuralism consists in looking behind visible phenomena or the world of appearances to discover the unobservable reality behind, like pulling aside a veil to see the truth behind it. The metaphor of visibility, though misleading, has been used many times. Godelier, for example, writes (1967, p. 91):

> For Marx, as for Claude Lévi-Strauss, 'structures' should not be confused with visible 'social relations' but constitute a level of reality invisible but present behind the visible social relations. The logic of the latter, and the laws of social practice more generally, depend on the functioning of these hidden structures.

While this implies that there is some kind of non-conceptual thought, a better distinction would be between the most immediate conceptualization and reality, rather than between conceptual and non-conceptual thought as such. There is a sense in which a newcomer to a situation will most readily conceptualize in a certain way: it is easier to see the relationship between capitalist and worker as based on the exchange of work and wage rather than on exploitation and surplus value. (In a similar way, someone listening to serial music for the first time seems to hear an unorganized mass of notes until he learns to perceive the internal structure of relationships between pitch, timbre, destiny, etc.) While structuralism does not imply the platonic distinction between appearance and reality, it does stress the importance of going beyond the first analysis. Nor is the transition from 'apparent' to 'real' structure a once for all step: the relationship between our mind and the object of study is not a standardized one but mediated in all sorts of ways. While some aspects of social reality are more obscured by ideology, others may be less resistant to analysis. The situation is more complex than the visual analogy implies, and the structuralist approach should rest on two distinctions: that between the most immediate conceptualization and reality, and that between ideology and reality.

Description and explanation

The hypothetico-deductive method of positivism distinguishes between description and explanation (in the sense of the application of theory to observations) as separate stages of analysis. However, the level at which structures are conceptualized confounds this distinction: the description of a structure simultaneously explains the phenomenon. In the example taken from Freud, cited above, the process of dream formation was not considered to be adequately comprehended until it had been described with reference to the superego, and this description counted as an explanation of the thought processes at work in the dream. In the same way the interaction between id, ego and superego, and between them and the external environment at the various levels of consciousness explained the individual psychic structure, and these terms were also used to describe the process.

Structuralists fuse explanation, which means essentially synchronic causation, with description in attempting to demonstrate the structure behind events, behaviour and processes and to establish the relations of determination between different levels and layers. Lévi-Strauss shows, in his earlier work at least, why a society possesses a particular kinship structure or myth by examining its universal features (for example, the need for social solidarity, the solution of intellectual problems) and demonstrating how its details are related to the religion, economy and political structure of the same society. The whole of Marx's *Capital* is to be understood as the description of the structure of capitalism as a social formation, a description which entails a synchronic explanation of the workings of the system.

For the structuralists, scientific activity involves conceptualizing society (or the phenomenon under investigation) as a totality, by defining its specific features, analysing it as a structure constituted by the interrelation of structural elements, and defining stages of social development as different combinations of these. Their concepts must correspond one by one with the elements of material reality, and reality is thought to have a structured form. Empirical generalizations and regularities are to be explained by reference to this underlying reality, and laws which hold for one historical context may well be false in another.

146

Synchronic causation

That the stages of description and explanation can be integrated in this way depends on a particular conception of cause. Essentially the structuralists' aim is limited and very simple: to show the synchronic principles of operation at work in the phenomena under consideration, so that the relations of determination between the elements and levels of a social formation, and the limits to which these apply, can be discovered. Structures may be synchronically explained in terms of their internal mechanisms.

This conception is based on the following theoretical premises:

(a) that the structure causes its effect synchronically;

(b) that the structure, though immanent, is manifested only in its effects—it is never immediately active so causation is mediated;

(c) the elements and levels of the structure and the relationships between them may be of different natures and weightings so that any structure consists of several types of determination;

(d) that there is no one to one relation between cause and effect, and that contradictions and elements are likely to be 'overdetermined';

(e) that although one of the levels may be 'determinant in the last instance', the dominant role in the structure may be taken by another level.

Two key terms designate this type of causality: *Darstellung* and metonymy.

Althusser calls the type of causality appropriate to structuralism 'metonymic', a term borrowed from Lacan. His rejection of a monist interpretation of society, such as Hegel's, in terms of ideas, technology or class, entails opposition to the simple conception of cause and effect which such approaches rely on, where causation is ultimately reduced to one agency or cause in two dimensional space or to homogeneous causations all of 'equal strength'. 'Metonymic' causality denotes a more complex type of causation in three dimensional space, where the elements of a structure may be related to each other in all sorts of links of autonomy and interdependence. This is associated with a focus on structures as relatively autonomous yet interrelating to make up a complete social formation in a complex but not predetermined way. The characteristics of the structuralist totality may be 'overdetermined'; that is, each is due to several causes and has more than one *raison d'être*. The term 'overdetermination' was originally introduced by Freud to denote how a single dream image expressed several unconscious desires. He wrote about condensation, one of the processes of dream formation that 'the elements of the dream are constructed out of the whole mass of

L

dream thoughts and each one of these elements is shown to have been determined many times over in relation to the dream thoughts' (Freud, 1954, p. 284).

The notion of overdetermination abandons the one to one relation between cause and effect. In the case of dreams, where it was relatively simple to distinguish causes from effects, a dream element represented the condensation of many dream thoughts, and the same dream thought could be expressed many times over in different ways by different dream elements.

I showed in the last chapter how Althusser uses overdetermination to indicate the complexity of any contradiction. For him, as for Marx, Lenin and Mao, the contradictions of capitalism and imperialism are never simple but multi-dimensional and over-determined, and there is no one general contradiction in any social formation (Althusser, 1969a, p. 100):

> If a vast 'accumulation of contradictions' come into play in the same court, some of which are radically heterogeneous—of different origins, different senses, different levels and points of application—but which nevertheless 'group themselves' into a ruptural unity, we can no longer talk of the sole, unique power of the general contradiction.

One example of the complexity of determination is the distinction made by Althusser between economic determinacy in the last instance, and the dominant role which may be taken by other levels of the social structure, which was discussed in chapter 4. This has obvious applicability to the analysis of complex societies. For example, social ownership of the economic system is a necessary but insufficient condition for the existence of socialism. In a socialist society the economy does not of itself dominate the rest of society but is subordinated to political decisions as to the allocation of resources; while the economic base is determinant in the last instance and is the precondition for socialism, other levels of structure are dominant at any given time. In non-capitalist social formations, the determinant role may be taken by another level of society than the economy: politics, religion or kinship. The concept of each sphere (ideology, polity, economy) must therefore be constructed for each mode of production. Dominance consists in setting limits to the independence of other levels, and defining the looseness of the degree of fit between structures compatible with the maintenance of a given state of the totality.

The other concept, *Darstellung*, was employed by Marx to charac-terize the mode of existence of the structure of a mode of production. Literally it means 'representation'. Althusser defines it as the 'space between the content and its forms of appearance'. It implies that the representation of, say, capitalism does not 'take the form of an emissary of some essence which remains behind'. Nothing remains behind or external to the representation; rather, the structure exists only in and through its representation. It is like a play whose latent structure cannot be grasped from the individual speeches or characters. The structure can be grasped only from the whole, never from the manifestations which merely hint at it. Althusser calls this 'un tout complexe déjà donné', and refers to *Darstellung* variously as the existence of a structure through its effects, or an absent cause. These terms are obscure but their meaning is clear: causation is not to be seen as something external to the phenomenon and willing it, but must be sought within its own internal organization.

Marx grappled with the problem of conceptualizing determination of this variety, and used several metaphorical expressions to describe it. One of the clearest of these refers to the relation between subordinate and dominant structures (Marx, 1904, p. 302):

Under all forms of society, there is a determinate production, and relations engendered by it, which assigns to all other productions and to the relations engendered by them, their rank and importance.

It is the universal light with which all the other colours are tinged and are modified through its peculiarity. It is a special ether which determines the specific gravity of everything that appears in it.

Althusser is the main theorist of structural causality, while Lévi-Strauss demonstrates it practically. Freud however attempted a formulation of structural causality in his lecture on 'The Anatomy of the Mental Personality' (1933). He argued that individual psychic structures and particular mental states were to be directly referred to two series existing in the mind, which determine them: the id, ego and superego, which are regions of the mind, and the unconscious, preconscious and conscious which are to be thought of as qualities rather than mental provinces. In Freud's terms, any psychic structure represented a compromise formation between the multitude of conflicts and contradictions existing at the structural level between id, ego and superego fought out over time. The exact nature of the compromises and repressions involved was discernible only at the unconscious level of the consciousness series.

The notions of determination by a structure, and synchronic causality are peculiar to structuralists. They are also very simple— explanation for them involves laying bare the internal mechanisms of a social formation or cultural item and the relationships between its different orders. This approach to causation is to be seen in relation to problems in explanation in the social sciences.

For example, the central problems of sociology could be held to embody a particular conception of cause. To answer questions about the existence and persistence of society, and about social order in terms of causes implies that 'cause' is an active agency embodied in values, technology or some other order that objectively determines social life. It is an anthropomorphic notion which conceives of cause as an active force, probably left over from the days when a religious explanation in terms of an active agency satisfied all questions. This role was of course, taken by only one agent. The secularization of philosophy abolished anthropomorphism to a large extent; man, society and history was now to be explained as emanating ultimately from one source whether mind, matter or ideas. Explanation also tends to be confined to external determination and assumes that the passage of time is evidence that an effect is the direct result of an earlier cause, which slides into the assumption that time itself is to be treated as a causal agency. J. S. Mill defined cause as 'the universal antecedent of a phenomenon' and MacIver, in his classic work on social causation, started by emphasizing that sequence and causality are not the same, but later postulated (1942, p. 3) as of the axioms for the study of causation, that 'every effect is the result of a prior cause and every effect is the cause of a posterior effect', and that 'causal relation is the nexus of things moving from the present to the future'—in this way the quest for social causation was assimilated to the study of social change. Functionalism is an exception to this; it does not explain by means of social development, but still relies on time for causal association: a function is explained by its role in the system of which it is a part, that is, according to the ends which determine its course. When explanation relies on the time factor, causality is restricted to linearity and to temporality, and this ignores the possibility of variations in the time scales of different phenomena, and that the relationship between cause and effect may be more complex than sequence. In other words, historical explanation is inadequate in itself: analysis of social institutions solely in terms of their genesis is necessarily partial in ignoring the synchronic dimension. Society is a structure which can be understood in terms of the interrelation of its parts and a process which can be understood in terms of its past. Exclusive concentration on the process aspect neglects that the meaning of each part is visible synchronically in the present. There is a third type of explanation, in terms of individual motivation, showing how the personality structure is articulated to and reinforces the social structure. These three types of explanation are not separate; individual motivation is determined by socialization which is rooted in the social structure, and in turn maintains it; social structure depends ultimately on the activity of individuals which has a historical aspect, and social change must be on the basis of a given social structure.

There are thus several problems involved in determining causes: anthropomorphism, the use of time as a causal agency, monism, external determination, different 'strengths' of causes, and different types of explanation.

Much recent sociological theory has avoided these problems, or transferred explanation to a plane where cause is irrelevant. The explanations of early functionalism were both tautological (phenomena exist because they have a function, everything that exists has a function), and teleological (phenomena exist because of the future ends they serve). Rigid empiricism documented empirical relationships (correlations) between data rather than analysing why and how the variables are related. Perspectivism (à la Mannheim) contended that the sum of all viewpoints will provide an adequate explanation, although each in itself is one-sided. Alternatively the problem was avoided by aiming for empathic understanding rather than causal explanation.

Recent attempts to introduce a systemic approach into functionalism promise to overcome the bias to teleology and the tendency to ignore structural antagonisms and contradictions. Lockwood's critique (1964) of 'normative functionalism', for example, leads to the systemic investigation of societal integration. He argues that attention should be focused on the relations between the parts of the social system in terms of the goodness of fit between the 'core institutional order' and its 'material substratum', rather than on the relations between the actors. But no content is given to system integration; he does not consider the sources of systemic contradiction nor is the approach integrated to a concept of the unity of a structured whole. Gouldner (1959) also draws attention to the inadequacies of traditional functionalism and argues that different parts of the social structure have a differential significance in social change. Once the interdependence of the parts and the equilibrium of the whole is taken as problematic rather than given, the prevalent emphasis on the role of shared values in the maintenance of social order must be abandoned. The interconnexion of the parts may be closer or weaker, and their relative independence must be established in each case. Lockwood and Gouldner both go far in subverting the notion of a homogeneous totality with the recognition that societies are constructed of parts or subsystems whose relative importance and interrelation vary from case to case. They divert attention from individuals and values to structures, and so enable analysis of, for instance, social conflict, to consider the various effects on a social system of conflicts occurring at its different levels.

151

Others, such as Parsons and Buckley, demonstrate a theoretical awareness of the significance of systemic analysis, and use terms from information theory to describe social systems. But, as they do not provide transformation rules to the data below, this is of limited practical use.

In so far as the structuralist approach solves some of the problems of explanation, it does so by pursuing only a very limited aim: the demonstration of internal principles of operation. Insights from psychology and linguistics as well as sociology are applied to the problems of explanation. One forerunner of this approach was Gregory Bateson, whose study of the Iatmul 'naven' ceremonies was intended as an attempt at non-teleological explanation; he explained the ceremonies by showing the logical network into which they fitted, and their interrelation with other aspects of Iatmul life on the structural, cultural, 'ethological' (affective), and 'eidological' (cognitive) planes, in addition to examining them developmentally (this last based, to a large extent, on cybernetics with an emphasis on feedback and metaperception). The explanation was structural in showing how and why the ceremonies operated, the significance of their different aspects and features for different levels of social organization, and the logic of their mechanism, with constant reference to the thought structures which underlie Iatmul culture and render observations comprehensible as part of a particular *Weltanschauung*. His distinction between cultural and social structure prefigured Lévi-Strauss's isolation of the cultural sphere as a relatively autonomous area and the principle of overdetermination pervaded the study as Bateson recognized that causation from one of these points of view was insufficient as an explanation.

The concepts of overdetermination, *Darstellung* and metonymy are extremely simple, and if they appear novel and complex, it can only be due to the theoretical weakness of sociological theory as regards explanation and causation. Far more complex notions have long been employed in linguistics, mathematics and the natural sciences.

The existence of structures

If real structures are to be discovered and their internal determinations revealed, it must be recognized that structures are distinct from models, in construction, logical status and purpose. As customarily conceived, a model is a heuristic device to simplify reality by expressing it in terms of a limited number of variables that can be algebraically manipulated or to deal with an unknown process by attributing to it a form known to operate elsewhere. Models are useful in certain situations to predict the effects on the system as a whole of altering one or more of the variables; but they do not attempt to explain social reality.

The structuralists take pains to avoid the tendency in both the natural and social sciences to use models to represent the field they are studying, where it is felt not to be capable of conceptualization in any other way. Such models typically involve the use of analogy, and run into the danger that what may be appropriate in one field of study will not necessarily be appropriate to all aspects of the field to which this 'proven' model is applied. A model in this sense will have dubious ability to predict and will be inadequate as a means of explanation. The structuralist approach to analogy, metaphor and models owes much to Bachelard, whose ideas were summarized in the section on Althusser's genealogy in chapter 4. He showed how, in eighteenth-century chemistry, the notions of 'coagulation' and 'spongeosity' were applied to all sorts of matter by means of analogy, with disastrous results for the development of scientific knowledge. Sociology too has suffered from the unwarranted extension of analogies; for example, the naturalism of late nineteenth century evolutionism and functionalism, to be found in the work of Spencer[2] among others. This is not to say that structuralists are themselves free of this tendency; Lévi-Strauss's misuse of the linguistic analogy in anthropology was discussed in chapter 3.

Thus, for the structuralists, structures are thought to have a real existence; the structure represents the fundamental elements of a phenomenon, their articulation, and the consequences of the interplay of their different levels. 'Structure' may apply to various degrees of generality: a particular historical period (the capitalist mode of production), unrelated societies (marriage as a form of exchange), or individual cultural forms. This assumes that there is only one structure to a field which is discoverable and has an objective existence. There is an isomorphic relation between structure and reality, in that the elements are matched one for one.

In this way, an implicit distinction is made between structures and models: structures are presumed to have an objective existence, whereas models function as a conceptual device to facilitate the handling of empirical material. For example, a model of social structure could describe a kinship system showing how patrilineal cross-cousin marriage tends to create social instability. As such it would function as a licence to infer propositions about phenomena in patrilineal societies and its utility would depend on its power in generating hypotheses about the phenomena in question; the model has no existential claim. Lévi-Strauss's 'structures' do have an existential claim; they refer not to the observed material of social relations but to the unconscious and hidden reality which is the 'real' social structure. This is reached by progressively disclosing the elements which are articulated in a formal 'structure', rather than by abstraction from the facts. So the representation is a description of the structure of the society and an explanation of how it works. It is unfortunate that the term 'structure' is used both for the representation and the reality it describes.

The differences between these views of model and reality have not been clearly understood in British anthropology. Lévi-Strauss and Radcliffe-Brown carried on a protracted correspondence on the topic of models, structures and structural models.[3] Radcliffe-Brown's emphasis was on structural description, on the inductive establishment of structural patterns, not on verification of deductively derived laws of structural association. The differences emanate from the connexions between structure, model and reality, expressed by Lévi-Strauss in his comments on Radcliffe-Brown's letter. He emphasized that for him models are the only reality, but they have to be reached by transcending observations. Some observable phenomena are nearer to their model than others; for example, sea shells as opposed to kinship relations. Needless to say, when Lévi-Strauss uses 'model' here he means structure, or representation of structure. The connexion between structure and reality it represents is isomorphic. The structure accounts for the phenomena as observed by showing their connexion with hitherto unrevealed relationships.

Conclusion and critique

Althusser, Lévi-Strauss and other structuralists such as Marx, Saussure, and Freud share a view about what the social sciences should aim to achieve and how they should set about it. They have a particular view of the sort of knowledge of the social world that should be sought, of what causation consists in, and of the difference between appearance and reality. In addition they share certain ideas about scientific procedure. Their epistemology implies a whole range of dangers which require a specific methodology if they are to be avoided. They emphasize for example that the object of study must be defined and concepts developed which are applicable to the sphere in question; the necessity of recognizing that the units of study are not immediately visible; that the correct units of study are social relations and not individuals; the value of proceeding through a critique of past theory which lays bare its ideological nature and increases objectivity; the danger of analogy especially as it affects the choice of methods; that the criterion for judging theories must be intelligibility rather than verification/falsification; the necessity of recognizing that only things, not concepts, are measurable. These postulates are implicit in the exposition of the ideas of Lévi-Strauss and Althusser in previous chapters.[4] Taken individually they are not necessarily characteristic of a structuralist outlook since they may all be found in the work of non-structuralist social scientists. However, they are not to be found in combination elsewhere, and the structuralists emphasize their necessary interrelation: for any discipline to establish itself as autonomous, it is essential that its sphere of study should be defined and concepts formulated which are applicable to it alone, and not just borrowed from older established disciplines by means of analogy. This requires a high degree of self-consciousness on the part of theorists about what they are doing at each stage of study. The analogy of the natural and social sciences brings with it assumptions about the nature of causation, and the idea that laws may be empirically established. When this has been rejected intelligibility necessarily replaces verification by observation.

There are certain problems in structuralist epistemology: although some areas are clearly worked out, the epistemology as a whole has been inadequately put to the test. Paradoxically, it has been developed theoretically in Marxism but least tested there, and where it has been most used in practice, by Lévi-Strauss, it has been the least theorized. Given this, there is the same problem as regards epistemology that I discussed in relation to Althusser in the last chapter—nothing is adequately specified. At a general level, all the notions presented above are highly suggestive, but when examined in detail it is unclear what they mean in practice. For example, the concept of overdetermination is certainly novel as regards the Marxist notion of contradiction, but does it mean anything more than multicausal explanation? In Freud's formulation it means that many phenomena, or symptoms, can be combined into one, or alternatively that one underlying phenomenon can be fragmented into a number of manifestations. Althusser takes over the former sense, but there is no indication as to which factors are necessary or sufficient, and what combination of factors is required for a revolution to occur. Again, the ideas about different types of determination and of the different weightings of elements are useful, and do represent a specifically structuralist approach to explanation, but they too have been inadequately specified and applied. As I suggested above, these ideas would not be so striking if sociological theory were more advanced.

A second problem relates to the distinction between appearance and reality. All concepts must depend on a theoretical or abstract reformulation of empirically perceived phenomena, however empiricist the approach, and the structuralists are mistaken in implying that some frameworks are 'empiricist' as opposed to 'theoretical', and that an absolute distinction can be drawn between conceptual thought and empirical observation. The difference is one of degree rather than kind: some procedures are more empiricist than others, and some concepts are reached by a greater process of abstraction and working through of empirical data than others. The structuralists are at the abstract end of this continuum, and their method involves reducing the phenomena they study to their bare skeletons, but this is not the difference in kind that they assume it to be.

The distinction between appearance and reality is associated with this. A dichotomous attitude towards this distinction is the inevitable result of their ideas about abstraction and conceptualization: probe through mystifying appearance far enough and you will arrive at reality. There are several unexplained implications of this conception: that there can be a once for all step between appearance and reality (and that the investigator can know when he has reached reality), that reality always appears in a mystified form, and that there is one authentic level of reality. By making an implicit *a priori* principle of the appearance/reality distinction, the structuralists fall into an idealism of which they are quite unaware: what they are aiming for in their search for the real level of reality is an ultimate essence in the phenomena they are investigating, a 'rational kernel in the mystical shell'. Althusser dismisses this conception of reality and appearance in his critique of Hegelianism, but in the absence of further explanation it is not at all clear how the search for structural elements differs radically from idealism.

This problem in turn affects the structuralist distinction between models and structures, which is based primarily on their different modes of existence, heuristic in the one case and ontological in the other. This may well be so, but this critique of the use of models is very weak if it does not actually criticize their function and method, and provide some alternative. The criticisms of metaphor and analogy are valuable, but there is more to models than this, and the use of models would seem to be a necessary means to the reduction of empirical phenomena to their structural elements.

These problems are rooted in the inability of structuralism to provide consistent and thoroughgoing alternatives to the approaches they criticize. Idealism is rejected, but Lévi-Strauss in particular seems unable to avoid the essentially idealist distinction between appearance and reality. Empiricism is rejected, but the alternatives they suggest differ in degree rather than in kind.

However, there are three points to be made against these criticisms and in defence of structuralist epistemology. First, it may not be fully worked out or systematic, but it is a distinctive approach which highlights certain areas and attempts to come to terms with them in a particular way; though they make no break with either idealism or empiricism in the way they think they do, the structuralists do occupy a specific position on both continua. Second, many of their ideas go some way at least to posing and answering persistent problems in the social sciences; about the nature of causation, the relation between description and explanation, the meaning of reality. Their ideas require considerable refinement and elaboration before they can be of general operational use, but they do promise a rigour which has so far been lacking. In time, the structuralists' epistemological strictures and suggestions may well be regarded as obvious. Then structuralism may be accepted as normal scientific procedure and will cease to be a distinctive approach.

To summarize, structuralist epistemology raises some important questions and attempts to answer them; it does not answer them sufficiently but this is better than nothing and provides the possibility for an adequate epistemology in the future.

6 Conclusion: the structuralist problematic

This chapter has several tasks: to decide whether or not structuralism constitutes a distinctive problematic, by comparing the thought structures of Althusser and Lévi-Strauss; to examine the most important differences between these two authors; to assess the contribution of structuralism to the social sciences; and, finally, to discuss the value of the structuralist approach to the analysis of theory.

Comparison of the thought structures of Althusser and Lévi-Strauss

In the first chapter I suggested a rigorous approach to the examination of theory, which would avoid the problems of relativism, and argued that theories could be examined in at least four ways: historically, in terms of their genesis and development; sociologically, in terms of their connexions with the social conditions under which they arose; evaluatively, in terms of their substantive validity, and morphologically, in terms of the structure of concepts on which they are based. The main focus of this work has been on the last of these approaches. I suggested five possible distinctive levels which might be found in any theoretical system and which should be analysed separately: epistemology, philosophy, theory, methodology and field of study.

Summary of the historical, sociological and evaluative approaches

I have examined the work of Althusser and Lévi-Strauss from all four points of view but paid more attention to some than to others. Their theories have been looked at developmentally so as to determine the genealogy of their central concepts. In this respect, I argued that while Lévi-Strauss borrows more from other theorists than Althusser, and while already established methods and procedures, particularly psychoanalytic and linguistic ones, are more important to Lévi-Strauss's approach, a sum of the separate elements of each does not amount in either case to an adequate account or explanation of their theory. The key to both authors is their own contribution rather than what they have borrowed from others. Neither can be sufficiently explained in historical terms but a developmental approach can clarify the derivation of many of their concepts.

The social referents of their theories have also been examined, and the relationship between their systems of ideas and the social conditions under which they were written, though not in detail. The reason for this is that in both cases it would be wrong to consider the relevant social conditions to be French society in the 1960s or, even more generally, late capitalist society. Lucien Goldmann (1964a and, with Piaget, 1967) has attempted to do this for Lévi-Strauss and views his structuralism as the ideology of neo-capitalist society in which the meaningful action and efficacy of individuals and humans is denied, and the structures of society presented as autonomous, both in development and perpetuation. This, he maintains, reflects and justifies the monolithic and bureaucratic character of neo-capitalism. However, such a crude sociology of knowledge approach does not really come to terms with the specific concepts used by Lévi-Strauss, and it is doubtful whether either theorist, or indeed any theorist, can fruitfully be examined in such a general way in relation to the whole social structure.

It is more meaningful to look at both theorists in relation to more particular conditions, especially to intellectual orthodoxy in both their areas of interest, and in the social sciences as a whole. Althusser says that his work was prompted by the postwar re-interpretation of Marxism as humanism which, he felt, had disastrous consequences for Marxist theory, epistemology and political action; so his writing attempts to distinguish Marxism from humanism and from the philosophical tradition from which modern humanism derives. Similarly, Lévi-Strauss's work is to be seen in relation to the impasse of contemporary anthropology: with decolonization and industrialization small scale primitive societies, which were its conventional raw data, are rapidly disappearing and it is no longer possible to go on accumulating information about empirical primitive societies. As Lévi-Strauss himself says in *Tristes Tropiques* (1955), he felt that an alternative approach based on generalizations about social organization and thought on the basis of existing data, was hindered by an empiricist methodology and classificatory approach to social reality. His anthropology represents an attempt to break out of this, to provide a new theoretical approach, capable of generalizing, which rests on an appropriate epistemology. Of course, Lévi-Strauss's demand for generalization is not original, but had been made earlier by Radcliffe-Brown and others. However, in Lévi-Strauss's case, the demand has a particular orientation: he wants to investigate the relationship between cultural invariants and the universal properties of the mind, as well as those of society. In this way, his approach is not only shaped by decolonization, but also reflects a discontent with the sociologism of post-Durkheimian British and French academic anthropology. With his increasing neglect of the study of social interaction, this discontent is taken to its logical conclusion. The particular areas Lévi-Strauss chooses to study, such as kinship, thought and cultural products, satisfy another aim, which is to break down the barriers between disciplines; not only between sociology and anthropology, but also between anthropology and linguistics, and anthropology and economics. In so far as his work has more general philosophical implications, it is to be seen as a reaction to existentialism, especially Sartre's emphasis on the individual and individual choice, on the primacy of history over structure and voluntarism over determinism.

In both cases, the social conditions are primarily intellectual, and the developments and conflicts that exist occur within theory rather than as a result of wider social conditions. Social conditions, understood as intellectual conditions, and history both help to explain the form and content of Althusser's and Lévi-Strauss's theories but do not explain them fully.

On the assumption that it was more rigorous and fruitful to evaluate theory in terms of its internal consistency, rather than risk an empiricism or theoretical relativism, by referring to empirical data or alternative theoretical approaches, I examined both theorists evaluatively, in terms of internal inconsistencies, contradictions and unsolved problems within their theories. In chapter 3, I isolated several important problems in the work of Lévi-Strauss: whether concepts borrowed from other disciplines were used metaphorically or substantively, particularly the concept of the phoneme and of the unconscious; whether the intellectual prowess of primitive men is due to cultural creativity or to the physiological structure of the brain; the psychological reductionism of his schema, which conflicts with his explicit anti-naturalism; his inadequate explanation of forms of thought, and the lack of autonomy attributed to social organization; the contradiction between his psychologism in which both structures of the mind and social organization are necessarily predetermined and his avowed Marxism in which men make history undeterred by 'human nature'; finally, his ambiguities about his own method and the relation of myth-science to the science of myth.

The main problems in Althusser's schema were the inadequate

linkage between the various practices and levels of the Marxist totality; lack of specification of his crucial concepts of determination in the last instance by the economy and relative autonomy; the relationship between theory and practice and the contradictory notions about theories of science; ambiguity about the relevance of economic struggle, class and consciousness, and the relationship between objective structure and lived experience.

Comparison of the thought structures

It is now time to tie together the results of the morphological analysis, and compare the main concepts of Althusser and Lévi-Strauss. This will be done in terms of the five component levels of a theoretical structure: epistemology, philosophy, theory, methodology and field of study (outlined above, p. 10). I have already substantiated and argued the points made below in chapters 2, 3 and 4. What follows is an attempt to summarize them, and compare them systematically, not to argue the points.

At the epistemological level, Lévi-Strauss upholds an anti-empiricist approach to the study of social reality. Since there is a possible distinction between the appearance of things and reality, he emphasizes that theoretical abstraction from the concrete observable is necessary if real structures are to be reached. There is a one-to-one relationship between reality and structures arrived at in this way.

Lévi-Strauss's framework is shaped by two further epistemological premises. The first is the stress on the development of concepts appropriate to the subject matter which are neither borrowed nor based on analogy. In Lévi-Strauss's view, correct concepts are the necessary basis for the comparative analysis by which the relationship between phenomena, distinct in time and space, can be analysed. The second is that structural explanation and causality should be the main focus of the social sciences, particularly anthropology. This is based on his anti-historicism which maintains the primacy of structure over history, and entails theoretical attention to the internal structure of social organization and forms of thought, and an attempt to elaborate types of internal construction and inter-relation between structural elements (for example contradiction, opposition, dominance, homology, inversion and symmetry).

Althusser's epistemology also embodies an anti-empiricist conception of reality, which emphasizes the need for the elaboration of concepts adequate to the data, which are neither borrowed nor based on analogy. Each region of reality, natural and social, has its concept, and eventually there is a one-to-one relationship between the concrete-real and the concrete-in-thought.

161

He stresses the importance of structural causal analysis in opposition to historicist and idealist approaches where the parts of the totality are seen as reflections or epiphenomena of a central core, and where history is understood as the continuous development of this system of relationships. Hence he pays attention to the internal structure of social formations and to the separate development of its elements based on concepts such as relative autonomy, determinance, dominance, weightings, metonymy and contradiction.

A third important epistemological proposition is that knowledge and theory are productive processes like any others, and that knowledge is produced within the order of thought and is not testable by reference to empirical reality; thus for Althusser, there are no external guarantees of theory.

The main similarities between Althusser and Lévi-Strauss appear at the epistemological level. Both uphold an anti-empiricist conception of reality and stress the need for elaborating adequate and appropriate concepts; for both, structure has primacy over history and their theories are based on an explicit anti-historicism; the concept of structure is central to both, and both concentrate their focus on the internal construction of social and cultural phenomena (layers, levels and weightings) and on structural causality. Finally, both have a realist approach to science: they maintain that structures have a real existence, though they differ as to the relationship between the theory and the object of theory.

Philosophically, Lévi-Strauss oscillates between idealism and psychologism. Although he maintains that he is a materialist, his structures are not tied to a material base. On the contrary, they are either apparently free-floating, with an *a priori* existence or caused by the physiological make-up of the brain. Both of these types of explanation have implications for the possibility of conscious social change: if forms of thought and social organization are predetermined, men cannot create society in accordance with their own values.

Althusser's philosophy is shaped by two characteristics; his materialism and his strategic problematic. For him, social formations are determined in the last instance by the economy, and all his structures are tied to a material base in the real world, in practice as well as in theory. Strategically, as a revolutionary socialist, Althusser's aim is to change the world, and philosophy is meaningful only in so far as it is a political intervention. Althusser believes in man's capacity to change the world in accordance with his own values, and theory represents an auxiliary weapon in this project.

The differences between the two are clearest at this level. Althusser is a materialist and the basic premiss of his theory is that the characteristic activity of man is production, in which a raw matter is transformed into a finished product, be it in the sphere of economics, politics or ideology. The structures that Marxism studies always have a base in the real material world, though they are relatively autonomous of it at any given historical moment. Lévi-Strauss's structures are not tied or bounded in this way, and are physiological and psychological rather than material.

This basic difference engenders another relating to the possibility of conscious social change; for Lévi-Strauss men always have a mystified comprehension of social reality which limits their ability to change the world. Althusser's strategic problematic and distinction between theory and ideology, as science and non-science, reflect his belief that theory is part of the structure of forces that men can use politically to change the world in a revolutionary way. Where Lévi-Strauss tends to be overcautious in this respect, Althusser tends to voluntarism.

At the theoretical level, the 'combinatory' is Lévi-Strauss's central concept. It implies that social organization is based on a limited number of structural elements which are combinable in a finite number of ways. Structure, in these terms, is the syntax of transformations which never exists in empirical form itself, but empirically existing phenomena are to be seen as different combinations and permutations of the same elements.

Similarly, the 'combination' is Althusser's central theoretical concept. He examines the social formation as a complex interrelation of structures and levels of relative autonomy where the economy is determinant in the last instance. All social formations are ultimately reducible to five invariant elements whose content and mode of interrelation differ according to the particular mode of production. This structural determination conflicts to some extent with the voluntarism of Althusser's philosophy, a contradiction which was discussed in chapter 4 as being due to inadequate linkage between the various levels and practices of his totality.

The concept of structure is thus central to both Althusser and Lévi-Strauss and there are substantial similarities between the combination and combinatory. Both believe that structures are based on a limited number of elements which may be combined in a finite number of ways to produce different but related empirical social realities. In both cases the elements are given, though their content may change according to the particular combination, and the particular mode of articulation between the elements gives the resultant structure its unique character.

I shall return in the next section to Althusser's denial of the similarity between the 'combination' and 'combinatory'. Despite his assertions, the similarities far outweigh the differences, which may

M

best be seen in terms of their very different fields of study, and his point does not undermine the present argument.

Lévi-Strauss's main canon of method is that structural elements and principles are to be arrived at by means of abstraction from concrete empirical phenomena. Both the structural skeleton of social and cultural phenomena, and the structural relation between them, are to be approached in this way.

The method that Althusser uses most consistently in his writings is the critique of past theory. He argues that concepts can be best elaborated and refined by examining and criticizing past ideology and by making explicit its latent ideas.

The difference in field of study makes comparison of the methodology of Althusser and Lévi-Strauss difficult. However, there are similarities at this level. Both aim at the elaboration of concepts appropriate to the area under investigation, and most of their general methodological postulates in relation to this are the same. Apart from emphasizing the importance of analysing past ideology, both stress that the correct units of study are relationships between structural elements, not individuals, and that the structural elements are not necessarily observable. Both warn against the danger of analogy and metaphor, especially as regards the construction of theory and method. They both consider intelligibility to be the criterion of validity of their theory.

I made the point in chapter 5 that none of these principles is unique to Lévi-Strauss or Althusser, but may be found in the work of Weber, Durkheim or Radcliffe-Brown. However, the particular combination is unique and is something that Althusser and Lévi-Strauss arrived at independently.

There is one apparent methodological difference, but this is more terminological than substantive. Lévi-Strauss associates the passage from observed empirical phenomena to the underlying structure with the transition from concrete to abstract so that the resultant knowledge has an abstract character. For Althusser, on the other hand, the passage is from abstract empirical reality or past ideological concepts to concrete structural concepts, and knowledge produces concrete theory, not abstraction. He rejects as ideological and idealist the view that knowledge passes from concrete to abstract. Most of the confusion disappears when it is realized that Althusser calls empirical reality abstract whereas Lévi-Strauss considers it concrete, and vice versa for the eventual theory and concepts. The similarity between them emerges in the fact that Althusser writes pejoratively of the abstract, and Lévi-Strauss of the concrete.

There are several fields of study to which Lévi-Strauss applies his theory and philosophy, the main ones being kinship, myth and cultural artefacts and activities such as art, cooking and language.

Althusser's field of study is the theory of historical materialism, and he undertakes a textual analysis of Marx's writings, particularly *Capital*, and also of Lenin's, particularly *Materialism and Empirio-criticism*.

The difference in field of study is fundamental. Not only do Lévi-Strauss and Althusser work in different disciplines, but one is primarily political and non-academic whereas the other is academic, and their immediate objects of study are divergent in both nature and scope.

It would be possible to continue listing the similarities and differences between Althusser and Lévi-Strauss almost endlessly, and if we are to reach a definitive conclusion, the point at which the comparison ends will necessarily appear arbitrary. So far, it appears that there are substantial similarities at the levels of epistemology, theory and method, that the levels of philosophy and field of study are markedly different and that there are minor differences at the levels of theory and method. Given that their total outlook is not the same, the problem is to weigh up the relative importance of the similarities and differences. Any conclusion must therefore be a qualified one, always open to contradictory evidence, either that there are similarities or differences at other levels.

Taken as a whole, it is clear that there is a structure to the similarities and differences between Althusser and Lévi-Strauss, and that all the important differences are concentrated at one level alone. The general epistemological approach is the same and so is the theoretical apparatus they rely on: the concept 'structure' has the same meaning for both, the conception of how social phenomena are constructed and internally organized is the same and so is the methodological approach to that reality. What does differ is—at the end of the analysis—what the structures are tied or reduced to. What I am arguing here is that the levels of a theoretical structure are interconnected but relatively autonomous of each other and that Althusser and Lévi-Strauss can have a similar epistemological and methodological approach despite their obvious philosophical differences. Thus, the fact that for Lévi-Strauss the process of construction and organization is largely an emanation from the mind performing transformations on social and natural raw material, while for Althusser there is an autonomous social process which can be explained in terms of social interaction, does not invalidate the present argument. Examined in terms of the levels I have defined, this is a philosophical difference, and a difference in field of study, but it does not affect the basic epistemological and theoretical approach from which their studies are undertaken.

In this way, the questions that define the area of study are very similar, as are the means of posing those questions. It is only when the answers are pushed to their logical conclusion that the differences between the two become paramount.

As defined in chapter 1, a theoretical structure is characterized essentially by the questions that it poses. To repeat Althusser, science or theory can only pose questions 'on the terrain and within the horizons of' a definite theoretical structure or problematic which 'constitutes the absolutely defined condition of possibility, and thus the absolute determination of the form in which any problem can be posed'. Now, in terms of the fundamental outlook and questions posed, the similarities between the two are unambiguous, and it is legitimate to consider that they share a problematic, and that this is a structuralist problematic. Both seek structured totalities composed of pre-given elements and maintain that these are to be discovered at a theoretical level. This is not to deny that the philosophies to which their theoretical postulates ultimately return are very different; indeed, if one were to conduct a philosophical comparison of the two, the conclusion would have to be that they have very little in common.

Thus, depending on the point of view from which the comparison is made and the questions on which it is based, the answer will be different. As the approach adopted here has been to examine the theoretical framework as a whole and its underlying problematic rather than its philosophy, the conclusion is that Lévi-Strauss and Althusser do share a common problematic. A problematic does not require that all the answers are the same or that the theoretical postulates in the various spheres are strictly analogous. So this conclusion is not invalidated by their philosophical differences.

Briefly then, the comparison of the various levels of the thought structures of Althusser and Lévi-Strauss shows that there are both similarities and differences. They share a common structuralist problematic defined in terms of the basic questions posed, the approach to social reality and centrality and similarity of the concept of structure. Their philosophical differences do not undermine the approach as a whole or the questions that define it.

This conclusion was reached by use of a structuralist problematic and suffers from the inadequacies entailed by such an approach. Just as Lévi-Strauss tends to draw theoretical conclusions from his method, so I have been led by the morphological analysis of theory to draw the theoretical conclusions that epistemology defines the structuralist problematic, and that epistemological similarities override other great differences between Lévi-Strauss and Althusser. The approach has produced similarities at the level of method and epistemology which differentiate structuralism as a general approach from empiricism and idealism. In time these may appear to be superficial, with the increasing divergence between the two theorists' substantive work, and with the development of a non-empiricist and non-humanist approach to the social sciences. In this sense, my findings are temporary and inconclusive: there are fundamental differences between Lévi-Strauss and Althusser, and between them and other structuralists such as Barthes and Foucault despite their common epistemology. It all depends on the perspective from which one examines them.

Combination, combinatory and history

In the introduction to the English edition of *Reading Capital* (1970), Althusser claims that structuralism is an unscientific ideology, and takes pains to differentiate himself from it, and particularly from Lévi-Strauss. The two main differences he refers to are the conception of the structured totality and history, and he concludes (p. 7): 'We believe that despite the terminological ambiguity, the profound tendency of our texts was not attached to the "structuralist" tendency.' However, these differences are more apparent than real, and the similarity of Althusser to Lévi-Straussian structuralism is very much greater than he would like to admit. The question of history is the more substantial one and I shall deal with it first.

In the chapters of *Reading Capital* on the Hegelian conception of history, Althusser criticizes a type of 'structuralist historicism', and the rigid distinction between synchrony and diachrony. It will be remembered that for him there is no history 'in general' but different histories, different temporalities specific to different levels of the complex structures of particular modes of production, and that the key to the understanding of the totality is its internal mode of articulation rather than its genesis. Althusser believes that this does not involve a radical distinction between synchrony and diachrony and attacks any kind of structural approach which reduces history to diachrony as the mere 'becoming' of the present or synchronic. He implies that Lévi-Straussian structuralism rests on the idea that structure is a configuration of elements that maintain external correlations with each other and reside in the contemporaneity of time. The specificity of the various levels is achieved at the expense of establishing a mode of articulation between them and the mode of articulation does not change through time or between one structure and the next, so that diachrony is merely the succession of the same synchronic structure. He accuses Lévi-Strauss of having a Hegelian conception of time and of seeing history as pure chance (Althusser and Balibar, 1970, p. 96):

> The synchronic is contemporaneity itself, the copresence of the essence with its determinations, the present being readable as a

167

structure in an 'essential section' because the present is the very existence of the essential structure. The synchronic therefore presupposes the ideological conception of a continuous-homogeneous time. It follows that the diachronic is merely the development of this present in the sequence of a temporal continuity in which the 'events' to which 'history' in the strict sense can be reduced (cf. Lévi-Strauss) are merely successive contingent presents in the time continuum. Like the synchronic, which is the primary concept, the diachronic therefore presupposes both of the very two characteristics I have isolated in the Hegelian conception of time: an ideological conception of historical time.

Later he clarifies his contention that the ideological conception of diachrony is based on the ideological conception of synchrony (ibid., p. 108):

Diachrony is reduced to the sequence of events (*à l'événementiel*), and to the effects of this sequence of events on the structure of the synchronic: the historical then becomes the unexpected, the accidental, the factually unique, arising or falling in the empty continuum of time, for purely contingent reasons. In this context, therefore, the project of a 'structural history' poses serious problems, and a laborious reflection of this can be found in the passages devoted to it by Lévi-Strauss in *Structural Anthropology*. Indeed, by what miracle could an empty time and momentary events induce de- and re-structurations of the synchronic? Once synchrony has been correctly located, diachrony loses its 'concrete' sense and nothing is left of it either but its epistemological use, on condition that it undergoes a theoretical conversion and is considered in its true sense as a category not of the concrete but of knowing.

How correct are these criticisms and how relevant are they? To answer this, we must look more closely at what Lévi-Strauss has to say about history. In *The Savage Mind* (1966b), he characterizes history as a modern myth: anthropology and history are complementary perspectives which focus on different aspects of human life, through space and time, and the preference for history in French philosophy is due to the fact that the time element restores continuity to the seeming diversity of social forms. Yet historical 'fact' is no more given than any other; it is made possible only by selection according to a particular code, that of chronology, so history consists in trying to understand the relation before/after. The general code of dates on which historical analysis depends is not a linear series but consists of discontinuous classes of dates (for instance, prehistory, millennia, centuries, years, days), each furnishing an autonomous frame of reference, and so history is a classificatory activity like any other. Events which are significant in one code are not significant in others, so that, for example, an event in modern history is insignificant if coded in the prehistoric system. There can be identity between anthropology and history only at the price of reducing other societies to anterior forms of development of our own.

Lévi-Strauss attempts to avoid the pure diversity resulting from the rejection of unification through history by seeking unity at the level of the conditions of possibility of all social organization. The difference between social organizations is due to the particular combination so that myths and kinship structures differ in actualizing one particular combination of elements rather than another. Thus whereas for Hegel and Sartre the most advanced society includes all others, for Lévi-Strauss the whole has no existence. Paradoxically, the diversity of societies is respected despite his focus on universal characteristics. If anthropology is concerned to account for the repertory of real and possible combinations, there is no problem of genesis or origins because the conditions of possibility are identical. The diversity of societies in time is only a particular case of diversity in space, and historical change is only one type of variation.

More recently, Lévi-Strauss (1963) has admitted the polemical nature of his critique of history. The final chapter of *The Savage Mind* was directed against the tendency in France to consider historical knowledge as superior to all other forms of knowledge, and particularly against Sartre's *The Critique of Dialectical Reason* (1960). While showing that history depends on a code like all other forms of knowledge and suffers from the same problems as them, he has neglected so he says, the important question of whether in fact men express themselves better in structural or historical terms, and has postponed the problem of elaborating 'diachronic structures'.

How does this relate to Althusser's charges? It is undoubtedly the case that for Lévi-Strauss structuralist explanation is essentially synchronic and anti-historical; however, there are specific reasons why this should be so, given his anthropological subject matter, and also it is not clear that the distinction between synchrony and diachrony is as rigid as Althusser suggests. In the first place, Lévi-Strauss is dealing with what are, in Marxist terms, pre-class societies in which there is very little cumulative change and where the time element has less effect on the social organization than in industrial societies. Cumulative change occurs even in isolated circumstances, but over a longer time span, so the time factor is relatively less important in primitive than in other types of society, particularly class societies, and a historical approach has little to add to a synchronic account which takes the present structure as its central focus. Lévi-Strauss (1958b; Charbonnier, 1969) makes an important distinction between 'hot' and 'cold' societies, and ones in which history is cumulative and stationary. The time factor is built into the structure of 'hot' societies and cumulative change occurs so that the passing of time influences social organization. In 'cold' societies the reverse is the case. Time is experienced differently in the two cases and is of objectively different significance (quoted in Charbonnier, 1969, p. 39):

> We should not, then, draw a distinction between 'societies with no history' and 'societies which have histories'. In fact, every human society has a history and they all go equally far back, since all history dates from the birth of mankind. But whereas so-called primitive societies are surrounded by the substance of history and try to remain impervious to it, modern societies interiorize history, as it were, and turn it into the motive power of their development.

The implication is that while 'cold' societies, the ones in which Lévi-Strauss is himself interested, do not require a developmental approach, the historical dimension must be an integral part of an explanation of 'hot' societies. Thus Lévi-Strauss is not saying, as Althusser contends, that history is always irrelevant or that there is no point in examining class societies historically. Rather the reverse: he is arguing for a flexible approach that takes account of the differential significance of time and change in different types of society. Just because he does not examine class societies himself does not mean that he rules out a historical approach towards them.

The second point is that when Lévi-Strauss does deal with the relationship between different types of society such as caste and totemic society, he compares the structural principles on which they are based rather than examining their relationship on an evolutionary scale. Thus he focuses on the transformation of the structure rather than on time and development: one society is not seen as developing out of another in any natural way, but both are taken as already constituted structured wholes which may be synchronically compared. This approach to the comparison of different social forms is very similar to Althusser's. Lévi-Strauss would not disagree that the history of each element should be examined separately, as Althusser and Balibar suggest, and indeed he does make the same point about different elements and structures having different temporalities and trajectories of development.

Another of Althusser's accusations is that Lévi-Strauss has a 'chance' theory of history, that is, one that assumes there is no necessary connexion between different and successive social formations. However, where Lévi-Strauss does ascribe to a 'roulette' theory of history (where there is an important chance element as to which particular structural elements combine to form a society and as to which combination emerges at a given point in time), this is always directed against an ethnocentric evolutionary theory which views societies as ranged on a developmental scale from the most primitive to the most advanced with predetermined stages and a necessary development from one to the next. Like Althusser, he is saying that it is not predetermined which particular sort of society emerges from a given preceding type of society; for example, that there is no necessary evolution from slavery to feudalism or from feudalism to a particular type of capitalist society. This does not mean that an investigation of the transition from feudalism to capitalism is irrelevant, but that it should concentrate on the development of particular elements, and not treat the total structure of one as emanating spontaneously from the other. This again is the same as Althusser maintains. The fact that Lévi-Strauss believes in the contingent convergence of different types of society; for example, caste and totemic society, while Althusser does not, does not affect this argument. For Lévi-Strauss, the convergence occurs in the order of theory, at the abstract structural level; it is not a real historical process of convergence and does not affect his approach to the study of history.

Finally, Lévi-Strauss does discuss the problems of diachrony and intimates that the clue to diachronic structures will come from structural linguistics, where recurrent sequences are examined in detail. Gaboriau (1963) has suggested that his writings contain several indications as to how change and history are to be integrated. A kind of 'thought experiment' is required to analyse the change of a society through a series of states in determinate time, which excludes external factors such as the natural milieu and other societies and uses the method of phonetics: it concentrates on one of the systems that constitute the society to see if it contains internal disequilibrium which tends towards a particular state. Kinship is looked at in this way in the *Elementary Structures of Kinship*. But this method is inadequate in itself and Lévi-Strauss makes additional suggestions: new elements are to be introduced into the theoretical representation to explain transformations and show why social structure is never reduced to a kinship system (or whatever is the dominant level of structure). A third clue is traits borrowed from neighbouring societies, for instance in the diffusion of myth. Extra-social influences are examined in *The Savage Mind* in the form of the demographic and environmental factors that underlie all society. Although structural history is not constituted, Lévi-Strauss does have some idea as to what is involved in it.

To summarize, Althusser and Lévi-Strauss are concerned with

171

class and pre-class societies respectively, and this explains why Lévi-Strauss does not pay much attention to historical transformations. Both make a principled criticism of theories which give historical explanation priority over structural causality. While Althusser and Balibar go some way, in theory at least, to elaborating a structuralist approach to history, Lévi-Strauss is less developed in this respect. If he makes a rigid distinction between synchrony and diachrony, it is because his particular subject matter enables him to distinguish empirically between stationary and cumulative history, and because much of his terminology derives from linguistics. If the distinction were pushed to its logical extreme, an undisguised formalism would emerge, but this is not the case. For Althusser's criticisms to be valid, Lévi-Strauss would have to see diachrony as little more than synchrony through time, where history makes little difference to synchronic structures which remain relatively stable through time. But it is precisely one of Lévi-Strauss's main contentions that different types of society have different internal structures.

In this way, Althusser's criticisms are either unfounded or irrelevant, being based on extrapolations of what he wrongly believes Lévi-Strauss to be arguing. This brings us back to his second way of trying to differentiate his Marxism from structuralism. All he says (Althusser and Balibar, 1970, p. 7) is that the 'combination' to be found in Marx 'has nothing to do with a combinatory' and that the categories he uses such as determination in the last instance, domination, overdetermination, and production process are 'foreign to structuralism'. As the statement is so brief there is little that can be said in reply but three points must be made. First, contrary to what Althusser maintains, there is nothing in those categories which is foreign to Lévi-Strauss, and if there is something specifically Marxist about them it is up to Althusser to prove his point by demonstration. Second, if what Althusser is getting at is the philosophical difference between materialism and idealism, then the difference is legitimate. However it does not affect the combination/combinatory apparatus. I argued above that structuralism is characterized by its questions and means of posing them, rather than by the philosophical viewpoint of the theorist, and that the final philosophical answers are not related in any necessary way to the means of posing the questions. The only differences that Althusser can point to to distinguish the combination from the combinatory are the question of history and of materialism/idealism. He does neither in an explicit way, and the issues he raises have little substance.

Despite his denials, Althusser is just as much of a structuralist as Lévi-Strauss in the respects he wishes to deny. This brings us to the third point: Althusser's assertions about his own philosophy and theoretical position are not to be taken too seriously. He has a tendency to change sides depending on his audience so as to maintain his superiority over all of them. Thus he attacks other versions of Marxism for being non-structuralist, but in discussion with non-Marxist structuralists emphasizes the political dimension of his work and his Marxism so that he can accuse them of being unscientific. In his terms, non-structuralist Marxists are unscientific because they are not structuralists, and non-Marxist structuralists are unscientific because they are not Marxist. But this attempt to establish his own scientific integrity is incoherent even in Althusser's own terms; he is making a political distinction between different kinds of theory while politics is for him, in theory at least, a practice quite independent of theory and theory contains its own guarantees of scientificity independent of political position.

The contribution of structuralism to the social sciences

The distinctive features of structuralism also constitute its contribution to the social sciences. These can be reduced to two essentially: the rigorous approach to social phenomena, and the analysis of the internal structure of social totalities. The former involves a particular attitude towards empirical phenomena, and raises and answers philosophical questions pertaining to the nature of social reality. The emphasis on the development of adequate concepts, at appropriate levels of abstraction, the attention paid to the possible knowledge of the social world that might be acquired, represent an attempt to put sociology and the social sciences more generally on a scientific footing. This is based on the premiss that a scientific approach does not use the same procedures in all spheres but that each region of life has its own specific procedures. Structuralism represents the search for the correct procedures for the analysis of social, as opposed to any other, phenomena.

The second distinctive feature is related to this. Althusser and Lévi-Strauss attempt to develop concepts adequate to analyse the internal composition of phenomena, which can demonstrate how they work as synchronic totalities, containing their own means of intelligibility. In this, structuralism is characterized by a 'geological' approach, describing the separate layers, levels and elements, and a synthetic orientation which shows how these are combined to form the phenomenon under investigation. The attention to the different weightings of the various elements, and the complex and multifarious way in which the levels are integrated, reveal the concern with structural causality and with demonstrating how it is that a social formation can exist as it does. In this way, a successful structuralist

173

analysis lays bare the underlying principles of operation of the object studied.

These characteristics distinguish structuralism from other theoretical approaches in the social sciences. Its emphasis on the interrelation of elements rather than on social action by individuals and groups or on the social relations between individuals implies an objectivist approach which does not take the actor's perception of his activity as valid or meaningful, and so structuralism differs in this respect from certain important aspects of Weber's theory and from the action theory that derives from it, which does take as basic the meaning of social action for the actor.

On the other hand, the stress on the distinction between appearance and reality, and the emphasis that the correct unit of study is not necessarily observable or amenable in any way to the senses, puts structuralism on the other side of the fence from those theoretical approaches in the social sciences which derive from behaviourism and positivism, and for which sense data is the raw material for the construction of theory. Structuralism is not alone in highlighting the discrepancy between appearance and reality, but does so in a particularly stringent way, and attempts to build this distinction into its epistemological and theoretical approach.

Again the attention to the different weightings of the elements of social structure and the number of possible modes of articulation, especially contradiction and opposition, distinguish structuralism from the functionalist predisposition to treat all elements as equivalent and hence unweighted or undifferentiated in terms of their relative determinacy.

Finally, structuralism is furthest methodologically from a purely historical approach to social phenomena, which examines genesis at the expense of structure. However, the historical dimension is always held to be complementary to the structuralist approach, though not in any way a substitute.

In this way, structuralism has a contribution to make both as method and theory. In use it is interdisciplinary: the objects that Lévi-Strauss examines are linguistic and psychological, as well as more properly sociological and anthropological, and he manages to integrate them all; similarly, Althusser follows the tradition of political economy that breaks down the barriers between sociology, politics, economics and philosophy. In this way, the contribution they have to make is to the social sciences as a whole rather than sociology alone. Coupled with this is the comparative nature of structuralism: the 'geological' attitude permits the comparison of phenomena at different stages of development and indeed of phenomena which are apparently unrelated in all ways, and so avoids the evolutionism that characterized early comparative sociology.

This is especially relevant when it comes to examining cultural products and forms of thought, where the structuralist approach is at its strongest.

But this contribution is not without qualifications (viz. the criticisms of specific points at the end of chapter 5). It is important to realize that at the moment the contribution is more potential than actual. The validity of structuralism still has to be proved in practice. Also, in so far as structuralism is a theory as well as a method, it is not unproblematic. The most important general problems of theory besetting it are the integration of the objective analysis of society with knowledge based on subjective experience, the danger of formalism, the question of the derivation of structures, and the assimilation of the historical dimension into structuralism. Again the way to settle these is in practice rather than by an even more elaborate metatheory.

From a more substantive point of view, Lévi-Strauss has contributed in a major way to the revitalization of anthropology. He has rescued it from ethnocentrism and evolutionism, and made it possible to use accumulated fieldwork data for theoretical rather than purely ethnographic purposes. What he has done for myths can now be done for other cultural products, without a division between the structuralist analyses of primitive and 'modern' culture. And this project can be pursued without the assumption of innate cognitive structures. The non-subjectivist and non-humanist approach to social relations marks a significant advance in sociological and anthropological theory.

The structuralist approach to theory

In one sense this work has been an empirical investigation of the fruitfulness of the structuralist approach, since its analysis of structuralism is based on the postulates and prescriptions of structuralism itself. In this way, I have attempted a case study in structuralism, or an application of structuralism to itself. The basic premiss was that thought systems were to be examined morphologically in terms of their internal structure, rather than historically, and that their constituent layers were to be separately analysed. These layers of structural elements, which were the various conceptual levels, were not treated as equivalent or of equal importance in the constitution of the structuralist problematic, but rather as linked by different relations of determination. Thus I tried to show the principles underlying structuralism, its skeletal structure of concepts. This was both comparative and interdisciplinary since Althusser and Lévi-Strauss are apparently unrelated as far as their subject matter is concerned, and work in different disciplines. One advantage of the morphological orientation is that by looking for a problematic consisting of several layers, it avoids a one-sided approach which asks whether structuralism is a method, a theory or a philosophy, where these are regarded implicitly as mutually exclusive. It is possible to reach conclusions about all of these, and not to see differences at the different levels as contradictory. Flexibility is, in this way, a major feature of the structuralist approach to theory. This work has attempted to show in practice all the advantages of the structuralist approach that were summarized in the preceding section.

Several substantive conclusions were reached with the aid of this approach:

(1) analysis of the concept of structure as used in traditional sociology and social anthropology on the one hand and in modern structuralism on the other, revealed that there is an important distinction between structural and structuralist thought (chapter 2);

(2) the similarities between Althusser and Lévi-Strauss, in terms of general epistemology as well as their conception of structure, amount to a structuralist problematic, or distinctive framework for the analysis of social and cultural phenomena (chapters 3 and 4);

(3) structuralist epistemology and methodology is shared by theorists working in disciplines other than sociology and anthropology, notably political economy, linguistics, semiology and psychoanalysis. Thus its relevance is of general import to the social sciences as a whole (chapter 5);

(4) the convergence or divergence of the systems of ideas of different theorists is not to be seen as an all-or-nothing issue. An examination of both the similarities and the differences between Althusser and Lévi-Strauss showed that both are structuralists, but that Althusser is a Marxist whereas Lévi-Strauss is not. In this way their structuralism is similar and their philosophy is different, and structuralist Althusserian concepts may also be part of a theory which is not historical materialist nor dedicated to the overthrow of capitalist society (chapter 6).

This final conclusion raises questions about the theory of theory which go beyond the scope of this work. In so far as the structuralist approach to the analysis of theory is a theory as well as a method, it raises theoretical problems, just as structuralism itself does. How is it that the levels of a theoretical framework can be dissociated from each other, as may be the case with epistemology and philosophy for Althusser and Lévi-Strauss? Is this characteristic peculiar to structuralist theory? Are alternative theoretical frameworks defined by levels other than epistemology? Can the uses and limitations of other social theories be explained in terms of the levels at which they operate and their degree of elaboration of the other levels?

The elaboration of the theory of theory and the answers to these questions will depend on further analysis of other theoretical approaches. This work has been confined to structuralism but it would be possible to look at other theories in the same way and thus arrive at more general conclusions about the internal construction of social theory.

I have analysed and evaluated structuralism at the same time, and applied it to itself. The advantages and limitations of this application are to be seen as part of the substantive contributions and problems of structuralism.

Notes

Chapter 1   The approach to structural and structuralist theory

1 I am thinking particularly of the work of Popper and Kuhn. While it
   is true that Parsons has analysed past sociological theory, in *The
   Structure of Social Action*, his reconstructions are teleological, and not
   based on an explicit method or theory other than his vague concept of
   'frame of reference'. The approach adopted here is derivative of
   Althusser's analysis of Marx and Lenin, as will become clear, in its
   concentration on the internal structure of the texts.
2 Marx had already drawn attention to this in *The German Ideology*
   (1965, p. 29): 'Not only in their answers, but in their very questions
   there was a mystification. Their dependence on Hegel is the reason why
   not one of these modern critics has even attempted a comprehensive
   criticism of the Hegelian system, however much each professes to have
   advanced beyond Hegel.'
3 I have been unable to find any published work by Jacques Martin, and
   this is the sole reference to him, apart from the dedication of *For Marx*.
   It seems, however, that although he may have coined the phrase, it is
   Althusser who has developed it in use.
4 In this sense 'problematic' is an updated and more systematic version
   of Mannheim's *Weltanschauung*, but it focuses solely on the internal
   and morphological aspects of theory.
5 His findings in the *Essays*, as opposed to his more theoretical works of
   1949 and 1951.
6 For example Lane (1970) and Runciman (1969).

Chapter 2   Meanings and uses of the term structure

1 Lévi-Strauss argues this most forcibly in his definition of social
   structure in R. Bastide (1962).
2 E.g. 'Direct observation does reveal to us that human beings are
   connected by a complex network of social relations. I use the term
   "social structure" to denote this framework of actually existing rela-

tions' (1952, p. 190); and again: 'In the study of social structure the concrete reality with which we are concerned is the set of actually existing relations, at a given moment of time, which link together certain human beings. It is on this that we can make direct observations' (ibid., p. 192).

3 In fact, Radcliffe-Brown tended to sociologism, expecially in his earlier writings, which were particularly influenced by Durkheim. In *The Andaman Islanders*, for example, he interpreted all practices, beliefs and customs as expressing the value of society to the individual and the external force of the society over its members.

4 Even then, as Meyer Fortes has pointed out, he errs in attempting to synthesize separate theoretical issues into one formula since time is not uniform in its incidence but has several functions.

5 Leach has assumed the role of radical dissenter from orthodox British social anthropology in several instances. In *Political Systems of Highland Burma* he demonstrated that the question of the stability of primitive social systems should be taken as problematic, and challenged the functionalist tendency to consider primitive societies as stable and in equilibrium. In *Pul Eliya*, he attempted to account for the continuity of the social system in terms other than unilineal descent group analysis, and drew attention to the importance of the local group and to statistical as opposed to ideal models.

6 For a discussion of this see my article in Rex, ed. (1974).

7 For a similar argument, see P. Anderson: 'Components of the National Culture', in R. Blackburn and A. Cockburn, eds, (1969).

8 See M. Mauss (1950, 1966), especially 'Une catégorie de l'esprit humain: la notion de personne, celle de "moi".'

9 But many of them were killed in the war. Mauss, who survived, was distracted from his own work to a large extent by the task of collecting and editing work left by them.

10 He congratulates them particularly for recognizing that there is more than one type of valid understanding, and for not being misled by Durkheim's quest for universal laws. See especially his Introduction to Hertz (1960).

11 See chapter 5 for a discussion of the difference between models and structures.

12 See 'Do Dual Organizations Exist?' in Lévi-Strauss (1969b).

13 See 'The Mother's Brother in South Africa' in Radcliffe-Brown (1952).

14 Althusser distinguishes terminologically between Lévi-Strauss's and his 'structure'. They are 'combinatoire' (combinatory) and do well to use this term to avoid the confusion of the structural elements and the structure as a whole.

Chapter 3   Claude Lévi-Strauss

1 For a biography see Lévi-Strauss (1961), and Leach (1970).

2 Lévi-Strauss refers most often to *The Critique of Political Economy*, with its methodological Introduction, and to the *18th Brumaire of Louis Bonaparte*, both of which reveal clearly that Marx was in no sense an economic determinist.

3 Lévi-Strauss's anthropology and Marxism will be dealt with in more detail in the critical section below.

4 E.g. Leach (1970) and K. Burridge, 'Lévi-Strauss and Myth' in Leach, ed. (1967).

5 See especially Lévi-Strauss (1962).

6 Metaphor and metonymy are opposed on a vertical and horizontal axis respectively. Take for example the word 'red': becoming red, redness, blue, green and yellow all stand in a metaphorical relation to red. Their content can be substituted for red. However 'The red flag is blowing in the wind' constitutes a syntagmatic or metonymic chain: 'flag' and 'red' stand in a metonymic relation to each other, forming part of a chain of meaning. To form a syntagm, 'red' requires a noun to complement it.

7 Lévi-Strauss (1969a) discusses in the introduction the analysis of both complex and intermediary structures of kinship.

8 In Lévi-Strauss (1949) there is one reference to linguistics, and one to Saussure and Jakobson.

9 See Lévi-Strauss (1961) on face painting and sculpture and (1968b) chapters 9, 10, 13 and 14.

10 For example, he says 'Although they belong to another order of reality, kinship phenomena are of the same type as linguistic phenomena. Can the anthropologist, using a method analogous in form (if not in content) to the method used in structural linguistics, achieve the same kind of progress in his own science as that which has taken place in linguistics?' (Lévi-Strauss, 1968b, p. 34).

11 In his critique of Lévi-Strauss on totemism, P. Worsley in Leach, ed. (1967) argues that binary discrimination is too limited a basis on which to construct the totemic compendium and suggests the relevance of other mental operations based on Vygotsky's psychology of child development (for example unorganized congeries of elements, and complexes of actually-present abstract relations).

12 See discussion of history in chapter 6.

13 'Running right through all his structural analyses is the belief that a kind of principle of Hegelian dialectic is at work' (Leach, 1965a, p. 778).

14 On this see Godelier (1971) who gives outlines for a materialist analysis of myth which could examine the historical and social conditions which give rise to mythical thought. From this perspective, the structural correspondences, found in myths from unrelated areas, do not derive from savage thought, pure and simple, nor from nature, but must be located in the very structure of primitive societies.

15 See note 13.

16 As Lévi-Strauss claims, see p. 53 above.

17 His work has no connexion with that of contemporary French Marxist-anthropologists, such as Meillassoux, Terray, Olivier de Sardan.

Chapter 4   Louis Althusser

1 His first published work was on Montesquieu.

2 Althusser is a member of the PCF and discusses the circumstances of his joining in (1969a) Introduction.

3 See (1969a) especially 'Introduction', 'On the Young Marx' and 'Marxism and Humanism', and (1971) 'The Object of Capital', especially chapters 6 and 7.

4 See chapter 5 for discussion of this in relation to the use of models and analogy.

5 This is discussed in 'Introduction' and 'On the Young Marx' in (1969a). The early period as a whole includes all Marx's writings from his doctoral dissertation to *The Holy Family* of 1844.

6 Althusser argues that this idealism-empiricism problematic, either empiricism of the essence and idealism of the subject or vice versa, characterized social theories from Hobbes to Rousseau, political economy from Petty to Ricardo, and theories of knowledge from Kant to Feuerbach.

7 In his discussion of the development of Marx's theory and elsewhere, Althusser hardly mentioned Engels as independent thinker or co-author.

8 See 'On Practice', Mao Tse Tung (1967).

9 Balibar notes the similarity between this and Freud's history of the libido where different stages of sexuality replace each other by displacement rather than evolution but all have the same function. Displacement occurs at the level of the erogenous zones, biological functions on which the sexual drive focuses, the object of desire, etc. Each variation is a system of organization of a complex drive consisting of several elements.

10 See Balibar in Althusser and Balibar (1970), pp. 212–16.

11 There is a more detailed discussion of the relation between synchrony, time and causality in chapter 5.

12 See on metonymy and *Darstellung* in chapter 5, and note 5 to chapter 3.

13 See 'On the Materialist Dialectic' in (1969a).

14 These diagrams are based on a series of lectures on 'The Sociology of Revolution' given by Robin Blackburn at the London School of Economics in 1968–9.

15 A blob of oil resting on water still retains its own specific molecular structure, as does the water, and yet it is not autonomous of the water. Or another example, psychological processes may have their own specificity, yet depend, as a precondition, on the physico-chemical functioning of the brain.

Chapter 5 Structuralist epistemology

1 See *The Phenomenology of Mind* and Lefebvre (1969).

2 Spencer compared telegraph wires to nerves, and communication in society to the nervous system in the body.

3 The correspondence is quoted in G. Murdock, article in Tax Sol (1953).

4 These similarities are not invalidated by Lévi-Strauss's ambiguities as regards science, nor by the different relation between theory and object of theory in Lévi-Strauss and Althusser.

Bibliography

ALBÉRÈS, R. (1967) 'Le Structuralisme en littérature', *Revue de Paris*, 7–8. Also published as 'Strukturalismus Diskussion', no. 54, Berlin, 1967.

ALTHUSSER, LOUIS

(1959) *Montesquieu, le politique et l'histoire*, Paris: PUF.

(1960) *Manifestes philosophiques de Feuerbach (1839–45) textes choisis*, Paris: PUF.

(1963) 'Philosophie et science humaines', *Revue de l'Enseignment Philosophique*, June–July.

(1964) 'Problèmes Etudiantes', *La Nouvelle critique*, no. 152, January.

(1965) *Pour Marx*, Paris: Maspéro. (See also Althusser, 1969a.)

(1966) 'Matérialisme historique et matérialisme dialectique', *Cahiers Marxistes-Léninistes*, no. 11, April.

(1967a) 'Sur le travail théorique', *La Pensée*, no. 132, March-April.

(1967b)' Sur le "Contrat Social": les décalages', *Cahiers pour l'analyse*, no. 8, Summer.

(1969a) *For Marx*, translated by Ben Brewster, London: Allen Lane, The Penguin Press.

Contains: Introduction; On the Young Marx (1961); Feuerbach's Philosophical Manifestoes (1960); Contradiction and Overdetermination (1962); The 'Picollox Teatro': Bertolazzi and Brecht (1962); The '1844 Manuscripts' of Karl Marx (1963); On the Materialist Dialectic (1963); Marxism and Humanism (1964).

(1969b) *Lénine et la philosophie*, Paris: Maspéro. (See also Althusser, 1971).

(1969c) 'Letters to Maria Macciocchi' in M. A. Macciocchi: *Lettre dall'interno del PCI a Louis Althusser*, Milan: Feltrinelli.

(1971) *Lenin and Philosophy and Other Essays*, trans. Ben Brewster, London: New Left Books.

Contains: Lenin and Philosophy (1968); Philosophy as a Revolutionary Weapon (1968); Preface to Capital Volume One (1968); Lenin Before Hegel (1969); Ideology and the Ideological State Apparatuses (1969); Freud and Lacan (1969); A Letter on Art in Reply to André Daspré (1966); Cremonini, Painter of the Abstract (1966).

182

ALTHUSSER, LOUIS AND BALIBAR, E.
  (1968) *Lire le Capital*, vols I and II, Paris: Maspéro. (See also Althusser and Balibar, 1970).
  (1970) *Reading Capital*, trans. Ben Brewster, London: New Left Books.
  Contains: Foreword to the Italian edition; From Capital to Marx's Philosophy (1965); The Object of Capital (1965); The Basic Concepts of Historical Materialism (Balibar).
ANZIEU, D. (1966) 'Oedipe avant le complexe ou de l'interprétation psychanalytique des mythes', *Les Temps Modernes*, 24–5, October.
L'*Arc*
  (1965) Aix-en Provence, no. 26, Lévi-Strauss.
  (1968) Aix-en Provence, no. 34, Freud.
AUZIAS, T. (1967) *Clefs pour le structuralisme*, Paris: Seghers.
BACHELARD, G.
  (1963) *Le Matérialisme rationnel*, Paris: PUF.
  (1967) *La Formation de l'esprit scientifique*, Paris: Vrin. (See notes to chapters 4 and 5.)
BACKÈS, C. (1968) 'Lacan ou le "porte-parole" ', *Critique*, February.
BADIOU, A.
  (1967) 'Le (re)commencement du matérialisme dialectique', *Critique*, March.
  (1969) *Le Concept de modèle*, Paris: Maspéro.
BARTHES, R.
  (1957) *Mythologies*, Paris: Seuil. (See also Barthes, 1972.)
  (1966a) Interviews, in *Alétheia*, 4.
  (1966b) 'Structuralist Activity', *Form*, I, Summer.
  (1967a) Interviews, *Les Lettres Françaises*, 1172, March.
  (1967b) *Systeme de la mode*, Paris: Editions du Seuil.
  (1967c) 'Le Discours de l'histoire', *Social Science Information*, vol. 6, no. 4.
  (1967d) 'The Structuralist Activity', *Partisan Review*, vol. 34, no. 1.
  (1967e) *Elements of Semiology*, London: Cape.
  (1972) *Mythologies*, London: Cape.
BASTIDE, R. (1962) *Sens et usages du terme structure*, The Hague: Mouton.
BATESON, G. (1936) *Naven*, Cambridge University Press.
BERSANI, L. (1967) 'From Bachelard to Barthes', *Partisan Review*, vol. 34, no. 2.
BERTHERAT, Y.
  (1967a) 'La Pensée folle', *Esprit*, 5, May.
  (1967b) 'Freud avec Lacan', *Esprit*, 12, December.
BLACKBURN, R. and COCKBURN, A. (1969) *Student Power*, Harmondsworth: Penguin.
BOUDON, P.
  (1967) 'Essai sur l'interprétation de la notion de l'échange', *L'Homme*, vol. 7, no. 2.
  (1968) *A quoi sert la notion de structure?*, Paris: Gallimard.
BUCKLEY, W. (1967) *Sociology and Modern Systems Theory*, Englewood Cliffs: Prentice Hall.

BURGHELIN, P. (1967) 'L'Archéologie de savoir', *Esprit*, 5, May.

Cahiers pour l'analyse

(1966) Paris, no. 3, Sur l'object de la psychanalyse.

(1966b) no. 4, Lévi-Strauss dans le XVIII siècle.

(1967a) no. 5, Ponctuation de Freud.

(1967b) No. 7, Du mythe au roman.

(1967c) no. 8, L'Impensée de J.-J. Rousseau.

CANGUILHEM, G.

(1965) *La Connaissance de la vie*, Paris: Vrin.

(1966) *Le Normal et le pathologique*, Paris: PUF.

(1968) *Etudes d'histoire et de philosophie des sciences*, Paris: Vrin.

CASTEL, R. (1964) 'Méthode structurale et idéologies structuralistes', *Critique*, 210, April.

CAWS, M. (1966) *Surrealism and the Literary Imagination—a Study of Breton and Bachelard*, The Hague: Mouton.

CERTEAU, M. DE (1967) 'Les Sciences humaines et la mort de l'homme', *Etudes*, March.

CHARBONNIER, G. (ed.)

(1961) *Entretiens avec Claude Lévi-Strauss*, Paris: Plon-Juillard. (See also Charbonnier, 1969.)

(1969) *Conversations with Claude Lévi-Strauss*, London: Cape.

CHATÊLET, F. (1967) 'Le Miel et le tabac', *La Quinzaine Littéraire*, I, January.

CHOMSKY, N.

(1957) *Syntactic Structures*, The Hague: Mouton.

(1964) 'Current Issues in Linguistic Theory', in J. Fodor and J. Katz (eds): *The Structure of Language*, Englewood Cliffs: Prentice Hall.

(1965) *Some Aspects of the Theory of Syntax*, London: MIT Press.

COHEN, P.

(1966) 'Models', *British Journal of Sociology*, vol. XVII, no. 1, March.

(1969) 'Theories of Myth', *Man*, vol. 4, no. 3.

CORVEZ, M.

(1968) 'Le Structuralisme de M. Foucault', *Revue Thomiste*, January.

(1969) *Les Structuralistes*, Paris: Aubier-Montaigne.

DAGOGNET, F. (1965) *Gaston Bachelard*, Paris: PUF.

DAVIS,K. (1959) 'The Myth of Functional Analysis', *American Sociological Review*, vol. 24, no. 6, December.

DERRIDA, J. (1966) 'Nature, culture, écriture (de Lévi-Strauss à Rousseau)', *Cahiers pour l'analyse*, no. 4, September–October.

DESCHAMPS, J. (1967) 'Psychanalyse et structuralisme', *La Pensée*, no. 135, October.

DOUGLAS, M. (1967) 'The Meaning of Myth', in Leach (ed.), 1967.

DUCROT, O. (1968) *Qu'est-ce que le structuralisme?* Paris: Seuil.

DUMEZIL, G.

(1941) *Jupiter, Mars, Quirinus*, Paris: Gallimard.

(1949) *L'Héritage indo-européen à Rome*, Paris: Gallimard.

(1952) *Les dieux des indo-européens*, Paris: PUF.

(1956) *Déesses latines et mythes védiques*, Bruxelles: Collection Latomus XXV.

(1966) *La religion romaine archaique*, Paris: Payot.

DUMONT, L. (1970) *Homo hierarchicus*, London: Weidenfeld and Nicolson.

DURKHEIM, E.

(1896–7) 'La prohibition de l'inceste et ses origines' in *Année Sociologique*, I.

(1915) *The Elementary Forms of Religious Life*, London: Allen & Unwin.

(1933) *The Division of Labour in Society*, Chicago: Free Press.

(1938 & 1966) *The Rules of Sociological Method*, Chicago and New York: Free Press.

(1952) *Suicide*, London: Routledge & Kegan Paul.

DURKHEIM, E. and MAUSS, M. (1963) *Primitive Classification*, London: Cohen & West.

EHRLICH, V. (1965) *The Russian Formalists*, The Hague: Mouton.

Esprit

(1963) Paris, November, Structuralism.

(1967) Paris, May, Structuralism.

EVANS-PRITCHARD, E. E.

(1940) *The Nuer*, London: Oxford University Press.

(1951) *Social Anthropology*, London: Cohen & West.

FEYERABEND, P. (1965) 'Problems of Empiricism' in R. Colodny, (ed.), *Beyond the Edge of Certainty*, Englewood Cliffs: Prentice Hall.

FICHANT, M. and PECHEUX, M. (1969) *Sur l'histoire des sciences*, Paris: Maspéro.

FIRTH, R. (1951) *Elements of Social Organization*, London: Watts.

FODOR, J. and KATZ, J. (1964) *The Structure of Language*, Englewood Cliffs: Prentice Hall.

FORGE, A. (1967) 'Claude Lévi-Strauss', *New Society*, no. 2, January.

FORTES, M.

(1945) *Dynamics of Clanship among the Tallensi*, London: International African Institute.

(1949) 'Time and Social Structure' in *Social Structure*, Oxford: Clarendon Press.

FOUCAULT, M.

(1966a) Interviews, *La Quinzaine Littéraire*, 5, May.

(1966b) *Les Lettres françaises*, 1125.

(1966c) *Les Mots et les choses*, Paris: Gallimard. (See also Foucault, 1970.)

(1967a) *Les Lettres françaises*, 1187.

(1967b) *Madness and Civilization*, London: Tavistock.

(1968a) Interviews, *La Quinzaine Littéraire*, 46/7, March,

(1968b) Interview, *La Pensée*, no. 140, February.

(1968c) 'MF definit sa methode', *Cahiers pour l'Analyse*, no. 9.

(1968d) 'Réponse au cercle d'epistemologie', *Les Lettres françaises*, 1240.

(1968e) 'Réponse à une question', *Esprit*, 5, May.

(1969) *L'Archéologie du savoir*, Paris: Gallimard.

(1970) *The Order of Things*, London: Tavistock.

FOX, R. (1967) *Kinship and Marriage*, Harmondsworth: Penguin.

FREUD, S.

(1922) *Introductory Lectures on Psychoanalysis*, London: Allen & Unwin.

(1933) *The New Introductory Lectures on Psychoanalysis*, London: Hogarth Press.

(1954) *The Interpretation of Dreams*, London: Allen & Unwin.

(1962) *Three Essays on Theory of Sexuality*, London: Hogarth Press.

GABORIAU, M. (1963) 'Anthropologie structurale et histoire', *Esprit*, 322.

GEORGE, F.

(1969a) 'Marx et le dogmatisme', *Les Temps Modernes*, 273.

(1969b) 'Lire Althusser', *Les Temps Modernes*, 275.

GERTH, HANS and MILLS, C. WRIGHT (eds) (1948) *From Max Weber*, London: Routledge & Kegan Paul.

GLUCKSMANN, A.

(1968) *Le Discours de la guerre*, Paris: L'Herne.

(1972) 'A ventriloquist Structuralism', *New Left Review*, 72, March–April.

GLUCKSMANN, C.

(1969a) 'A propos de la théorie marxiste de l'état capitalist', *L'Homme et la Société*, 11.

(1969b) 'A propos d'Althusser', *La Nouvelle Critique*, 23.

GLUCKSMANN, M.

(1969) 'Lucien Goldmann: Humanist or Marxist?' *New Left Review*, 56, July–August.

(1971) Review article on structuralism, *British Journal of Sociology*, vol. 22, no. 2, June.

(1974) 'Lévi-Strauss, Althusser and Structuralism', in J. Rex (ed.), *Approaches to Sociology*, London: Routledge & Kegan Paul.

GODEL, R. (ed.) (1957) *Les Sources manuscriptes du 'cours de linguistique générale'*, Paris: Société des Publications Romanes et Françaises.

GODELIER, M.

(1966) *Rationalité et irrationalité en economie*, Paris: Seuil.

(1967) 'System, Structure and Contradiction in Capital', in J. Savile and R. Miliband (eds), *The Socialist Register*, London: Merlin Press.

(1971) 'Myth and History', *New Left Review*, 69, September–October.

GOLDMANN, L.

(1964a) *The Hidden God*, London: Routledge & Kegan Paul.

(1964b) *Pour une sociologie du roman*, Paris: NRF.

(1968) 'Criticism and Dogmatism in Literature' D. Cooper (ed.), *The Dialectics of Liberation*, Harmondsworth: Penguin.

GOLDMANN, L. and PIAGET, J.

(1964) *Génèse et structure*, The Hague: Mouton.

(1967) *Logique et connaissance scientifique*, Paris: NRF.

GOULDNER, A. (1959) 'Autonomy and reciprocity' in L. Gross (ed.), *Symposium on Sociological Theory*, Evanston: Row and Peterson.

(1967) *Enter Plato*, London: Routledge & Kegan Paul.

GRANET, M. (1920) 'Quelques peculiarités de la langue et de la pensée chinoise', *Revue Philosophique*, LXXXIX.

GREIMAS, A.
(1956) 'L'Actualité du saussurisme', *Le Français Moderne.*
(1963) 'La Description de la signification et la mythologie comparée', *L'Homme,* vol. 3, no. 3, September–December.

GURVITCH, G.
(1955) 'Le Concept de Structure Sociale', *Cahiers Internationaux de Sociologie,* XIX.
(1957) 'Une source oubliée des concepts de structure sociale, fonction sociale, et institution: H. Spencer', *Cahiers Internationaux de Sociologie,* XXIII.

HAMMEL, E. (1968) 'Anthropological Explanations: Styles in Discourse', *Southwestern Journal of Anthropology,* vol. 24, no. 2.

HAYES, E. and T. (1970) *Claude Lévi-Strauss: the Anthropologist as Hero,* London: MIT Press.

HEGEL, F. (1931) *The Phenomenology of Mind,* London: Allen & Unwin.

HERTZ, R. (1960) *Death and the Right Hand,* London: Cohen & West.

HJELMSLEV, L. (1947) 'Structural Analysis of Language', *Studia Linguistica.*

HOMANS, G. and SCHNEIDER, M. (1955) *Marriage, Authority and Final Causes,* Chicago: Free Press.

HUBERT, H. (1905) *Etude sommaire de la représentation du temps dans la religion et la magie,* Ecole Pratique des Hautes Etudes (Sciences Religieuses).

HUBERT, H. and MAUSS, M.
(1902–3) 'Esquisse d'une théorie générale de la magie', *Année Sociologique,* 8.
(1909) *Mélanges d'histoire des religions,* Paris.
(1964) *Sacrifice,* London: Cohen & West.

JAKOBSON, R.
(1962) *Selected Writings,* The Hague: Mouton.
(1963) *Essais de linguistique générale,* The Hague: Mouton.
(1966) Interviews, *Les Lettres françaises,* 1157.
(1968a) Interviews, *Les Lettres françaises,* 1221.
(1968b) *La Quinzaine Littéraire,* no. 51.

JAKOBSON, R. and HALLE, M. (1956) *Fundamentals of Language,* The Hague: Mouton.

KALIDOVA, R. (1968) 'Marx et Freud', *L'Homme et la Société,* nos 7 and 8.

KANT, I. (1952) *The Metaphysics of Morals,* University of Chicago Press.

KIRK, G. (1970) *Myth: Its Meaning and Functions,* Cambridge University Press.

KUHN, T. S. (1962) *The Structure of Scientific Revolutions,* University of Chicago Press.

LACAN, J.
(1953) 'Some Reflections on the Ego', *International Journal of Psychoanalysis,* XXXIV.
(1966a) *Ecrits,* Paris: Seuil.
(1966b) Interviews, *Les Lettres françaises,* 1159.
(1966c) Interviews, *Le Figaro Littéraire,* 29, December.
(1968) 'The Mirror Phase', *New Left Review,* 51, September–October.

LACAN, J. (ed.) (annually) *La Psychanalyse,* Paris: PUF.

BIBLIOGRAPHY

LANE, M. (1970) *Structuralism—A Reader*, London: Cape.

LAPLANTE, J. and LECLAIRE, S. (1961) 'L'inconscient', *Les Temps Modernes*, 183.

LEACH, E. R.

(1954) *Political Systems of Highland Burma*, London: LSE.

(1961a) *Pul Eliya*, Cambridge University Press.

(1961b) *Rethinking Anthropology* London: Athlone Press.

(1964) 'Telstar et les aborigènes ou la pensée sauvage', *Annales*, 6.

(1965a) 'Review of *Le Cru et le Cuit*', *American Anthropologist*, vol. 67, 3, June.

(1965b) 'Claude Lévi-Strauss: Anthropologist and Philosopher', *New Left Review*, 34, November–December.

(1967) *Structural Study of Myth and Totemism*, London: Tavistock.

(1969) *Genesis as Myth and Other Essays*, London: Cape.

(1970) *Lévi-Strauss*, London: Fontana-Collins.

LEFEBVRE, H.

(1967) 'C. Lévi-Strauss et le nouvel éléatisme', *L'Homme et la Société*, 1.

(1968) 'Forme, fonction et structure dans le Capital', *L'Homme et la Société*, 7.

(1969) *Dialectical Materialism*, London: Cape.

LENIN, V. I. (1947) *Materialism and Empirio-criticism*, Moscow: FLPH.

Les Lettres françaises

(1968a) No. 1126, Au structuralisme.

(1968b) Nos 1238, 1239, Structure du structuralisme.

LÉVI-STRAUSS, CLAUDE

(1946) 'French Sociology' in W. Moore and G. Gurvitch (eds), *Twentieth Century Sociology*, New York: Philosophical Library.

(1948) *La vie familiale et sociale des indiens Nambikwara*, Paris: Société des Americanistes.

(1949) *Les Structures élémentaires de la parenté*, Paris: PUF. (See also Lévi-Strauss, 1969a.)

(1950) 'Introduction à l'œuvre de Marcel Mauss' in M. Mauss: *Sociologie et anthropologie*, Paris: PUF.

(1952a) *Conference on Anthropology and Linguistics*, Bloomington: Indiana University Press.

(1952b) *Race et histoire*, Paris: UNESCO. (See also Lévi-Strauss, 1958b.)

(1955) *Tristes Tropiques*, Paris: Plon. (See also Lévi-Strauss, 1961.)

(1956) 'The Family' in Harry L. Shapiro (ed.), *Man, Culture and Society*, London: Oxford University Press.

(1958a) *Anthropologie structurale*, Paris: Plon. (See also Lévi-Strauss, 1968b.)

(1958b) *Race and History*, Paris: UNESCO.

(1960a) 'La Geste d'Asdiwal', *Annuaire*, Ecole Pratique des Hautes Etudes (Sciences Religieuses), Paris. (See also Lévi-Strauss, 1967b.)

(1960b) *Leçon inaugurale*, 5 January, Collège de France, Chaire d'Anthropologie Sociale, Paris. (See also Lévi-Strauss, 1967c.)

(1960c) 'La Structure et la forme: reflexions sur un ouvrage de

Vladimir Propp' Cahiers de l'Institut des Sciences Economiques Appliquées, series M, no. 7, March.

(1961) *A World on the Wane*, trans. John Russell, London: Hutchinson.

(1962a) *La Pensée sauvage*, Paris: Plon. (See also Lévi-Strauss, 1966b.)

(1962b) *Le totémisme aujourd'hui*, Paris: PUF. (See also Lévi-Strauss 1964c.)

(1962c) 'Jean-Jacques Rousseau, fondateur des sciences de l'homme' in *Jean-Jacques Rousseau*, Neuchâtel: La Baconnière.

(1963) 'Réponses à quelques questions', *Esprit*, 322, November.

(1964a) 'Critères scientifiques dans les disciplines sociales et humaines', *Revue Internationale des Sciences Sociales*, vol. 16, no. 4, Paris: UNESCO.

(1964b) *Mythologiques I: le cru et le cuit*, Paris: Plon. (See also Lévi-Strauss, 1969b.)

(1964c) *Totemism*, trans. R. Needham, London: Merlin Press.

(1965a) 'The Future of Kinship Studies', the Huxley Memorial Lecture, in *Proceedings of the Royal Anthropological Institute*, London.

(1965b) 'Le triangle culinaire', *L'Arc*; Aix-en-Provence, no. 26, pp. 19–29.

(1966a) *Mythologiques II: du miel aux cendres*, Paris: Plon.

(1966b) *The Savage Mind*, London: Weidenfeld & Nicolson.

(1966c) 'The Culinary Triangle', *New Society*, 22, December.

(1966d) 'Philosophie et anthropologie', *Cahiers de philosophie*, 1, January.

(1967a) 'Vingt ans après': introduction to new edition of *Les Structures élémentaires de la parenté*, Paris: Mouton.

(1967b) 'The Story of Asdiwal', trans. N. Mann, in E. R. Leach (ed.), *The Structural Study of Myth and Totemism*, ASA Monographs No. 5, London: Tavistock.

(1967c) *The Scope of Anthropology*, London: Cape.

(1967d) Interview with R. Bellour, *Les Lettres françaises*, 1165, January.

(1967e) Interview 'A contre courant', *Le Nouvel Observateur*.

(1967f) 'Une lettre de Claude Lévi-Strauss', *Cahiers pour l'analyse*, no. 8, October.

(1968a) *Mythologiques III: l'Origine des manières de table*, Paris: Plon.

(1968b) *Structural Anthropology*, trans. C. Jakobson and B. G. Schoepf, London: Allen Lane, The Penguin Press.

(1969a) *The Elementary Structures of Kinship*, trans. J. Bell, J. von Sturmer and R. Needham, London: Eyre and Spottiswoode.

(1969b) *The Raw and the Cooked*, London: Cape.

(1971) *Mythologiques IV: L'Homme nu*, Paris: Plon.

LÉVI-STRAUSS, CLAUDE and JAKOBSON, R. (1962) 'Les Chats de Charles Baudelaire', *L'Homme*, vol. 2, no. 1.

LOCKWOOD, D. (1964) 'Social Integration and System Integration', in (eds), W. Hirsch and G. Zollschan, *Explorations in Social Change*, London: Routledge & Kegan Paul.

LUKÁCS, G. (1971) *History and Class Consciousness*, London: Merlin Press.

LYOTARD, J. (1965) 'Les indiens ne cueillent pas les fleurs', *Annales*, vol. 20, no. 1.

MACHEREY, P. (1967) *Pour une théorie de la production littéraire*, Paris: Maspéro.

MACIVER, R. (1942) *Social Causation*, Boston: Ginn.

MALMBERG, B. (1966) 'F. de Saussure et l'école de Genève, le structuralisme', *Les Nouvelles Tendances de la Linguistique*.

MANNHEIM, K. (1952) *Essays on the Sociology of Knowledge*, London: Routledge & Kegan Paul.

MANSUY, M. (1967) *Gaston Bachelard et les éléments*, Paris: Corti.

MAO TSE TUNG (1967) *Selected Works*, 4 vols, Peking: Foreign Languages Press.

MARTINET, A. (1953) 'Structural Linguistics' in A. Kroeber (ed.), *Anthropology Today*, University of Chicago Press.

MARX, K.

(1904) *Introduction to the Critique of Political Economy*, Chicago: Charles Kerr.

(1951) *Capital*, Moscow: FLPH.

(1956) *Poverty of Philosophy*, London: Lawrence & Wishart.

(1959) *Economic and Philosophical Manuscripts*, London: Lawrence & Wishart.

(1963) 'Critique of Hegel's Philosophy of Right' in T. Bottomore (ed.), *Early Writings*, London: Watts.

(1965) *The German Ideology*, London: Lawrence & Wishart.

(1971) *Contribution to the Critique of Political Economy*, London: Lawrence & Wishart.

MARX, K. and ENGELS, F. (1951) *Selected Works*, Vols I and II, Moscow: FLPH.

MAUSS, M.

(1950) *Anthropologie et sociologie*, Paris: PUF.

(1966) *The Gift*, London: Cohen & West.

MAUSS, M. and FAUCONNET, P. (1887) 'Sociologie' in *La Grande Encyclopédie*, Paris.

MEILLASSOUX, C.

(1964) *Anthropologie économique des Gouru de Côte d'Ivoire*, Paris: Mouton.

(1972) 'From Production to Reproduction', *Economy and Society*, vol. I, no. 1, February.

MERLEAU-PONTY, M. (1965) 'De Mauss à Lévi-Strauss', in *Eloge de la philosophie*, Paris: NRF.

MORGAN, L. (1971) *Systems of Consanguinity and Affinity of the Human Family*, Washington.

MOULOUD, N. (1967) 'La méthode des sciences de structures et les problèmes de la connaissance rationnelle', *La Pensée*, 135, October.

MOUNIN, G.

(1967a) 'Linguistique, structuralisme et marxisme', *La Nouvelle critique*, 6.

(1967b) *Ferdinand de Saussure, ou le structuraliste sans le savoir,* Paris: Seghers.

NADEL, S. (1957) *The Theory of Social Structure,* London: Cohen & West.

NEEDHAM, R. (1962) *Structure and Sentiment,* University of Chicago Press.

OLIVIER DE SARDAN, J. P. (1969) *Systèmes des relations sociales chez les Wogo* (Niger), Institut d' Ethnologie, Mem 3, Paris.

PARETO, V. (1935) *The Mind and Society,* London: Cape.

PARIS, R. (1966) 'En deça du marxisme', *Les Temps Modernes,* 240.

PARSONS, T.

(1949) *The Structure of Social Action,* Chicago: Free Press.

(1951) *The Social System,* Chicago: Free Press.

(1954) *Essays in Sociological Theory,* Chicago: Free Press.

La Pensée (1967) No. 135, October, Structuralism.

PIAGET, J.

(1971) 'Mécanismes communs dans les sciences de l'homme', *L'Homme et la Société,* 2.

(1971) *Structuralism,* London: Routledge & Kegan Paul.

PIAGET, J. and GOLDMANN, L.

(1964) *Génèse et structure,* The Hague: Mouton.

(1967) *Logique et connaissance scientifique,* Paris: NRF.

PIGUET, J. (1965) 'Les Conflits de l'analyse et de la dialectique', *Annales,* vol. 20, no. 3.

PIVIDAL, J. C. (1965) 'Peut-on acclimatiser la pensée sauvage?' *Annales,* vol. 20, no. 3.

PONTALIS, J.

(1956) 'Freud aujourd'hui', *Les Temps Modernes,* 124, 125, 126.

(1965) *Après Freud,* Paris: Juillard.

POPPER, K.

(1962) *The Logic of Scientific Discovery,* London: Hutchinson.

(1963) *Conjectures and Refutations,* London: Routledge & Kegan Paul.

POUILLON, J.

(1965) 'Sartre et Lévi-Strauss', *L'Arc,* 26.

(1966a) 'L'analyse des mythes', *L'Homme,* vol. 6, no. 1.

(1966b) 'Du côté de chez Marx', *Les Temps Modernes,* 240.

POULANTZAS, N.

(1966) 'Vers une théorie marxiste', *Les Temps Modernes,* 240.

(1970) *Pouvoir politique et classes sociales,* Paris: Maspéro.

PROPP, V. (1958) 'Morphology of the Folktale', *International Journal of American Linguistics,* vol. 24, no. 4.

RADCLIFFE-BROWN, A.R.

(1922) *The Andaman Islanders,* Chicago: Free Press.

(1948) *A Natural Science of Society,* Chicago: Free Press.

(1951) 'The Comparative Method in Anthropology', *Journal of the Royal Anthropological Institute,* 81.

(1952) *Structure and Function in Primitive Society,* London: Cohen & West.

REBOUL, J. (1962) 'Jacques Lacan et les fondements de la psychanalyse', *Critique,* XVII.

RICHARD, P.
(1969) 'A propos de l'origine des manières de table de C. Lévi-Strauss', *L'Homme et la Société*, 11.

RICOEUR, P.
(1963) 'Structure et hermeneutique', *Esprit*, 11.
(1966) 'La philosophie à l'age des sciences humaines', *Cahiers de Philosophie*, 1.

ROUSSEAU, J. J.
(1954) *Confessions*, Harmondsworth: Penguin.
(1955) *Discourse on the Inequality of Mankind*, London: Dent.
(1970) 'Essai sur l'origine des langues', *Cahiers pour l'analyse*, 8.

ROUSSEL, J. (1968) 'Introduction to Jacques Lacan', *New Left Review*, 51, September–October.

RUNCIMAN, W. (1969) 'What is Structuralism?' *British Journal of Sociology*, vol. 20, no. 3.

RUWET, N. (1963) 'Linguistique et science de l'homme', *Esprit*, 11.

SARTRE, J. P.
(1960) *Critique de la raison dialectique*, Paris: Bibliothèque des Idées.
(1966) 'L'Anthropologie', *Cahiers de Philosophie*, 2–3.

SAUSSURE, F. DE (1959) *Course in General Linguistics*, New York: Philosophical Library.

SEBAG, L.
(1962) 'Histoire et structure', *Les Temps modernes*, 195.
(1964) *Marxisme et structuralisme*, Paris: Payot.
(1965) 'Le mythe: code et message', *Les Temps* Modernes, 226.

SÈVE, L.
(1967a) 'Marxisme et sciences de l'homme', *La Nouvelle Critique*, 2.
(1967b) 'Méthode structurale et méthode dialectique', *La Pensée*, 135.

SIMONIS, Y. (1968) *Claude Lévi-Strauss ou la 'passion de l'inceste'*, Paris: Aubier-Montaigne.

SPENCER, H. (1969) *The Principles of Sociology*, London: Macmillan.

STEINER, G. (1966) 'Conversations with Lévi-Strauss', *Encounter*, April.

SURET-CANALE, J. (1967) 'Structuralisme et anthropologie économique', *La Pensée*, 135.

TAX, S. *et al.* (1953) *An Appraisal of Anthropology Today*, University of Chicago Press.

Les Temps Modernes (1966) No. 246, November, Structuralism.

TERRAY, E. (1969) *Le marxisme devant les sociétés primitives*, Paris: Maspéro.

TODOROV, T.
(1965) 'L'héritage méthodologique du formalisme', *L'Homme*, vol. 5, no. 1.
(1967a) 'De la semiologie à la rhétorique', *Annales*, 6.
(1967b) *Littérature et signification*, Paris: Larousse.

TORRANCE, J. (1967) 'Rationality and the Structural Study of Myth', *European Journal of Sociology*, vol. 8, no. 2.

TROUBETZKOI, N. (1949) *Principes de phonologie*, Paris: Les Belles Lettres.

TURNER, V. (1969) *The Ritual Process*, London: Routledge & Kegan Paul.

VACHEK, J.

(1966a) *Prague School Reader in Linguistics*, Bloomington: Indiana University Press.

(1966b) *The Prague School of Linguistics*, Bloomington: Indiana University Press.

VERRET, M. (1967) *Théorie et politique*, Paris: Editions Sociales.

VIET, J. (1968) 'La notion de structure et les méthodes structuralistes dans les sciences sociales', *Methodology and Science*, January.

DELLA VOLPE, G.

(1964) *Marx e Rousseau*, Milan: Riuniti.

(1970) 'Rousseau and Marx', *New Left Review*, 59, January–February.

Yale French Studies (1966) Structuralism, J. Ehrmann (ed.) nos 36, 37, New Haven.

Index

195

197

International Library of Sociology

Edited by
John Rex
University of Warwick

Founded by
Karl Mannheim

as The International Library of Sociology
and Social Reconstruction

*This Catalogue also contains other Social Science
series published by Routledge*

Routledge & Kegan Paul   London and Boston

68-74 Carter Lane London EC4V 5EL
9 Park Street Boston Mass 02108

Contents

● *Books so marked are available in paperback*
All books are in Metric Demy 8vo format (216 × 138mm approx.)

GENERAL SOCIOLOGY

Belshaw, Cyril. The Conditions of Social Performance. *An Exploratory Theory. 144 pp.*

Brown, Robert. Explanation in Social Science. *208 pp.*

● Rules and Laws in Sociology.

Cain, Maureen E. Society and the Policeman's Role. *About 300 pp.*

Gibson, Quentin. The Logic of Social Enquiry. *240 pp.*

Gurvitch, Georges. Sociology of Law. *Preface by Roscoe Pound. 264 pp.*

Homans, George C. Sentiments and Activities: *Essays in Social Science. 336 pp.*

Johnson, Harry M. Sociology: *a Systematic Introduction. Foreword by Robert K. Merton. 710 pp.*

Mannheim, Karl. Essays on Sociology and Social Psychology. *Edited by Paul Keckskemeti. With Editorial Note by Adolph Lowe. 344 pp.*

Systematic Sociology: *An Introduction to the Study of Society. Edited by J. S. Erös and Professor W. A. C. Stewart. 220 pp.*

Martindale, Don. The Nature and Types of Sociological Theory. *292 pp.*

● **Maus, Heinz.** A Short History of Sociology. *234 pp.*

Mey, Harald. Field-Theory. *A Study of its Application in the Social Sciences. 352 pp.*

Myrdal, Gunnar. Value in Social Theory: *A Collection of Essays on Methodology. Edited by Paul Streeten. 332 pp.*

Ogburn, William F., and **Nimkoff, Meyer F.** A Handbook of Sociology. *Preface by Karl Mannheim. 656 pp. 46 figures. 35 tables.*

Parsons, Talcott, and **Smelser, Neil J.** Economy and Society: *A Study in the Integration of Economic and Social Theory. 362 pp.*

● **Rex, John.** Key Problems of Sociological Theory. *220 pp.*

Urry, John. Reference Groups and the Theory of Revolution.

FOREIGN CLASSICS OF SOCIOLOGY

● **Durkheim, Emile.** Suicide. *A Study in Sociology. Edited and with an Introduction by George Simpson. 404 pp.*

Professional Ethics and Civic Morals. *Translated by Cornelia Brookfield. 288 pp.*

● **Gerth, H. H.,** and **Mills, C. Wright.** From Max Weber: *Essays in Sociology. 502 pp.*

Tönnies, Ferdinand. Community and Association. *(Gemeinschaft und Gesellschaft.) Translated and Supplemented by Charles P. Loomis. Foreword by Pitirim A. Sorokin. 334 pp.*

SOCIAL STRUCTURE

Andreski, Stanislav. Military Organization and Society. *Foreword by Professor A. R. Radcliffe-Brown. 226 pp. 1 folder.*

Coontz, Sydney H. Population Theories and the Economic Interpretation. *202 pp.*

Coser, Lewis. The Functions of Social Conflict. *204 pp.*

Dickie-Clark, H. F. Marginal Situation: *A Sociological Study of a Coloured Group. 240 pp. 11 tables.*

Glass, D. V. (Ed.). Social Mobility in Britain. *Contributions by J. Berent, T. Bottomore, R. C. Chambers, J. Floud, D. V. Glass, J. R. Hall, H. T. Himmelweit, R. K. Kelsall, F. M. Martin, C. A. Moser, R. Mukherjee, and W. Ziegel. 420 pp.*

Glaser, Barney, and **Strauss, Anselm L.** Status Passage. *A Formal Theory. 208 pp.*

Jones, Garth N. Planned Organizational Change: *An Exploratory Study Using an Empirical Approach. 268 pp.*

Kelsall, R. K. Higher Civil Servants in Britain: *From 1870 to the Present Day. 268 pp. 31 tables.*

König, René. The Community. *232 pp. Illustrated.*

● **Lawton, Denis.** Social Class, Language and Education. *192 pp.*

McLeish, John. The Theory of Social Change: *Four Views Considered. 128 pp.*

Marsh, David C. The Changing Social Structure of England and Wales, 1871-1961. *288 pp.*

Mouzelis, Nicos. Organization and Bureaucracy. *An Analysis of Modern Theories. 240 pp.*

Mulkay, M. J. Functionalism, Exchange and Theoretical Strategy. *272 pp.*

Ossowski, Stanislaw. Class Structure in the Social Consciousness. *210 pp.*

SOCIOLOGY AND POLITICS

Hertz, Frederick. Nationality in History and Politics: *A Psychology and Sociology of National Sentiment and Nationalism. 432 pp.*

Kornhauser, William. The Politics of Mass Society. *272 pp. 20 tables.*

Laidler, Harry W. History of Socialism. *Social-Economic Movements: An Historical and Comparative Survey of Socialism, Communism, Co-operation, Utopianism; and other Systems of Reform and Reconstruction. 992 pp.*

Mannheim, Karl. Freedom, Power and Democratic Planning. *Edited by Hans Gerth and Ernest K. Bramstedt. 424 pp.*

Mansur, Fatma. Process of Independence. *Foreword by A. H. Hanson. 208 pp.*

Martin, David A. Pacificism: *an Historical and Sociological Study. 262 pp.*

Myrdal, Gunnar. The Political Element in the Development of Economic Theory. *Translated from the German by Paul Streeten. 282 pp.*

Wootton, Graham. Workers, Unions and the State. *188 pp.*

FOREIGN AFFAIRS: THEIR SOCIAL, POLITICAL AND ECONOMIC FOUNDATIONS

Mayer, J. P. Political Thought in France from the Revolution to the Fifth Republic. *164 pp.*

CRIMINOLOGY

Ancel, Marc. Social Defence: *A Modern Approach to Criminal Problems. Foreword by Leon Radzinowicz. 240 pp.*

Cloward, Richard A., and **Ohlin, Lloyd E.** Delinquency and Opportunity: *A Theory of Delinquent Gangs. 248 pp.*

Downes, David M. The Delinquent Solution. *A Study in Subcultural Theory. 296 pp.*

Dunlop, A. B., and **McCabe, S.** Young Men in Detention Centres. *192 pp.*

Friedlander, Kate. The Psycho-Analytical Approach to Juvenile Delinquency: *Theory, Case Studies, Treatment. 320 pp.*

Glueck, Sheldon, and **Eleanor.** Family Environment and Delinquency. *With the statistical assistance of Rose W. Kneznek. 340 pp.*

Lopez-Rey, Manuel. Crime. *An Analytical Appraisal. 288 pp.*

Mannheim, Hermann. Comparative Criminology: *a Text Book. Two volumes. 442 pp. and 380 pp.*

Morris, Terence. The Criminal Area: *A Study in Social Ecology. Foreword by Hermann Mannheim. 232 pp. 25 tables. 4 maps.*

● **Taylor, Ian, Walton, Paul,** and **Young, Jock.** The New Criminology. *For a Social Theory of Deviance.*

SOCIAL PSYCHOLOGY

Bagley, Christopher. The Social Psychology of the Epileptic Child. *320 pp.*

Barbu, Zevedei. Problems of Historical Psychology. *248 pp.*

Blackburn, Julian. Psychology and the Social Pattern. *184 pp.*

● **Brittan, Arthur.** Meanings and Situations. *224 pp.*

● **Fleming, C. M.** Adolescence: Its Social Psychology. *With an Introduction to recent findings from the fields of Anthropology, Physiology, Medicine, Psychometrics and Sociometry. 288 pp.*

● The Social Psychology of Education: *An Introduction and Guide to Its Study. 136 pp.*

Homans, George C. The Human Group. *Foreword by Bernard DeVoto. Introduction by Robert K. Merton. 526 pp.*

Social Behaviour: *its Elementary Forms. 416 pp.*

Klein, Josephine. The Study of Groups. *226 pp. 31 figures. 5 tables.*

Linton, Ralph. The Cultural Background of Personality. *132 pp.*

Mayo, Elton. The Social Problems of an Industrial Civilization. *With an appendix on the Political Problem. 180 pp.*

Ottaway, A. K. C. Learning Through Group Experience. *176 pp.*

Ridder, J. C. de. The Personality of the Urban African in South Africa. *A Thematic Apperception Test Study. 196 pp. 12 plates.*

● **Rose, Arnold M.** (Ed.). Human Behaviour and Social Processes: *an Interactionist Approach. Contributions by Arnold M. Rose, Ralph H. Turner, Anselm Strauss, Everett C. Hughes, E. Franklin Frazier, Howard S. Becker, et al. 696 pp.*

Smelser, Neil J. Theory of Collective Behaviour. *448 pp.*
Stephenson, Geoffrey M. The Development of Conscience. *128 pp.*
Young, Kimball. Handbook of Social Psychology. *658 pp. 16 figures. 10 tables.*

SOCIOLOGY OF THE FAMILY

Banks, J. A. Prosperity and Parenthood: *A Study of Family Planning among The Victorian Middle Classes. 262 pp.*
Bell, Colin R. Middle Class Families: *Social and Geographical Mobility. 224 pp.*
Burton, Lindy. Vulnerable Children. *272 pp.*
Gavron, Hannah. The Captive Wife: *Conflicts of Household Mothers. 190 pp.*
George, Victor, and **Wilding, Paul.** Motherless Families. *220 pp.*
Klein, Josephine. Samples from English Cultures.
   1. Three Preliminary Studies and Aspects of Adult Life in England. *447 pp.*
   2. Child-Rearing Practices and Index. *247 pp.*
Klein, Viola. Britain's Married Women Workers. *180 pp.*
   The Feminine Character. *History of an Ideology. 244 pp.*
McWhinnie, Alexina M. Adopted Children. *How They Grow Up. 304 pp.*
Myrdal, Alva, and **Klein, Viola.** Women's Two Roles: *Home and Work. 238 pp. 27 tables.*
Parsons, Talcott, and **Bales, Robert F.** Family: Socialization and Interaction Process. *In collaboration with James Olds, Morris Zelditch and Philip E. Slater. 456 pp. 50 figures and tables.*

SOCIAL SERVICES

Bastide, Roger. The Sociology of Mental Disorder. *Translated from the French by Jean McNeil. 260 pp.*
Carlebach, Julius. Caring For Children in Trouble. *266 pp.*
Forder, R. A. (Ed.). Penelope Hall's Social Services of England and Wales. *352 pp.*
George, Victor. Foster Care. *Theory and Practice. 234 pp.*
   Social Security: *Beveridge and After. 258 pp.*
● **Goetschius, George W.** Working with Community Groups. *256 pp.*
Goetschius, George W., and **Tash, Joan.** Working with Unattached Youth. *416 pp.*
Hall, M. P., and **Howes, I. V.** The Church in Social Work. *A Study of Moral Welfare Work undertaken by the Church of England. 320 pp.*
Heywood, Jean S. Children in Care: *the Development of the Service for the Deprived Child. 264 pp.*
Hoenig, J., and **Hamilton, Marian W.** The De-Segration of the Mentally Ill. *284 pp.*
Jones, Kathleen. Mental Health and Social Policy, 1845-1959. *264 pp.*

King, Roy D., Raynes, Norma V., and **Tizard, Jack.** Patterns of Residential Care. *356 pp.*

Leigh, John. Young People and Leisure. *256 pp.*

Morris, Mary. Voluntary Work and the Welfare State. *300 pp.*

Morris, Pauline. Put Away: *A Sociological Study of Institutions for the Mentally Retarded. 364 pp.*

Nokes, P. L. The Professional Task in Welfare Practice. *152 pp.*

Timms, Noel. Psychiatric Social Work in Great Britain (1939-1962). *280 pp.*

●   Social Casework: *Principles and Practice. 256 pp.*

Young, A. F., and **Ashton, E. T.** British Social Work in the Nineteenth Century. *288 pp.*

Young, A. F. Social Services in British Industry. *272 pp.*

SOCIOLOGY OF EDUCATION

Banks, Olive. Parity and Prestige in English Secondary Education: a Study in Educational Sociology. *272 pp.*

Bentwich, Joseph. Education in Israel. *224 pp. 8 pp. plates.*

● **Blyth, W. A. L.** English Primary Education. *A Sociological Description.*
    1. Schools. *232 pp.*
    2. Background. *168 pp.*

Collier, K. G. The Social Purposes of Education: *Personal and Social Values in Education. 268 pp.*

Dale, R. R., and **Griffith, S.** Down Stream: *Failure in the Grammar School. 108 pp.*

Dore, R. P. Education in Tokugawa Japan. *356 pp. 9 pp. plates*

Evans, K. M. Sociometry and Education. *158 pp.*

Foster, P. J. Education and Social Change in Ghana. *336 pp. 3 maps.*

Fraser, W. R. Education and Society in Modern France. *150 pp.*

Grace, Gerald R. Role Conflict and the Teacher. *About 200 pp.*

Hans, Nicholas. New Trends in Education in the Eighteenth Century. *278 pp. 19 tables.*

●   Comparative Education: *A Study of Educational Factors and Traditions. 360 pp.*

Hargreaves, David. Interpersonal Relations and Education. *432 pp.*

●   Social Relations in a Secondary School. *240 pp.*

Holmes, Brian. Problems in Education. *A Comparative Approach. 336 pp.*

King, Ronald. Values and Involvement in a Grammar School. *164 pp.*
    School Organization and Pupil Involvement. *A Study of Secondary Schools.*

● **Mannheim, Karl,** and **Stewart, W. A. C.** An Introduction to the Sociology of Education. *206 pp.*

Morris, Raymond N. The Sixth Form and College Entrance. *231 pp.*

● **Musgrove, F.** Youth and the Social Order. *176 pp.*

● **Ottaway, A. K. C.** Education and Society: An Introduction to the Sociology of Education. *With an Introduction by W. O. Lester Smith. 212 pp.*

Peers, Robert. Adult Education: *A Comparative Study. 398 pp.*

Pritchard, D. G. Education and the Handicapped: *1760 to 1960. 258 pp.*
Richardson, Helen. Adolescent Girls in Approved Schools. *308 pp.*
Stratta, Erica. The Education of Borstal Boys. *A Study of their Educational Experiences prior to, and during Borstal Training. 256 pp.*

SOCIOLOGY OF CULTURE

Eppel, E. M., and **M.** Adolescents and Morality: *A Study of some Moral Values and Dilemmas of Working Adolescents in the Context of a changing Climate of Opinion. Foreword by W. J. H. Sprott. 268 pp. 39 tables.*
● **Fromm, Erich.** The Fear of Freedom. *286 pp.*
  The Sane Society. *400 pp.*
  Mannheim, Karl. Essays on the Sociology of Culture. *Edited by Ernst Mannheim in co-operation with Paul Kecskemeti. Editorial Note by Adolph Lowe. 280 pp.*
  Weber, Alfred. Farewell to European History: *or The Conquest of Nihilism Translated from the German by R. F. C. Hull. 224 pp.*

SOCIOLOGY OF RELIGION

Argyle, Michael. Religious Behaviour. *224 pp. 8 figures. 41 tables.*
Nelson, G. K. Spiritualism and Society. *313 pp.*
Stark, Werner. The Sociology of Religion. *A Study of Christendom.*
  Volume I. *Established Religion. 248 pp.*
  Volume II. *Sectarian Religion. 368 pp.*
  Volume III. *The Universal Church. 464 pp.*
  Volume IV. *Types of Religious Man. 352 pp.*
  Volume V. *Types of Religious Culture. 464 pp.*
Watt, W. Montgomery. Islam and the Integration of Society. *320 pp.*

SOCIOLOGY OF ART AND LITERATURE

Jarvie, Ian C. Towards a Sociology of the Cinema. *A Comparative Essay on the Structure and Functioning of a Major Entertainment Industry. 405 pp.*
Rust, Frances S. Dance in Society. *An Analysis of the Relationships between the Social Dance and Society in England from the Middle Ages to the Present Day. 256 pp. 8 pp. of plates.*
Schücking, L. L. The Sociology of Literary Taste. *112 pp.*

SOCIOLOGY OF KNOWLEDGE

Mannheim, Karl. Essays on the Sociology of Knowledge. *Edited by Paul Kecskemeti. Editorial Note by Adolph Lowe. 353 pp.*

Remmling, Gunter W. (Ed.). Towards the Sociology of Knowledge. *Origins and Development of a Sociological Thought Style.*

Stark, Werner. The Sociology of Knowledge: *An Essay in Aid of a Deeper Understanding of the History of Ideas. 384 pp.*

URBAN SOCIOLOGY

Ashworth, William. The Genesis of Modern British Town Planning: *A Study in Economic and Social History of the Nineteenth and Twentieth Centuries. 288 pp.*

Cullingworth, J. B. Housing Needs and Planning Policy: *A Restatement of the Problems of Housing Need and 'Overspill' in England and Wales. 232 pp. 44 tables. 8 maps.*

Dickinson, Robert E. City and Region: *A Geographical Interpretation. 608 pp. 125 figures.*

The West European City: *A Geographical Interpretation. 600 pp. 129 maps. 29 plates.*

● The City Region in Western Europe. *320 pp. Maps.*

Humphreys, Alexander J. New Dubliners: *Urbanization and the Irish Family. Foreword by George C. Homans. 304 pp.*

Jackson, Brian. Working Class Community: *Some General Notions raised by a Series of Studies in Northern England. 192 pp.*

Jennings, Hilda. Societies in the Making: *a Study of Development and Re-development within a County Borough. Foreword by D. A. Clark. 286 pp.*

● **Mann, P. H.** An Approach to Urban Sociology. *240 pp.*

Morris, R. N., and **Mogey, J.** The Sociology of Housing. *Studies at Berinsfield. 232 pp. 4 pp. plates.*

Rosser, C., and **Harris, C.** The Family and Social Change. *A Study of Family and Kinship in a South Wales Town. 352 pp. 8 maps.*

RURAL SOCIOLOGY

Chambers, R. J. H. Settlement Schemes in Tropical Africa: *A Selective Study. 268 pp.*

Haswell, M. R. The Economics of Development in Village India. *120 pp.*

Littlejohn, James. Westrigg: *the Sociology of a Cheviot Parish. 172 pp. 5 figures.*

Mayer, Adrian C. Peasants in the Pacific. *A Study of Fiji Indian Rural Society. 248 pp. 20 plates.*

Williams, W. M. The Sociology of an English Village: *Gosforth. 272 pp. 12 figures. 13 tables.*

9

SOCIOLOGY OF INDUSTRY AND DISTRIBUTION

Anderson, Nels. Work and Leisure. *280 pp.*

● **Blau, Peter M.,** and **Scott, W. Richard.** Formal Organizations: *a Comparative approach. Introduction and Additional Bibliography by J. H. Smith. 326 pp.*

Eldridge, J. E. T. Industrial Disputes. *Essays in the Sociology of Industrial Relations. 288 pp.*

Hetzler, Stanley. Applied Measures for Promoting Technological Growth. *352 pp.*

Technological Growth and Social Change. *Achieving Modernization. 269 pp.*

Hollowell, Peter G. The Lorry Driver. *272 pp.*

Jefferys, Margot, *with the assistance of Winifred Moss.* Mobility in the Labour Market: *Employment Changes in Battersea and Dagenham. Preface by Barbara Wootton. 186 pp. 51 tables.*

Millerson, Geoffrey. The Qualifying Associations: *a Study in Professionalization. 320 pp.*

Smelser, Neil J. Social Change in the Industrial Revolution: *An Application of Theory to the Lancashire Cotton Industry, 1770-1840. 468 pp. 12 figures. 14 tables.*

Williams, Gertrude. Recruitment to Skilled Trades. *240 pp.*

Young, A. F. Industrial Injuries Insurance: *an Examination of British Policy. 192 pp.*

DOCUMENTARY

Schlesinger, Rudolf (Ed.). Changing Attitudes in Soviet Russia.

2. The Nationalities Problem and Soviet Administration. *Selected Readings on the Development of Soviet Nationalities Policies. Introduced by the editor. Translated by W. W. Gottlieb. 324 pp.*

ANTHROPOLOGY

Ammar, Hamed. Growing up in an Egyptian Village: *Silwa, Province of Aswan. 336 pp.*

Brandel-Syrier, Mia. Reeftown Elite. *A Study of Social Mobility in a Modern African Community on the Reef. 376 pp.*

Crook, David, and **Isabel.** Revolution in a Chinese Village: *Ten Mile Inn. 230 pp. 8 plates. 1 map.*

Dickie-Clark, H. F. The Marginal Situation. *A Sociological Study of a Coloured Group. 236 pp.*

Dube, S. C. Indian Village. *Foreword by Morris Edward Opler. 276 pp. 4 plates.*

India's Changing Villages: *Human Factors in Community Development. 260 pp. 8 plates. 1 map.*

Firth, Raymond. Malay Fishermen. *Their Peasant Economy. 420 pp. 17 pp. plates.*

Gulliver, P. H. Social Control in an African Society: a Study of the Arusha, Agricultural Masai of Northern Tanganyika. *320 pp. 8 plates. 10 figures.*

Ishwaran, K. Shivapur. *A South Indian Village. 216 pp.*
Tradition and Economy in Village India: *An Interactionist Approach. Foreword by Conrad Arensburg. 176 pp.*

Jarvie, Ian C. The Revolution in Anthropology. *268 pp.*

Jarvie, Ian C., and **Agassi, Joseph.** Hong Kong. *A Society in Transition. 396 pp. Illustrated with plates and maps.*

Little, Kenneth L. Mende of Sierra Leone. *308 pp. and folder.*
Negroes in Britain. *With a New Introduction and Contemporary Study by Leonard Bloom. 320 pp.*

Lowie, Robert H. Social Organization. *494 pp.*

Mayer, Adrian C. Caste and Kinship in Central India: *A Village and its Region. 328 pp. 16 plates. 15 figures. 16 tables.*

Smith, Raymond T. The Negro Family in British Guiana: *Family Structure and Social Status in the Villages. With a Foreword by Meyer Fortes. 314 pp. 8 plates. 1 figure. 4 maps.*

SOCIOLOGY AND PHILOSOPHY

Barnsley, John H. The Social Reality of Ethics. *A Comparative Analysis of Moral Codes. 448 pp.*

Diesing, Paul. Patterns of Discovery in the Social Sciences. *362 pp.*

Douglas, Jack D. (Ed.). Understanding Everyday Life. *Toward the Reconstruction of Sociological Knowledge. Contributions by Alan F. Blum. Aaron W. Cicourel, Norman K. Denzin, Jack D. Douglas, John Heeren, Peter McHugh, Peter K. Manning, Melvin Power, Matthew Speier, Roy Turner, D. Lawrence Wieder, Thomas P. Wilson and Don H. Zimmerman. 370 pp.*

Jarvie, Ian C. Concepts and Society. *216 pp.*

Roche, Maurice. Phenomenology, Language and the Social Sciences. *About 400 pp.*

Sahay, Arun. Sociological Analysis.

Sklair, Leslie. The Sociology of Progress. *320 pp.*

International Library of Anthropology
General Editor Adam Kuper

Brown, Paula. The Chimbu. *A Study of Change in the New Guinea Highlands.*
Van Den Berghe, Pierre L. Power and Privilege at an African University.

11

International Library
of Social Policy
General Editor Kathleen Jones

Holman, Robert. Trading in Children. *A Study of Private Fostering.*
Jones, Kathleen. History of the Mental Health Services. *428 pp.*
Thomas, J. E. The English Prison Officer since 1850: *A Study in Conflict.*
   258 pp.

Primary Socialization, Language
and Education
General Editor Basil Bernstein

Bernstein, Basil. Class, Codes and Control. *2 volumes.*
   1. *Theoretical Studies Towards a Sociology of Language. 254 pp.*
   2. *Applied Studies Towards a Sociology of Language. About 400 pp.*
Brandis, Walter, and **Henderson, Dorothy.** Social Class, Language and
   Communication. *288 pp.*
Cook-Gumperz, Jenny. Social Control and Socialization. *A Study of Class
   Differences in the Language of Maternal Control.*
Gahagan, D. M., and **G. A.** Talk Reform. *Exploration in Language for Infant
   School Children. 160 pp.*
Robinson, W. P., and **Rackstraw, Susan, D. A.** A Question of Answers.
   2 volumes. 192 pp. and 180 pp.
Turner, Geoffrey, J., and **Mohan, Bernard, A.** A Linguistic Description and
   Computer Programme for Children's Speech. *208 pp.*

Reports of the Institute of Community Studies

Cartwright, Ann. Human Relations and Hospital Care. *272 pp.*
   Parents and Family Planning Services. *306 pp.*
   Patients and their Doctors. *A Study of General Practice. 304 pp.*
● **Jackson, Brian.** Streaming: *an Education System in Miniature. 168 pp.*
Jackson, Brian, and **Marsden, Dennis.** Education and the Working Class:
   *Some General Themes raised by a Study of 88 Working-class Children
   in a Northern Industrial City. 268 pp. 2 folders.*
Marris, Peter. The Experience of Higher Education. *232 pp. 27 tables.*
Marris, Peter, and **Rein, Martin.** Dilemmas of Social Reform. *Poverty and
   Community Action in the United States. 256 pp.*
Marris, Peter, and **Somerset, Anthony.** African Businessmen. *A Study of
   Entrepreneurship and Development in Kenya. 256 pp.*
Mills, Richard. Young Outsiders: *a Study in Alternative Communities.*

12

Runciman, W. G. Relative Deprivation and Social Justice. *A Study of Attitudes to Social Inequality in Twentieth Century England. 352 pp.*

Townsend, Peter. The Family Life of Old People: *An Inquiry in East London. Foreword by J. H. Sheldon. 300 pp. 3 figures. 63 tables.*

Willmott, Peter. Adolescent Boys in East London. *230 pp.*
The Evolution of a Community: *a study of Dagenham after forty years. 168 pp. 2 maps.*

Willmott, Peter, and **Young, Michael.** Family and Class in a London Suburb. *202 pp. 47 tables.*

Young, Michael. Innovation and Research in Education. *192 pp.*

● **Young, Michael,** and **McGeeney, Patrick.** Learning Begins at Home. *A Study of a Junior School and its Parents. 128 pp.*

Young, Michael, and **Willmott, Peter.** Family and Kinship in East London. *Foreword by Richard M. Titmuss. 252 pp. 39 tables.*
The Symmetrical Family.

Reports of the Institute for Social Studies in Medical Care

Cartwright, Ann, Hockey, Lisbeth, and **Anderson, John L.** Life Before Death.
Dunnell, Karen, and **Cartwright, Ann.** Medicine Takers, Prescribers and Hoarders. *190 pp.*

Medicine, Illness and Society
General Editor W. M. Williams

Robinson, David. The Process of Becoming Ill.
Stacey, Margaret. *et al.* Hospitals, Children and Their Families. *The Report of a Pilot Study. 202 pp.*

Monographs in Social Theory
General Editor Arthur Brittan

Bauman, Zygmunt. Culture as Praxis.
Dixon, Keith. Sociological Theory. *Pretence and Possibility.*
Smith, Anthony D. The Concept of Social Change. *A Critique of the Functionalist Theory of Social Change.*

Routledge Social Science Journals

The British Journal of Sociology. *Edited by Terence P. Morris. Vol. 1, No. 1, March 1950 and Quarterly. Roy. 8vo. Back numbers available. An international journal with articles on all aspects of sociology.*

Economy and Society. *Vol. 1, No. 1. February 1972 and Quarterly. Metric Roy. 8vo. A journal for all social scientists covering sociology, philosophy, anthropology, economics and history. Back numbers available.*

Year Book of Social Policy in Britain, The. *Edited by Kathleen Jones. 1971. Published Annually.*

Printed in Great Britain by Lewis Reprints Limited
Brown Knight & Truscott Group, London and Tonbridge   1373